ABOUT THINGS THAT MATTER

FOUNDATION BUILDING

Change That Matters

Time That Matters

Goals That Matter

Relationships That Matter

A SELF-IMPROVEMENT SERIES FOR SUCCESS

From Bestselling Author

JC RYAN

Copyright

Copyright © 2025 JC Ryan

All rights reserved. No part of this publication may be reproduced, distributed, or transmitted in any form or by any means, including photocopying, recording, or other electronic or mechanical methods, without the prior written permission of the publisher, except in the case of brief quotations embodied in critical reviews and certain other noncommercial uses permitted by copyright law.

Your Gift

As a way of saying thanks for your purchase, I'm offering you the first book in the series **About Things That Matter** as a gift.

This book is exclusive to my readers. You will not find this book anywhere else.

You're invited to pause, reflect, and reconsider what truly defines a meaningful life. In a world conditioned to chase money, status, and material achievements, this book challenges the conventional yardsticks of success. Through incisive insight and refreshing authenticity, it guides readers to shift their focus from external validation to the internal foundations that cultivate real fulfillment, purpose, and enduring happiness. It's a call to eliminate distractions, clarify values, and build a life anchored in what matters most.

Visit this link to download your free copy of **About Things That Matter** or type this address into your browser **https://BookHip.com/HLAJBFP**

Introduction

I first met JC Ryan some years ago when, as publisher, I interviewed him for Books & Pieces Magazine. We hit it off and became friends. Through his health issues at the time, and the changes he made to his life for the better, we came to discuss this extensive body of work he created, which detailed his journey and served as a blueprint for anyone wanting to improve their lives, both personally and professionally.

Thus came "About Things That Matter," a comprehensive 12-book series that can completely transform your thinking and your successes.

JC wanted my help in putting it all together, and we decided the best way was to offer a series of email courses to complement the books. And to really get it kick-started, JC decided to offer the first course, "Change That Matters," totally free to participants.

Having seen the entirety of this series, I can attest to its robust nature and that it truly is a solid plan for anyone wishing to better their lives, whether personally or in business.

The books and the course(s) have been designed to be followed easily at your own pace and include many additional resources that can be downloaded.

If you've found yourself asking the question: "Is there nothing more I can do with my life?" then this series is definitely for you. It is "About Things That Matter."

Yours in health,

William Gensburger
Publisher & Author
Books & Pieces Magazine (bnpmag.com)
B&P Books (bnpbooks.com)

In Every Life, It's The Things That Matter That Count

About Things That Matter

The Complete Transformation Series
Your Science-Based Roadmap to a Life of Meaning, Momentum, and Purposeful Living

Most people drift through life reacting to circumstances instead of creating them. They work hard but not strategically. They set goals but struggle to achieve them. They want deeper relationships but don't know how to build them. They feel busy but not fulfilled.

What if there was a better way?

The **About Things That Matter** series is your research-backed, implementation-focused system for transforming intention into achievement and dreams into reality. Based on decades of psychological research and tested by thousands of high achievers, this series provides the specific tools, strategies, and mindsets that separate those who merely wish for better lives from those who actually create them:

The complete "About Things That Matter" series provides a comprehensive, science-based system for transforming every area of your life while reclaiming the fundamental human capacities that have become luxuries in our modern world.

Each book builds on the previous ones, creating a compound effect of growth and transformation. You don't need to read them in order, but starting with your biggest challenge area will create the most immediate impact.

The Research Foundation:
- Harvard's 80-year Grant Study on human flourishing
- Stanford's research on the growth mindset and achievement
- MIT's findings on habit formation and behavioral change
- Decades of organizational psychology research on high performance

Foundation Building

Book 1: Change That Matters
Stop Drifting. Start Directing.

Master the psychology of lasting personal transformation through 8 proven principles that turn intention into achievement.

What You'll Gain:
- The neuroscience-based principles that make change stick
- A systematic approach to breaking limiting patterns
- Proven strategies for overcoming resistance and fear
- The mindset shifts that accelerate personal growth

Readers report feeling more in control of their lives within the first week of implementation.

Book 2: Goals That Matter
Turn Dreams into Done.

Create and achieve meaningful goals through purpose-driven planning that delivers real fulfillment, not just external success.

What You'll Gain:
- The SMART goals framework increases achievement rates by 42%
- How to align goals with your deepest values for sustained motivation
- Systems for maintaining momentum through obstacles and setbacks
- The art of celebrating progress to fuel continued success

Goal completion rates increase by 65% when shared with others using these methods.

Book 3: Time That Matters
Make Every Moment Count.

Transform your relationship with time through proven systems that create freedom, focus, and alignment with what matters most.

What You'll Gain:
- The 80/20 principle applied to daily and weekly planning
- Energy management strategies that multiply your effective working hours
- Digital tools and analog systems that enhance rather than distract

- The art of saying "no" to create space for what matters most

Users gain an average of 8-12 productive hours per week within 30 days.

Book 4: Relationships That Matter
Build Your Social Wealth.

Create deep, meaningful connections through authentic communication and relationship skills that enrich every area of your life.

What You'll Gain:
- The five essential relationship roles that every successful person needs
- Communication skills that transform surface connections into deep bonds
- Digital relationship strategies for authentic connection in a virtual world
- Community-building skills that create belonging and mutual support

Noticeable improvements in relationship quality and communication effectiveness within the first conversations.

Skill Development

Book 5: Emotional Intelligence That Matters
Feel Deeply, Respond Wisely.

Master the art of understanding and managing emotions to enhance relationships, decision-making, and personal effectiveness.

What You'll Gain:
- Advanced emotional awareness and regulation techniques
- Skills to read and respond to others' emotions effectively
- Tools for transforming emotional triggers into growth opportunities
- Leadership abilities rooted in emotional wisdom

Improved emotional responses and relationship dynamics within days of applying core techniques.

Book 6: Happiness That Matters
Choose Joy, Create Fulfillment.

Discover the science of sustainable happiness and build daily practices that create lasting contentment independent of circumstances.

What You'll Gain:
- Evidence-based strategies for cultivating genuine happiness
- Tools to break free from comparison and external validation
- Gratitude and mindfulness practices that rewire your brain for joy
- How to find meaning and purpose in everyday moments

Measurable improvements in mood and life satisfaction within two weeks of consistent practice.

Book 7: The 24-Hour Miracle That Matters
Transform Your Day, Transform Your Life.

Design perfect days that compound into an extraordinary life through intentional morning, work, and evening routines.

What You'll Gain:
- Hour-by-hour blueprints for days that energize rather than drain
- Morning routines that set you up for success and clarity
- Evening practices that restore and prepare you for tomorrow
- Weekend rhythms that rejuvenate and reconnect you to purpose

Dramatic improvements in energy, focus, and life satisfaction within one week of implementation.

Book 8: From Stressful to Successful
Stress Less, Achieve More.

Transform stress from a life-draining force into a success-driving advantage through proven resilience and performance strategies.

What You'll Gain:
- Stress reframing techniques that turn pressure into performance fuel
- Resilience-building practices for bouncing back from any setback
- Peak performance strategies used by top athletes and executives
- Recovery and restoration methods that prevent burnout

Significant reduction in stress levels and improved performance under pressure within days.

Advanced Integration

Book 9: The Connection Code
Crack the Code to Meaningful Relationships.

One-line Summary: Master advanced relationship dynamics, conflict resolution, and influence techniques that create lasting bonds and positive impact.

What You'll Gain:
- Advanced empathy and emotional attunement skills
- Conflict transformation strategies that strengthen rather than damage relationships
- Influence and persuasion techniques rooted in genuine care
- Leadership approaches that inspire and unite rather than divide

Enhanced ability to navigate difficult conversations and deepen existing relationships immediately.

Book 10: Procrastination
Stop Putting Off Your Potential.

Overcome procrastination forever through understanding its root causes and implementing systems that make action inevitable.

What You'll Gain:
- The psychology behind procrastination and how to interrupt the cycle
- Environmental design strategies that make good choices automatic
- Motivation techniques that work even when you don't feel like it
- Completion systems that turn started projects into finished successes

Immediate breakthrough on stuck projects and tasks that have been delayed for weeks or months.

Book 11: Self-Esteem That Matters
Build Unshakable Confidence from the Inside Out.

Develop authentic self-worth through proven strategies that transform self-doubt into genuine confidence and self-respect.

What You'll Gain:
- Tools to overcome negative self-talk and limiting beliefs
- Habits that reinforce your sense of worth daily
- Assertiveness skills to express needs and set boundaries

- The ripple effect of healthy self-esteem on relationships

Noticeable shifts in self-talk and confidence levels within the first week of practice.

Book 12: Thoughts That Matter
Your Brain Is Not Your Boss.

Harness the neuroscience of conscious living to master your mind, emotions, and purpose through proven mental training protocols.

What You'll Gain:
- How to rewire your brain for resilience, clarity, and growth
- Digital detox strategies to reclaim your attention
- Emotional intelligence tools for wise decision-making
- Daily practices to align thoughts with purpose

Mental clarity and emotional regulation improve within days of implementing the core exercises.

Table of Contents

Copyright 2

Your Gift 2

Introduction 3

About Things That Matter 4

Table of Contents 10

PART I - CHANGE THAT MATTERS 13

About Change That Matters 15

What's Driving You? 16

Chapter 1 – Prepare for Change 17

Chapter 2 – A Change Strategy 26

Chapter 3 – How to Effect Permanent Change 37

Chapter 4 – Mastering The Art Of Self-Talk 46

Chapter 5 – Know Thyself 57

Chapter 6 – SWOT Analysis 69

Chapter 7 – Your Journey Begins Now 80

Bibliography 90

PART 2 - GOALS THAT MATTER 92

About Goals That Matter 94

What Matters To You? 95

The Horse in the Granite 96

Chapter 1 – The Foundations of Goal Achievement 98

Chapter 2 – Vision: The First Step 106

Chapter 3 – Preparation: Choosing the Right Goals 114

Chapter 4 – Setting Goals That Matter 122

Chapter 5 – Planning for Success 130

Chapter 6 – Executing Your Plan 138

Chapter 7 – Your Journey Begins Now 145

Chapter 8 – Reflect, Refine, and Celebrate 158

Reflection and Action 165

Appendices & Resources 172

Bibliography 176

PART 3 - TIME THAT MATTERS 179

About Time That Matters 181

Life Is Like A Jar 183

Chapter 1 – Why Time Matters More Than Ever 185

Chapter 2 – Critical Concepts and Commandments 192

Chapter 3 - What's Causing Unnecessary Crises 203

Chapter 4 – Time, Change, and the Power of Prioritization 210

Chapter 5 – Setting Goals That Fit Your Life 219

Chapter 6 – Habits, Routines, and Systems for Time Mastery 226

Chapter 7 – Conquering Procrastination and Overwhelm 233

Chapter 8 – Stress, Energy, and Sustainable Productivity 243

Chapter 9 – Tools and Technology 250

Chapter 10 – Real-World Case Studies 257

Chapter 11 – Putting It All Together 265

Appendices & Resources 272

Bibliography 279

PART 4 - RELATIONSHIPS THAT MATTER 282

About Relationships That Matter 284

It's About Social Wealth 285

The Power of Social Wealth 286

Chapter 1 – Why Relationships Are the Ultimate Wealth 287

Chapter 2 – Mapping Your Relationship Landscape 293

Chapter 3 – Foundations of Lasting Connection 300

Chapter 4 – Communication Mastery 307

Chapter 5 – Boundaries, Energy, and Healthy Relationships 314

Chapter 6 – Community, Belonging, and Social Capital 321

Chapter 7 – Relationships in the Digital Age 329

Chapter 8 – Giving, Receiving, and Growing Together 338

Chapter 9 – Navigating Change, Conflict, and Life Transitions 346

Chapter 10 – Your Relationship Mastery Plan 354

Final Reflection 363

Appendices & Resources 365

Bibliography 369

Your Journey Continues 371

The Complete Transformation System 372

Your Gift 378

Also by JC Ryan 379

About JC Ryan 383

PART I - CHANGE THAT MATTERS

To those who dare to dream and to those who act on their dreams.

"We are products of our past, but we don't have to be prisoners of it.—**Rick Warren.**

Change That Matters

8 PRINCIPLES TO TRANSFORM YOUR LIFE

About Things That Matter

A SELF-IMPROVEMENT SERIES FOR SUCCESS

Book 1

JC Ryan

About Change That Matters

Change is inevitable. Growth is intentional.

Change That Matters guides you through eight foundational principles to transform your life, one step at a time. Drawing on proven strategies, timeless wisdom, and practical exercises, this book serves as your guide for navigating change, cultivating lasting habits, and grounding your life in what truly matters.

Whether you're seeking clarity, motivation, or a roadmap for personal growth, this book offers actionable tools and reflective insights to help you move from intention to achievement. Start your journey today because the things that matter deserve your best effort.

What's Driving You?

The pace of the world is accelerating, and you might feel the pressure to keep up or even stay afloat. You may be seeking deeper meaning in your life, striving to make each day more significant. Though it may seem like circumstances control you, you can choose what drives your life—everyone is guided by something.

The word "drive" implies guidance, control, or direction. For example, when you hammer a nail, you guide, control, and direct it into the wood. When you operate a vehicle, you guide, control, and direct it along the road. So, what's driving you?

At this moment, you might be driven by a problem that needs solving, the pressure of deadlines, or immediate demands. Or perhaps you're driven by less visible forces, such as feelings of guilt or resentment, anxieties, a focus on material possessions, or the need for others' approval. Many different situations, values, and emotions can drive your life, and each one can leave you feeling drained. You might be driven by current events, searching for meaning in things that are temporary. You feel the strain of societal divisions and rapidly advancing technology, and you've taken on an emotional burden that wasn't yours to carry. Even devotion can drive your life, leaving you exhausted and without a true sense of direction. Why? Because it can become about human efforts to reach a higher power, focusing on rules and restrictions, and thought to earn favor. True connection, however, is about that higher power reaching out to humanity.

Many forces can drive your life, but they all tend to lead to the same result: undeveloped potential, unnecessary stress, and a life lacking fulfillment. You need a purpose greater than yourself to direct your life. Nothing can compensate for moving through life without knowing your purpose, not achievement, wealth, recognition, or pleasure. Without purpose, your life will always feel like an activity without meaning and movement without true direction. When your purpose isn't clear, you lack a roadmap to guide your decisions, manage your time, and allocate your resources. You might repeatedly change direction—your career, relationships, or beliefs—hoping that each change will resolve the confusion or fill the emptiness within.

Chapter 1 – Prepare for Change

Embrace Change, Embrace Growth

Key Insight: Change is not a threat but an invitation to grow. Stepping outside your comfort zone doesn't mean leaping into a panic—growth happens in the "stretch zone," where challenge meets possibility.

Why Change?

Change is often sparked by a desire for something different or better in our lives. We might feel stuck in a job that no longer fulfills us, trapped in unhealthy habits, or simply yearning for personal growth. Whatever the reason, the decision to change usually comes when we realize that our current situation no longer serves us.

Change happens when the pain of staying the same is greater than the pain of change. — **Tony Robbins.**

This insight highlights a crucial aspect of human nature—we often resist change until the discomfort of our current situation becomes unbearable.

Common Scenarios:
- A person continues in an unfulfilling job until the stress affects their health.
- Someone remains in a toxic relationship until their self-esteem is severely damaged.
- An individual ignores health warnings until they face a serious medical condition.

In each case, change becomes necessary when the pain of the status quo outweighs the fear of the unknown.

Change is a Natural Process

It's important to recognize that change isn't just something we choose. It's an inherent part of life itself. Our bodies are in a constant state of renewal:
- Skin cells are replaced every 30 days.
- Bones regenerate every 3 months.
- Blood cells are refreshed every 4 months.

This biological process, known as *allostasis*, demonstrates that change is not only natural but essential for survival. Just as our bodies embrace change, our minds and habits must do the same to achieve personal growth.

The Fear of Change vs The Necessity of Change

Despite the necessity of change, many people resist it due to fear. The comfort zone, while not always ideal, feels safe and familiar.

Common fears about change include:
- Fear of failure
- Worry about things getting worse
- Concern about losing relationships
- Self-doubt about abilities
- Anxiety about commitment
- Overwhelmed at the perceived effort required

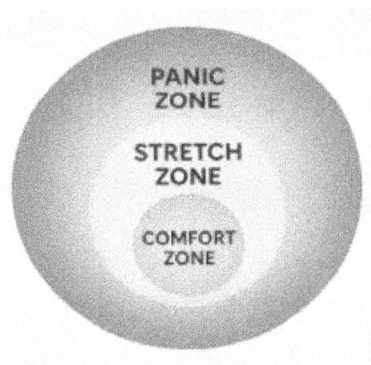

These fears are normal and understandable. However, it's crucial to recognize that avoiding change can be more detrimental in the long run. Just as species that fail to evolve become extinct, people who resist personal growth risk stagnation and unfulfilment.

The Comfort Zone, Stretch Zone, and Panic Zone. Growth happens in the stretch zone—just outside your comfort zone, but not so far that you enter panic.

Redefining Success

To embrace change, we often need to reexamine our definition of success. Society often equates success with external achievements: wealth, career status, or material possessions. However, true success is much deeper and more personal.

Success Is About The Things That Matter To YOU

Success is not a universal concept. It's unique to each individual based on their values, priorities, and goals.

For some, success might mean:
- Raising a loving family
- Running a business on their own terms
- Achieving personal growth and lifelong learning
- Making a positive impact on their community

The key is to define success on your own terms, not by society's standards.

Consider two individuals with similar professional achievements:
- Person A feels successful because their career provides freedom and fulfillment
- Person B feels unsuccessful despite similar accomplishments because they're measuring against society's expectations of constant advancement and wealth accumulation.

The difference is not in their circumstances but in their definition of success.

Success is a Journey

Many people view success as a destination, a final goal to be achieved. However, success is more accurately described as a journey of continuous growth and improvement. This perspective aligns with Earl Nightingale's definition:

Success is the progressive realization of a worthy goal.

By viewing success as a journey:
- You can celebrate small victories along the way.
- You remain motivated even when facing setbacks.
- You're more likely to enjoy the process, not just the end result.

Success and the Pursuit of Happiness

The United States Declaration of Independence states that all people are endowed with certain unalienable rights: "Life, Liberty, and the Pursuit of Happiness."

But what does Happiness mean in this context? Is it not a success?

When the Founding Fathers wrote about the pursuit of Happiness, they were referring to the right of every individual to define and pursue what success means to them—to set their own goals, to follow their passions, and to strive for fulfillment in whatever way they choose.

Success, then, is not something imposed on you by society. It is a deeply personal pursuit of what brings you meaning and satisfaction. It is your right to determine what a successful life looks like for you.

Understanding Your 'Why'

To successfully navigate change, it's crucial to understand your motivation—your 'why.' Your 'why' is the driving force behind your desire for change. It's what will keep you going when things get tough or when you face setbacks.

Identifying Your 'Why'

To identify your 'why,' ask yourself:
- What truly matters to me?
- What kind of life do I want to live?
- What impact do I want to have on the world?
- What would I regret not doing or becoming?

Your 'why' should be deeply personal and emotionally resonant. It's not about what others expect of you but what you expect of yourself.

Step	Prompt	Your Answer
1	What change do you want to make?	
2	Why?	
3	Why?	
4	Why?	
5	Why?	

Instructions: Write down a change you want to make (e.g., "I want to lose weight"). Ask yourself, "Why?" and write your answer. Repeat this process five times to uncover your core motivation.

The Power of a Strong 'Why'

A clear and compelling 'why' can:
- Provide motivation during challenging times
- Help you make decisions aligned with your goals
- Give you a sense of purpose and direction
- Increase your resilience in the face of obstacles

He who has a why to live can bear almost any how. — **Friedrich Nietzsche.**

Chapter Summary

- Change is natural and essential for growth, just as our bodies constantly renew themselves.

- Change often occurs when the pain of staying the same exceeds the pain of change.
- Define success on your own terms, not by society's standards of wealth or status.
- See success as a journey of continuous improvement, not a destination.
- Understand your 'why' to stay motivated during challenging times.
- Embrace discomfort as a sign of growth and expansion.

Reflection Questions

Question 1: What area of your life are you feeling the most discomfort with right now?

Former Student Responses:
- Career dissatisfaction or feeling stuck in a dead-end job
- Health issues like weight gain, lack of energy, or poor fitness
- Financial stress and inability to save money
- Relationship problems or loneliness
- Work-life balance struggles
- Lack of purpose or direction in life

Possible Solutions:
- **Career Issues**: Start with small steps like updating your resume, networking for 15 minutes daily, or taking one online course related to your desired field
- **Health Concerns**: Begin with a 10-minute daily walk, or replace one unhealthy snack with fruit
- **Financial Stress**: Track expenses for one week to identify spending patterns, then automate saving just $5 per week
- **Relationships**: Practice active listening in one conversation daily or reach out to one person weekly
- **Work-Life Balance**: Set one clear boundary, like not checking emails after 8 PM
- **Lack of Purpose**: Spend 10 minutes daily journaling about what brings you joy and meaning

Question 2: How would you define success in your own terms, regardless of society's expectations?

Former Student Responses:
- Having strong, loving relationships with family and friends
- Feeling peaceful and content with daily life
- Making a positive impact on others, even in small ways
- Having financial security without needing to be wealthy
- Pursuing creative passions and personal interests
- Maintaining good health and energy
- Having flexibility and freedom in how they spend their time

Possible Solutions:
- **Relationship-Focused Success**: Schedule regular quality time with loved ones and practice expressing gratitude to them
- **Peace-Seeking Success**: Develop a daily mindfulness practice or create calming routines
- **Impact-Oriented Success**: Volunteer monthly or find ways to help others in your current role
- **Security-Focused Success**: Create a realistic budget and savings plan aligned with your actual needs
- **Creative Success**: Dedicate 30 minutes weekly to a creative pursuit without pressure for perfection
- **Health Success**: Focus on one healthy habit at a time rather than dramatic lifestyle overhauls

Question 3: What is your personal 'why' that will drive you through the challenges of change?

Former Student Responses:
- Wanting to be a better role model for their children
- Desire to break generational patterns of dysfunction
- Fear of regret in later life
- Wanting to feel proud of themselves
- Desire to reduce stress and anxiety
- Wanting to contribute meaningfully to the world
- Seeking authentic happiness and fulfillment

Possible Solutions:

- **Role Model Motivation**: Write a letter to your future children about the person you want to be for them
- **Breaking Patterns**: Identify one specific pattern to change and create a plan with small, manageable steps
- **Avoiding Regret**: List three things you'd regret not trying, and choose one to begin this month
- **Self-Pride**: Set small, achievable goals that build confidence and self-respect
- **Stress Reduction**: Practice one stress-management technique daily, like deep breathing or brief meditation
- **Meaningful Contribution**: Identify one way to help others that aligns with your skills and interests

Question 4: What fears are currently holding you back from embracing necessary changes?

Former Student Responses:
- Fear of failure and looking foolish
- Worry about disappointing others or losing relationships
- Concern about financial instability
- Fear of the unknown and uncertainty
- Perfectionism and fear of not doing things "right"
- Imposter syndrome and self-doubt
- Fear of success and increased responsibility

Possible Solutions:
- **Fear of Failure**: Reframe failures as learning opportunities; start with low-risk experiments
- **Relationship Concerns**: Communicate your goals to loved ones and seek their support; find new supportive communities
- **Financial Fears**: Create a safety net plan and make changes gradually while maintaining stability
- **Fear of the Unknown**: Research and plan thoroughly; break changes into smaller, predictable steps
- **Perfectionism**: Set "good enough" standards and celebrate progress over perfection

- **Imposter Syndrome**: Keep a record of accomplishments and positive feedback; seek mentorship
- **Fear of Success**: Visualize positive outcomes and prepare mentally for new responsibilities

Question 5: When have you successfully navigated change in the past, and what helped you succeed?

Former Student Responses:
- Successfully completed school or training programs
- Overcame health challenges or addiction
- Navigated job changes or career transitions
- Moved to new cities or countries
- Ended toxic relationships or started healthy ones
- Developed new skills or hobbies
- Managed financial difficulties

Possible Solutions:
- **Academic Success**: Apply the same study habits and persistence to current goals; break tasks into manageable chunks
- **Health Victories**: Use the same support systems and gradual approach that worked before
- **Career Transitions**: Leverage networking skills and preparation strategies from previous successes
- **Relocation Success**: Apply the same adaptability and openness to new experiences
- **Relationship Changes**: Use the same courage and boundary-setting skills in other areas
- **Skill Development**: Apply the same patience and practice routine to new challenges
- **Financial Recovery**: Use the same budgeting and discipline strategies for other goals

Universal Solutions Across All Questions:
- **Start Small**: Whatever the area of discomfort or change needed, begin with tiny, manageable steps that build momentum without overwhelming your system.

- **Find Your Tribe**: Seek out others who share similar goals or have successfully made the changes you're pursuing.
- **Track Progress**: Keep a simple journal or use apps to monitor your advancement and celebrate small wins.
- **Practice Self-Compassion**: Treat yourself with the same kindness you'd show a good friend facing similar challenges.
- **Focus on Process Over Outcome**: Concentrate on building consistent habits rather than fixating on end results.

Take Action

1. Take 10 minutes to write down your personal definition of success.
2. Identify one small change you can make this week toward your goals.
3. Share your 'why' with someone you trust for additional accountability.
4. Schedule regular check-ins with yourself to assess your progress.
5. Practice reframing fears about change into opportunities for growth.

The secret of change is to focus all of your energy not on fighting the old but on building the new. — **Socrates**

In the next chapter, we'll explore how to develop a practical change strategy using the principles of Kaizen (continuous improvement) and create lasting habits that support your personal growth journey.

Chapter 2 – A Change Strategy

Small Steps, Big Changes: Your Journey Starts Here

Key Insight: Change doesn't have to be a daunting mountain to climb. Instead, imagine it as a series of small steps, each one bringing you closer to your goals. The Kaizen philosophy—continuous improvement—shows us that tiny changes, consistently applied, lead to big results.

Kaizen in Action

Kaizen, the Japanese philosophy of continuous improvement, demonstrates that small, consistent changes over time create significant transformation. Here are examples of Kaizen at work:

- Technology Evolution: The progression from early mobile phones to today's smartphones happened through countless small improvements over time.
- Auto Industry: Japanese car manufacturers used Kaizen to make incremental improvements to production processes, resulting in highly efficient and reliable vehicles.
- Personal Growth: A person who begins reading for 10 minutes a day may eventually develop a lifelong reading habit, greatly expanding their knowledge over time.

Key Insight: In Japanese, "Kai" means change, and "zen" means good. Kaizen is literally "good change" or "improvement." The philosophy emphasizes that small, consistent improvements compound over time, eventually leading to massive transformation.

Kaizen in Personal Change

Rather than overwhelming yourself with massive changes, start with small, manageable steps:

- Instead of trying to lose 50 pounds in three months, start by walking 10 minutes a day.
- Instead of attempting to wake up at 5 AM immediately, shift your wake-up time 15 minutes earlier each week.

- Dedicate 15 minutes a day, five days a week, to work on your goals—whether it's reading, meditating, exercising, or developing a new skill.

Kaizen Progress Chart

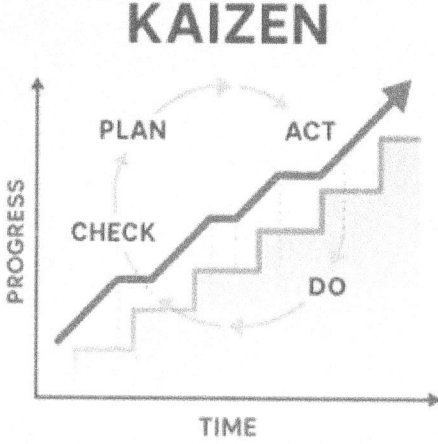

Overcoming Obstacles to Change

Even with a strong 'why' and a commitment to change, you're likely to encounter obstacles along the way. Here are some common challenges and strategies to overcome them:

1. Lack of Time

Many people cite a lack of time as a reason for not making changes. However, it's often more about priorities than actual time constraints.

Strategies:
- Use time-blocking to schedule important activities.
- Eliminate or reduce time-wasting activities.
- Wake up 30 minutes earlier to work on your goals.

2. Fear of Failure

Fear of failure can be paralyzing, preventing us from taking the first step towards change.

Strategies:
- Reframe failure as a learning opportunity.
- Set small, achievable goals to build confidence.
- Celebrate small victories along the way.

Real-Life Example: Thomas Edison made thousands of unsuccessful attempts before inventing a working light bulb. When asked about his failures, he famously said, "I have not failed. I've just found 10,000 ways that won't work." This mindset transformed what others would see as failures into valuable steps toward his ultimate success.

3. Lack of Support

Sometimes, the people around us may not understand or support our desire for change.

Strategies:
- Seek out like-minded individuals or support groups.
- Communicate your goals and reasons for change to loved ones.
- Consider working with a coach or mentor.

4. Overwhelm

The prospect of significant change can feel overwhelming, leading to procrastination or giving up.

Strategies:
- Break big goals into smaller, manageable tasks.
- Focus on one change at a time.
- Use the Kaizen approach of small, continuous improvements.

The Role of Habits in Change

Habits play a crucial role in our ability to create lasting change. Our daily habits, whether good or bad, shape our lives over time.

Understanding Habit Formation

Habits consist of three components:
1. Cue: The trigger that initiates the behavior.
2. Routine: The behavior itself.
3. Reward: The benefit you gain from the behavior.

To create new habits or break old ones, it's helpful to understand and manipulate these components.

Strategies for Habit Change

- Start Small: Begin with tiny habits that are easy to maintain.
- Stack Habits: Attach new habits to existing ones.
- Make It Easy: Remove obstacles to good habits and create barriers to bad ones.

- Track Progress: Use a habit tracker to maintain consistency.
- Be Patient: It takes time for new habits to become automatic.

Key Insight: The goal is progress, not perfection. Small, consistent changes in your habits can lead to significant transformations over time.

Exercise: Habit Stacking

Step	Prompt	Example
1	Identify a new habit you want to establish	"Stretch for 1 minute."
2	Choose an existing habit you already do consistently	"Brushing teeth"
3	Connect them: "After I [current habit], I will [new habit]."	"After I brush my teeth, I will stretch for one minute."
4	Keep the new habit extremely small at first	"Just one stretch."

More Examples
- "After I pour my morning coffee, I will write down three things I'm grateful for."
- "After I sit down for lunch, I will take one deep breath, hold it for four slow counts, and exhale in four short counts."
- "After work, on my way home, I will listen to an audiobook."

Embracing Discomfort for Growth

Change often requires stepping out of your comfort zone. While this can feel uncomfortable, it's in this space of discomfort that real growth occurs.

The Growth Zone Model

The Growth Zone Model typically consists of three main components:

	Comfort Zone: Safe, familiar, and in control. No significant growth or learning.
	Stretch Zone: Initial resistance and fear when stepping out of comfort.
	Anxiety/Panic Zone: Challenges become too intense, leading to stress or overwhelm.
	Growth/Stretch Zone: Just beyond comfort, where you face challenges that stretch your abilities without overwhelming you.

Strategies for Embracing Discomfort

- Start with small challenges and gradually increase difficulty.
- Reframe discomfort as a sign of growth.
- Practice mindfulness to manage anxiety about change.
- Celebrate your courage in facing discomfort.

Every time you step out of your comfort zone, it expands, making future changes easier.

Measuring Progress and Celebrating Success

Tracking your progress and celebrating your successes, no matter how small, is essential for motivation.

Tracking Progress

- Keep a journal to record your experiences and insights.
- Use apps or spreadsheets to track measurable goals.
- Regularly review and reflect on your progress.

Celebrating Success

- Acknowledge small wins along the way.
- Share your achievements with supportive friends or family.
- Reward yourself for reaching milestones.

Warning: Be careful not to use rewards that undermine your goals. For example, if your goal is to eat healthier, don't reward yourself with unhealthy food. Instead, choose rewards that align with or at least don't conflict with your objectives.

Embracing Change as a Way of Life

Change is not just something that happens to us—it's a skill we can develop and a mindset we can cultivate. By understanding the nature of change, redefining success on our own terms, applying the principle of Kaizen, identifying our 'why,' overcoming obstacles, forming positive habits, embracing discomfort, and celebrating our progress, we can harness the power of change to transform our lives.

"Progress is impossible without change, and those who cannot change their minds cannot change anything." — **George Bernard Shaw.**

Chapter Summary

- Small changes can lead to significant transformations when applied consistently.
- Kaizen—the Japanese principle of continuous improvement—provides a framework for sustainable change.
- Common obstacles to change include lack of time, fear of failure, lack of support, and overwhelm.
- Habit formation is essential for creating lasting change.
- Growth happens when we step out of our comfort zone into the "stretch zone."
- Tracking progress and celebrating small wins reinforces positive change.

Reflection Questions

Question 1: What area of your life could benefit from applying the Kaizen principle of small, continuous improvements?

Former Student Responses:
- Health and fitness - wanting to exercise regularly but finding it overwhelming
- Career development - feeling stuck but not knowing where to start
- Financial management - struggling with budgeting and saving money
- Learning new skills - wanting to develop professionally, but lacking time
- Relationships - wanting to improve communication with family or friends

- Organization and productivity - feeling overwhelmed by clutter and poor time management
- Mental health - wanting to reduce stress and anxiety

Possible Solutions:
- **Health and Fitness**: Start with 5-minute daily walks, add one healthy meal per week, or do 2 push-ups each morning
- **Career Development**: Spend 15 minutes daily reading industry articles, update one section of your resume weekly, or network with one new person monthly
- **Financial Management**: Save $1 per day, track expenses for just one category weekly, or read one financial tip daily
- **Skill Learning**: Practice for 10 minutes daily, watch one educational video weekly, or complete one online lesson per week
- **Relationships**: Send one appreciative text daily, practice active listening in one conversation, or have one meaningful check-in weekly
- **Organization**: Declutter one drawer per week, use a simple daily to-do list with just 3 items, or organize one area for 10 minutes daily.

Question 2: Which of the common obstacles to change do you find most challenging, and why?

Former Student Responses:
- **Lack of Time**: "I'm too busy with work and family responsibilities."
- **Fear of Failure**: "What if I try and don't succeed? I'll look foolish."
- **Overwhelm**: "The change seems too big and complicated."
- **Lack of Support**: "Nobody around me understands or encourages my goals."
- **Perfectionism**: "If I can't do it perfectly, why bother starting?"
- **Past Failures**: "I've tried before and failed, so why would this time be different?"
- **Comfort Zone**: "Change feels scary and uncertain."

Possible Solutions:
- **Lack of Time**: Use time-blocking for just 15 minutes daily, wake up 10 minutes earlier, or replace one time-wasting activity with goal-focused action
- **Fear of Failure**: Reframe failure as learning, start with extremely low-risk experiments, or focus on effort rather than outcome
- **Overwhelm**: Break goals into tiny steps, focus on just one change at a time, or use the "2-minute rule" for starting tasks.

- **Lack of Support**: Join online communities, find one accountability partner, or seek professional guidance through books or courses
- **Perfectionism**: Set "good enough" standards, celebrate progress over perfection, or commit to imperfect action
- **Past Failures**: Analyze what you learned from previous attempts, start smaller this time, or change your approach based on past experience
- **Comfort Zone**: Take tiny steps outside the comfort zone, practice gradual exposure, or reframe discomfort as growth

Question 3: What small habit could you start today that would move you toward your larger goals?

Former Student Responses:
- "I want to get healthier, but don't know where to start."
- "I want to advance my career, but feel stuck."
- "I want to improve my relationships, but don't know how."
- "I want to be more organized and productive."
- "I want to learn something new, but I never find time."
- "I want to improve my financial situation."
- "I want to reduce stress and be happier."

Possible Solutions:
- **Health Goals**: Drink one extra glass of water daily, take the stairs instead of the elevator, or do 5 jumping jacks each morning
- **Career Goals**: Read one industry article daily, update LinkedIn weekly, or practice one new skill for 10 minutes daily
- **Relationship Goals**: Give one genuine compliment daily, put phone away during conversations, or ask one thoughtful question per day
- **Organization Goals**: Make bed every morning, clear desk at the end of each day, or use a simple daily planning routine
- **Learning Goals**: Listen to educational podcasts during commute, read for 10 minutes before bed, or watch one tutorial weekly
- **Financial Goals**: Track daily expenses in a simple app, save loose change, or review one financial account weekly
- **Stress Reduction**: Take three deep breaths when stressed, write down one thing you're grateful for daily, or step outside for 5 minutes

Question 4: How comfortable are you with discomfort? When was the last time you deliberately stepped out of your comfort zone?

Former Student Responses:
- "I avoid discomfort at all costs - it's been years since I tried something truly new."
- "I'm somewhat comfortable with small challenges but avoid big risks."
- "I used to take more risks when I was younger, but now I play it safe."
- "I want to be more adventurous but fear judgment from others."
- "I'm comfortable with physical discomfort but struggle with emotional vulnerability."
- "I take professional risks but avoid personal ones."
- "I'm paralyzed by the fear of making the wrong choice."

Possible Solutions:
- **Extreme Comfort Zone Dwellers**: Start with tiny challenges like trying a new food, taking a different route to work, or introducing yourself to one new person
- **Moderate Risk-Takers**: Gradually increase challenge level, set monthly "stretch goals," or join groups that encourage growth
- **Former Risk-Takers**: Reflect on what changed, start with familiar but slightly challenging activities, or reconnect with your adventurous side through small steps
- **Fear of Judgment**: Practice self-compassion, remember most people are focused on themselves, or start with anonymous challenges
- **Selective Comfort**: Identify why certain areas feel safer, apply successful strategies from comfortable areas to challenging ones, or work with a coach
- **Professional vs. Personal**: Recognize the skills transfer between domains, apply professional confidence to personal growth, or start with low-stakes personal challenges
- **Decision Paralysis**: Practice making small decisions quickly, set decision deadlines, or use the "good enough" principle

Question 5: How might you effectively track progress toward your current goals?

Former Student Responses:
- "I've tried tracking before, but I always give up after a few days."
- "I'm not sure what metrics to use for my goals."
- "I prefer simple methods, but don't know what works best."
- "I get obsessed with tracking, and it becomes counterproductive."
- "I forgot to track consistently."

- "I don't know how often I should review my progress."
- "I want accountability, but don't know how to set it up."

Possible Solutions:
- **Tracking Dropouts**: Use extremely simple systems (one number daily), set phone reminders, or link tracking to existing habits
- **Metric Confusion**: Focus on input metrics (actions taken) rather than just outcomes, use both quantitative and qualitative measures, or start with one simple metric
- **Simplicity Seekers**: Use basic tools like paper calendars, simple phone apps, or photo progress journals
- **Over-Trackers**: Limit to 1-3 key metrics, track weekly instead of daily, or focus on trends rather than daily fluctuations
- **Forgetful Trackers**: Set consistent daily alarms, use habit stacking (track after existing routine), or place visual reminders in obvious places
- **Review Frequency Uncertainty**: Start with weekly reviews, schedule specific review times, or use monthly deeper assessments with weekly check-ins
- **Accountability Seekers**: Find one reliable accountability partner, join online communities, or use apps with social features

Universal Solutions Across All Chapter 2 Questions:
- **Start Ridiculously Small**: Whatever the challenge, begin with steps so small they seem almost trivial - this builds momentum without triggering resistance.
- **Use Habit Stacking**: Attach new behaviors to existing strong habits to increase consistency and reduce mental load.
- **Focus on Systems Over Goals**: Build processes and routines that naturally lead to desired outcomes rather than fixating on end results.
- **Embrace the Growth Zone**: Seek challenges that stretch you without overwhelming you, just outside your comfort zone, but not in panic territory.
- **Track Leading Indicators**: Monitor the actions you take (inputs) rather than just the results you achieve (outputs) for better motivation.
- **Celebrate Small Wins**: Acknowledge and reward progress regularly to maintain motivation and reinforce positive behavior patterns.
- **Prepare for Setbacks**: Expect obstacles and have specific plans for getting back on track when you inevitably face challenges.

- **Find Your Tribe**: Connect with others who share similar goals or have successfully made the changes you're pursuing for support and inspiration.

Take Action

1. Choose one small change to implement this week (so small it seems almost too easy).
2. Identify a current habit you can "stack" a new positive habit onto.
3. Create a simple tracking system for your new habit.
4. Schedule regular check-ins to review your progress.
5. Plan appropriate rewards for reaching your milestones.

"The journey of a thousand miles begins with a single step." — **Lao Tzu.**

In the next chapter, we'll explore how to effect permanent change by replacing negative patterns with positive alternatives and finding support systems to help you succeed in your transformation journey.

Chapter 3 – How to Effect Permanent Change

Reframe, Replace, Renew: The Power of Positive Habits

Key Insight: Lasting change is not about willpower alone. It's about replacing old patterns with new, supportive ones, reframing your thinking, and building a network that sustains your transformation.

Overcoming the Overwhelm of Change

Change can feel overwhelming, especially if you try to tackle too much at once. Our brains are naturally resistant to change because familiar patterns require less energy. When we attempt too many changes at once, our brain's "alarm system" activates, creating feelings of overwhelm.

Key Insight: Breaking change into small, manageable steps keeps us below this threshold, allowing progress without triggering resistance.

Eliminate the Negative: Replacing Bad Habits with Good Ones

Simply removing a negative habit creates a void. Nature abhors a vacuum, and your mind is no different. The most effective strategy is to replace negative habits with positive alternatives.

Examples:'
- Instead of "I won't eat junk food," say, "I'll eat fruit instead of junk food."
- If you want to stop watching TV late at night, replace it with reading or listening to calming music.

This approach addresses the same trigger but with a healthier response.

How to Reframe Negative Thinking

Negative self-talk is a common barrier to permanent change. Here's how to reframe it:

1. Identify the negative thought pattern.
2. Challenge its accuracy and helpfulness.
3. Create a more realistic and positive alternative.
4. Practice the new thought consistently.

Example:
- Old Thought: "I always mess up presentations."
- New Thought: "I can improve my presentation skills with practice and preparation."

Exercise: Thought Reframing
- Step 1: Write down three negative thoughts you frequently have about yourself.
- Step 2: For each, ask: Is it completely true? Is it helpful? What evidence contradicts this thought?
- Step 3: Create a more balanced, realistic alternative.
- Step 4: Practice saying these new thoughts whenever the old ones appear.

You Are Not Alone: Finding Support in Your Journey

You don't have to go through the process of change alone. There are numerous resources and support systems available to help you.

The Power of Community
Every month, thousands search for help with self-development. This means:
- Someone has experienced the very issue you want to change.
- Someone has studied the science behind it.
- Someone has written helpful tips and created tools to assist you.

Finding Support
- Seek out an accountability partner to check in with regularly.
- Join online communities focused on personal growth.
- Consider working with a professional coach or therapist.
- Use self-help books, blogs, and podcasts.

The Power of Accountability: Research shows you have a 95% chance of completing a goal if you have a specific accountability appointment with someone you've committed to.

Types of Support
- Informational Support: Resources that provide knowledge and guidance.
- Emotional Support: People who offer encouragement and understanding.
- Tangible Support: Practical assistance with specific tasks.
- Accountability Support: Someone who holds you to your commitments.

Warning: Not everyone in your life will support your desire to change. Some may feel threatened by your growth. Look beyond your immediate circle if needed.

Strategies for Specific Types of Change

Health and Fitness Changes
- Start with baseline measurements to track progress.
- Focus on consistency rather than intensity.
- Build a supportive environment (e.g., healthy food at home).
- Use visual reminders of your goals.

Financial Habits
- Automate positive financial behaviors when possible.
- Create systems that make saving easier than spending.
- Track expenses to increase awareness.
- Celebrate financial milestones appropriately.

Relationship Improvements
- Begin with self-awareness about your patterns.
- Practice active listening and empathy.
- Start with small positive interactions.
- Focus on changing your behavior, not your partner's.

Career Development
- Break larger goals into smaller skill-building activities.
- Seek mentors who have achieved what you aspire to.
- Create a learning routine that fits your schedule.
- Document progress to stay motivated during plateaus.

The Role of Self-Compassion in Change

One often overlooked aspect of successful, permanent change is self-compassion. Being kind to yourself during the process makes you more likely to persist through challenges.

Why Self-Compassion Matters
- Reduces the shame and negative emotions that can derail progress.

- Helps you bounce back from inevitable setbacks.
- Creates a positive emotional environment for growth.
- Builds resilience for the long-term journey.

Exercise: Self-Compassion Practice
- Step 1: Mindfulness – Acknowledge your feelings without judgment ("I notice I'm feeling disappointed about missing my workout today.")
- Step 2: Common Humanity – Recognize you're not alone ("Many people struggle with consistency when building new habits. This is normal.")
- Step 3: Self-Kindness – Speak to yourself with encouragement ("It's okay. One missed day doesn't erase my progress. I can get back on track tomorrow.") Practice this response whenever you face challenges in your change journey.

Chapter Summary

1. Change becomes less overwhelming when approached in small, manageable steps.
2. Replacing negative habits with positive alternatives is more effective than elimination alone.
3. Reframing negative self-talk creates a more supportive internal environment for change.
4. Support systems dramatically increase the likelihood of successful, permanent change.
5. Different types of changes may require specific strategies and approaches.
6. Self-compassion is a crucial but often overlooked component of lasting transformation.

Reflection Questions

Question 1: What negative habit would you like to replace with a positive one?

Former Student Responses:
- "I constantly check social media and waste hours scrolling mindlessly."
- "I eat junk food when I'm stressed or bored."
- "I procrastinate on important tasks until the last minute."

- "I stay up too late watching TV or browsing my phone."
- "I complain and focus on negative aspects of situations."
- "I avoid difficult conversations and let problems build up."
- "I spend money impulsively on things I don't really need."

Possible Solutions:
- **Social Media Addiction**: Replace mindless scrolling with reading for 10 minutes, taking a short walk, or practicing deep breathing exercises
- **Stress Eating**: When stressed, drink a glass of water first, then eat a piece of fruit or take five deep breaths before choosing food
- **Procrastination**: Use the "2-minute rule" - if something takes less than 2 minutes, do it immediately; for larger tasks, commit to working for just 15 minutes
- **Poor Sleep Habits**: Replace late-night screen time with reading a physical book, journaling, or gentle stretching
- **Negative Focus**: When catching yourself complaining, immediately identify one thing you're grateful for in that moment
- **Conflict Avoidance**: Practice having one small, honest conversation per week about minor issues before they become major problems
- **Impulse Spending**: Before any non-essential purchase, wait 24 hours and write down three reasons why you need it

Question 2: What recurring negative thoughts undermine your confidence and progress?

Former Student Responses:
- "I'm not smart enough to succeed in my career goals."
- "Everyone else has it figured out except me."
- "I always mess things up when it matters most."
- "People will discover I'm a fraud and don't deserve my success."
- "I'm too old/young to make significant changes in my life."
- "I don't have enough willpower to stick with anything."
- "Bad things always happen to me - I have terrible luck."

Possible Solutions:
- **Intelligence Doubts**: Reframe to "I'm capable of learning and growing in my field," and keep a record of problems you've solved and skills you've developed

- **Comparison Trap**: Remember that everyone struggles privately; focus on your own progress rather than others' highlight reels
- **Perfectionism**: Reframe mistakes as learning opportunities; create a "lessons learned" journal to track growth from setbacks
- **Imposter Syndrome**: Keep a "wins folder" with positive feedback, accomplishments, and evidence of your competence
- **Age Limitations**: Research examples of people who made major changes at your age or older; focus on the advantages your life stage brings
- **Willpower Beliefs**: Replace with "I can build habits gradually" and start with tiny changes that require minimal willpower
- **Victim Mentality**: Practice identifying one thing you can control in each challenging situation; focus on your response rather than the circumstances

Question 3: Who in your current circle could support your change journey? Who might resist your changes?

Former Student Responses:
- **Potential Supporters**: "My spouse is always encouraging," "My best friend has similar goals," "My mentor at work believes in personal growth."
- **Potential Resisters**: "My family thinks I'm fine as I am and don't understand why I want to change," "Some friends might feel threatened if I improve myself," "My coworkers are comfortable with the status quo."
- **Mixed Responses**: "I'm not sure who would support me - I haven't talked about my goals with anyone," "I think people care about me but might not understand my specific changes."

Possible Solutions:
- **Identifying Supporters**: Reach out to one person who has shown interest in personal growth; share your goals with someone who has been encouraging in the past; join online communities or local groups focused on your area of change
- **Managing Resisters**: Communicate your goals clearly and explain how the changes will benefit your relationships; set boundaries with people who consistently discourage your growth; find new supportive relationships to balance negative influences
- **Building Your Support Network**: Start conversations about personal growth to identify like-minded people; be a supportive friend to others working on changes; consider hiring a coach or joining a mastermind group.

- **Dealing with Family Resistance**: Help family understand that your growth benefits everyone; involve them in appropriate ways; reassure them that changing yourself doesn't mean rejecting them

Question 4: What external resources (books, courses, communities) might help you with your specific goals?

Former Student Responses:
- "I want to improve my health, but don't know where to start with reliable information."
- "I need to develop better communication skills for my career."
- "I want to learn about personal finance and investing."
- "I struggle with anxiety and need practical coping strategies."
- "I want to start a side business, but I lack business knowledge."
- "I need help with time management and productivity."
- "I want to improve my relationships and social skills."

Possible Solutions:
- **Health Goals**: Start with reputable sources like Mayo Clinic or Harvard Health; consider apps like MyFitnessPal for tracking; join local walking groups or fitness classes
- **Communication Skills**: Read books like "Crucial Conversations" or "How to Win Friends and Influence People"; join Toastmasters International; take online courses through platforms like Coursera
- **Financial Education**: Use free resources like Khan Academy's personal finance course; read "The Total Money Makeover" or "The Simple Path to Wealth"; follow reputable financial educators on YouTube
- **Anxiety Management**: Try apps like Headspace or Calm; read "The Anxiety and Worry Workbook"; consider online therapy platforms like BetterHelp
- **Business Development**: Take advantage of free resources from SCORE mentors; read "The Lean Startup"; join local entrepreneur meetups or online communities
- **Productivity**: Read "Getting Things Done" or "Atomic Habits"; use apps like Todoist or Notion; follow productivity experts like Cal Newport.
- **Social Skills**: Read "The Like Switch" or "Never Eat Alone"; practice in low-stakes social situations; join clubs or volunteer organizations

Question 5: How do you typically respond to setbacks? How could you be more self-compassionate?

Former Student Responses:
- "I beat myself up and tell myself I'm a failure when things go wrong."
- "I give up completely after one mistake and think 'what's the point?'"
- "I get angry and blame other people or circumstances."
- "I feel ashamed and hide from people when I mess up."
- "I catastrophize and think one setback means I'll never succeed."
- "I compare myself to others and feel even worse about my situation."
- "I pretend everything is fine and don't acknowledge the setback."

Possible Solutions:
- **Self-Criticism**: Practice talking to yourself like you would to a good friend; write yourself a compassionate letter after a setback; use phrases like "This is difficult right now, and that's okay."
- **All-or-Nothing Thinking**: Reframe setbacks as data points, not verdicts; create a comeback plan before you need it; remember that progress isn't linear
- **Blame and Anger**: Take responsibility for what you can control while accepting what you can't; use setbacks as opportunities to problem-solve rather than assign fault
- **Shame and Hiding**: Share your struggles with trusted friends; remember that everyone faces setbacks; practice vulnerability in small, safe ways
- **Catastrophizing**: Challenge extreme thoughts by asking, "Will this matter in 5 years?"; focus on what you can learn from the experience; keep perspective on the bigger picture
- **Comparison**: Remember that you only see others' highlight reels; focus on your own progress over time; celebrate small wins regularly
- **Denial**: Acknowledge setbacks honestly without judgment; treat them as information about what needs adjustment; create a simple process for reviewing and learning from challenges

Universal Solutions Across All Chapter 3 Questions:
- **Practice the 3-Step Self-Compassion Response**: When facing setbacks, practice mindfulness (acknowledge what happened), common humanity (remember others face similar challenges), and self-kindness (speak to yourself with care).

- **Create Replacement Strategies**: For every negative habit or thought pattern you want to eliminate, have a specific positive alternative ready to implement immediately.
- **Build Your Support Ecosystem**: Actively cultivate relationships with people who support your growth while setting boundaries with those who don't.
- **Develop a Learning Mindset**: View every setback as valuable information about what works and what doesn't, rather than evidence of personal failure.
- **Start Small and Stack Success**: Begin with tiny changes that are almost impossible to fail at, then build momentum through consistent small wins.
- **Plan for Obstacles**: Anticipate likely challenges and have specific strategies ready, so you're not caught off-guard when difficulties arise.
- **Celebrate Progress**: Acknowledge and reward yourself for effort and progress, not just outcomes, to maintain motivation during the change process.

Take Action

- Identify one negative habit to replace with a positive one this week.
- Practice reframing one negative thought into a positive statement daily.
- Reach out to one person who could provide accountability or support.
- Research one online community, book, or resource related to your change goal.
- Write a self-compassionate response to use when you face inevitable setbacks.

"Never doubt that a small group of thoughtful, committed citizens can change the world; indeed, it is the only thing that ever has." – ***Margaret Mead.***

In the next chapter, we'll explore the crucial role that self-talk plays in personal transformation. You'll learn how to master the conversation in your mind to create a supportive internal environment for lasting change.

Chapter 4 – Mastering The Art Of Self-Talk

Change Your Words, Change Your World

Key Insight: The way you talk to yourself shapes your reality. Self-talk is not just background noise; it is the script that directs your emotions, your actions, and, ultimately, your outcomes.

Understanding and Reframing Self-Talk

Self-talk is the ongoing internal dialogue that runs through your mind at all times. At an astonishing rate—up to 1,300 words per minute—your self-talk shapes your perceptions, emotions, and behaviors. Most of us are unaware of the sheer volume and power of this inner conversation.

Self-talk is as essential as breathing. It is automatic, constant, and deeply influential. The quality of your self-talk determines the quality of your life.

Key Insight: Your mind processes images 60,000 times faster than words. This is why your self-talk creates mental pictures that influence your emotions almost immediately. When you change your self-talk, you change the mental imagery that drives your emotional responses and behaviors.

The Nature of Self-Talk

Self-talk, the constant stream of thoughts running through our minds, often tends to skew toward negativity. Many individuals, like Job in the Bible, find themselves trapped in a cycle of self-condemnation, where every thought seems to reinforce negative beliefs about oneself. Job 9:20 states, "Everything I say seems to condemn me."

This tendency to be our own harshest critics can manifest in various forms of negative self-talk, including:

- Self-Criticism: Constantly evaluating and judging one's actions and choices, leading to feelings of inadequacy and low self-esteem.
- Catastrophizing: Automatically assuming the worst possible outcome in any situation, resulting in excessive worry and anxiety.
- Perfectionism: Setting impossibly high standards and being overly critical of one's performance, leading to chronic stress and dissatisfaction.

- Personalization: Taking responsibility for external events beyond one's control, leading to undue self-blame and guilt.

The Impact of Negative Self-Talk

The consequences of persistent negative self-talk can be far-reaching and detrimental to one's mental health and overall well-being. Some of the most significant impacts include:

- Low Self-Esteem: Continuous self-criticism perpetuates a cycle of self-doubt, making it challenging to recognize one's worth and potential.
- Anxiety and Depression: Catastrophizing and persistent self-judgment can contribute to the development of anxiety disorders and depression.
- Relationship Struggles: Negative self-talk often spills over into interactions with others, affecting personal and professional relationships.
- Decreased Productivity: Self-doubt and perfectionism can hinder focus and the achievement of goals.
- Physical Health Consequences: Chronic stress resulting from negative self-talk can lead to sleep disturbances, digestive issues, and even cardiovascular problems.

Warning: Research has shown that the average person has between 12,000 and 60,000 thoughts per day, and up to 80% of these thoughts may be negative in people with high levels of negative self-talk. This continuous stream of negativity creates a significant mental and emotional burden that affects every aspect of life.

Reframing Negative Self-Talk

Recognizing the power of our internal dialogue is the first step toward positive change. The Bible offers guidance in this area, encouraging us to:

> *"Fix your thoughts on what is true and good and right. Think about all you can thank God for and be glad about it. — **Philippians 4:8 (TLB)***

This principle of replacement aligns with modern psychological approaches to reframing negative self-talk.

Techniques for Reframing Self-Talk

Self-Compassion and Understanding
- Treat yourself with the same kindness and empathy you would offer a friend facing challenges.
- Acknowledge that making mistakes is part of being human.
- Use gentle, supportive language when addressing yourself.

Exercise: The Self-Compassion Letter

- Step 1: Think of a situation where you've been particularly hard on yourself.
- Step 2: Imagine a friend coming to you with exactly the same issue.
- Step 3: Write a letter to yourself from the perspective of this kind, understanding friend.
- Step 4: Note the tone and words you use when writing to yourself as a friend.
- Step 5: Practice using this same compassionate tone in your daily self-talk.

Identifying Negative Thought Patterns

- Become aware of your typical negative thoughts and triggers that set them off.
- Notice when and where these thoughts occur most frequently.
- Pay attention to the specific language you use internally.

Challenging Negative Thoughts

- Question the validity of your self-talk: Is this thought 100% true, or is it based on an assumption?
- Look for evidence that contradicts your negative thoughts.
- Consider alternative explanations or perspectives.

Example: The ABCD Method

Step	Description	Example
A	Activating Event	You make a mistake during a presentation
B	Belief/Thought	"I'm so stupid. Everyone thinks I'm incompetent now."
C	Consequence	Feelings of shame, embarrassment, and anxiety
D	Dispute	"Everyone makes mistakes occasionally. One error doesn't define my competence. Most people probably didn't even notice or will soon forget."

Positive Affirmations

- Replace negative thoughts with realistic, positive statements about yourself.
- Create affirmations that are believable and specific.
- Repeat them regularly, especially when negative thoughts arise.

Mindfulness
- Practice being present in the moment, observing your thoughts without judgment.
- Notice thoughts as they arise, but don't attach to them.
- Label negative thoughts as "just thoughts," not facts.

Cognitive Behavioral Therapy (CBT)
- This therapeutic approach helps in identifying and modifying negative thought patterns.
- Learn to recognize cognitive distortions (e.g., black-and-white thinking, overgeneralization).
- Work with a professional to develop personalized strategies.

The Power of Positive Self-Talk
Cultivating positive self-talk leads to numerous benefits:

- Enhanced Self-Confidence: A more realistic and compassionate self-view boosts self-esteem.
- Improved Mental Health: Reducing negative self-talk alleviates symptoms of anxiety and depression.
- Increased Problem-Solving Skills: A positive mindset enhances creativity and resilience in facing challenges.
- Better Physical Health: Positive thinking is associated with improved cardiovascular health and overall well-being.

Practical Applications of Positive Self-Talk

In Goal Achievement
- Use encouraging self-talk when facing challenges.
- Create a personalized mantra for difficult moments.
- Celebrate small wins with affirming self-talk.

In Relationships
- Positive self-talk improves how you interact with others.
- Self-compassion helps you extend compassion to others.
- Healthy internal dialogue reduces the projection of insecurities.

In Stress Management
- Supportive self-talk can calm your nervous system.
- Reframe stressors as challenges rather than threats.
- Use self-talk to activate problem-solving rather than rumination.

Exercise: Creating a Self-Talk Toolkit

- Step 1: Identify 3–5 situations where negative self-talk is most common for you.
- Step 2: For each situation, create 2–3 positive, realistic statements to counter the negative thoughts.
- Step 3: Write these statements on small cards or save them on your phone.
- Step 4: Review these statements regularly, especially before entering triggering situations.
- Step 5: After using a statement, note its effectiveness and refine it as needed.

Example:

Situation: Before giving a presentation.

Negative thought: "I'm going to mess up, and everyone will judge me."

Replacement statements:
- "I've prepared well and know my material."
- "Even if I make a mistake, I can recover gracefully."
- "My worth isn't determined by a perfect performance."

Chapter Summary

- Self-talk shapes your perceptions, emotions, and actions at a rate of 1,300 words per minute.
- Negative self-talk patterns include self-criticism, catastrophizing, perfectionism, and personalization.
- The impact of negative self-talk extends to mental health, relationships, productivity, and physical well-being.
- Reframing techniques include self-compassion, challenging thoughts, positive affirmations, and mindfulness.
- Positive self-talk benefits include enhanced confidence, improved mental health, better problem-solving, and physical well-being.

- Practical applications extend to goal achievement, relationships, and stress management.

Reflection Questions

Question 1: What are the most common negative thoughts you have about yourself?

<u>Former Student Responses:</u>
- "I'm not smart enough to succeed in my career or achieve my goals."
- "I always mess things up when it really matters."
- "I'm too lazy and lack the discipline to stick with anything."
- "Everyone else has their life figured out except me."
- "I'm not attractive/talented/worthy enough to deserve good things."
- "I'm a failure because I haven't accomplished what I thought I would by now."
- "People will discover I'm a fraud and don't really know what I'm doing."

<u>Possible Solutions:</u>
- **Intelligence Doubts**: Keep a "learning log" of new skills acquired and problems solved; reframe to "I'm capable of learning and growing"; focus on effort and progress rather than innate ability
- **Perfectionism**: Create a "lessons learned" journal; practice the "good enough" principle; celebrate attempts and progress, not just perfect outcomes
- **Discipline Concerns**: Start with tiny habits that require minimal willpower; track small wins; reframe as "I'm building my discipline muscle gradually."
- **Comparison Trap**: Limit social media exposure; keep a personal progress journal; remember that everyone struggles privately
- **Self-Worth Issues**: Write down three things you're grateful for about yourself daily; ask trusted friends what they value about you; practice self-compassion exercises
- **Achievement Pressure**: Redefine success based on your values, not external timelines; celebrate non-traditional accomplishments; focus on your unique journey
- **Imposter Syndrome**: Keep a "wins folder" with positive feedback and accomplishments; remember that competent people often feel this way; seek mentorship

Question 2: How have these thoughts impacted your confidence, relationships, and goals?

<u>Former Student Responses:</u>
- "I avoid taking on new challenges at work because I'm afraid I'll fail."
- "I don't speak up in meetings or social situations because I think my ideas aren't good enough."
- "I procrastinate on important goals because I'm convinced I'll mess them up anyway."
- "I push people away or don't form deep relationships because I think they'll eventually reject me."
- "I settle for less than I want because I don't believe I deserve better."
- "I give up on goals quickly when I face the first obstacle."
- "I constantly seek validation from others instead of trusting my own judgment."

<u>Possible Solutions:</u>
- **Avoidance Behaviors**: Start with low-risk challenges; break big tasks into smaller, manageable steps; practice the "2-minute rule" for getting started
- **Social Withdrawal**: Practice one small act of participation daily; prepare conversation starters; focus on being curious about others rather than self-focused
- **Procrastination**: Use implementation intentions ("When X happens, I will do Y"); set up accountability systems; focus on starting rather than finishing
- **Relationship Sabotage**: Practice vulnerability in small, safe ways; communicate your fears to trusted people; work on self-acceptance to reduce the need for external validation
- **Settling**: Identify your core values and non-negotiables; practice asking for what you want in low-stakes situations; build evidence of your worthiness through small achievements
- **Quick Abandonment**: Expect obstacles and plan for them; reframe setbacks as information, not verdicts; create comeback strategies before you need them
- **Validation Seeking**: Practice making decisions without consulting others; keep a decision journal to track your judgment accuracy; build internal validation through self-reflection

Question 3: What would happen if you challenged and reworded those thoughts to be more positive and supportive?

Former Student Responses:
- "I think I'd feel more confident to try new things, but I'm not sure I'd believe the positive thoughts."
- "It might help me take more risks and pursue opportunities I've been avoiding."
- "I'd probably be less anxious and stressed about making mistakes."
- "I might have better relationships because I wouldn't be so defensive or needy."
- "I could focus more on my goals instead of getting stuck in negative spirals."
- "I'd probably be kinder to other people, too, not just myself."
- "I'm worried it would make me overconfident or unrealistic about my abilities."

Possible Solutions:
- **Believability Concerns**: Start with neutral thoughts rather than extremely positive ones; use evidence-based reframes; practice gradual belief building through small experiments
- **Risk-Taking**: Create a "courage ladder" with progressively challenging actions; celebrate attempts regardless of outcomes; reframe failure as valuable data
- **Anxiety Reduction**: Practice thought-stopping techniques; use breathing exercises when negative thoughts arise; develop a toolkit of calming self-talk phrases
- **Relationship Improvement**: Practice giving compliments and positive feedback to others; work on active listening; focus on what you can give rather than what you need
- **Goal Focus**: Use positive self-talk as fuel for action, not replacement for it; create vision boards with supportive affirmations; practice daily goal-oriented self-talk
- **Compassion Transfer**: Notice how self-compassion naturally extends to others; practice loving-kindness meditation; volunteer or help others to reinforce a positive self-view
- **Overconfidence Fears**: Balance positive self-talk with realistic assessment; focus on a growth mindset rather than fixed abilities; maintain humility while building confidence

Question 4: What affirmations can you use to replace negative beliefs about yourself?

Former Student Responses:
- "I want to replace 'I'm not smart enough' but 'I'm brilliant' doesn't feel true."
- "I need something for when I'm feeling overwhelmed and want to give up."
- "I want to stop calling myself lazy and unmotivated."
- "I need affirmations for when I'm comparing myself to others."

- "I want to feel more confident in social situations."
- "I need something to help me believe I deserve good things."
- "I want affirmations that help me bounce back from setbacks."

Possible Solutions:
- **Intelligence Affirmations**: "I am capable of learning and growing"; "I have solved problems before and can do it again"; "My worth isn't determined by my intelligence alone"
- **Overwhelm Affirmations**: "I can handle this one step at a time"; "I have overcome challenges before"; "It's okay to rest and then continue"
- **Motivation Affirmations**: "I am building my discipline through small actions"; "I choose to take one small step forward"; "My past doesn't define my future actions"
- **Comparison Affirmations**: "I am on my own unique journey"; "Everyone has struggles I can't see"; "My progress matters, regardless of others' achievements"
- **Social Confidence Affirmations**: "I have valuable perspectives to share,"; "I belong in this conversation,"; "People appreciate my authentic self."
- **Self-Worth Affirmations**: "I deserve love and respect, including from myself"; "I am worthy of good things simply because I exist"; "I treat myself with the same kindness I show others"
- **Resilience Affirmations**: "Setbacks are temporary and informative"; "I am stronger than my challenges"; "Every obstacle teaches me something valuable"

Question 5: How can you incorporate mindfulness and self-compassion into your daily routine?

Former Student Responses:
- "I'm always rushing and never take time to check in with myself."
- "I notice my negative thoughts, but don't know how to respond to them differently."
- "I'm very self-critical and don't know how to be gentler with myself."
- "I want to be more present, but my mind is always racing."
- "I feel guilty when I try to be kind to myself, like I'm being self-indulgent."
- "I don't have time for long meditation sessions."
- "I want to stop the constant mental chatter and criticism."

Possible Solutions:

- **Rushing Lifestyle**: Set three daily "mindfulness bells" (phone alarms) for 30-second check-ins; practice mindful transitions between activities; use routine activities (brushing teeth, washing dishes) as mindfulness anchors
- **Thought Response**: Practice the STOP technique (Stop, Take a breath, Observe thoughts, Proceed mindfully); label thoughts as "thinking" without judgment; use the "friend test" (would I say this to a good friend?)
- **Self-Criticism**: Write yourself a compassionate letter after difficult days; practice the self-compassion break (mindfulness, common humanity, self-kindness); speak to yourself using your own name for more objectivity
- **Racing Mind**: Try the 4-7-8 breathing technique; practice single-tasking; use guided meditations for beginners; focus on physical sensations to anchor attention
- **Self-Kindness Guilt**: Reframe self-compassion as fuel for helping others; remember that self-criticism doesn't motivate positive change; practice treating yourself as you would a beloved friend
- **Time Constraints**: Use micro-meditations (1-3 minutes); practice mindful breathing during daily activities; try walking meditation; use apps for short guided sessions
- **Mental Chatter**: Practice the "noting" technique (simply noting "thinking" when the mind wanders); try loving-kindness meditation; use mantras or positive phrases to redirect attention

Universal Solutions Across All Chapter 4 Questions:
- **Create a Self-Talk Toolkit**: Develop a collection of realistic, positive statements for different situations and practice them regularly until they become automatic.
- **Practice the 3-Step Self-Compassion Response**: When facing difficulties, practice mindfulness (acknowledge what's happening), common humanity (remember others face similar challenges), and self-kindness (speak to yourself with care).
- **Use Evidence-Based Reframing**: Challenge negative thoughts by looking for evidence that contradicts them and developing more balanced, realistic perspectives.
- **Start Small with Mindfulness**: Begin with just 1-2 minutes of daily mindfulness practice and gradually increase as the habit becomes established.
- **Track Your Progress**: Keep a simple journal noting negative thought patterns and your efforts to reframe them, celebrating small improvements in self-talk.
- **Build a Support Network**: Share your self-talk goals with trusted friends who can gently remind you to be kinder to yourself when they notice self-criticism.

- **Practice Patience**: Remember that changing ingrained thought patterns takes time and consistent effort - be patient with yourself as you develop new mental habits.
- **Focus on Progress, Not Perfection**: Celebrate any movement toward more positive self-talk rather than expecting immediate transformation.

Take Action

- Track your self-talk for 24 hours—write down recurring negative thoughts.
- Identify and challenge one negative belief you've been telling yourself.
- Write and repeat three affirmations that align with your goals and strengths.
- Practice speaking kindly to yourself, as you would to a friend.
- Commit to replacing negativity with encouragement for the next week.

*"Watch your thoughts, they become your words; watch your words, they become your actions; watch your actions, they become your habits; watch your habits, they become your character; watch your character, it becomes your destiny. — **Lao Tzu**.*

In the next chapter, you'll explore the essential foundation to lasting change: understanding yourself. You'll learn how to recognize your unique personality traits, strengths, and tendencies as the basis for authentic personal growth.

Chapter 5 – Know Thyself

Self-Awareness: The Foundation of Growth

Key Insight: Self-knowledge is the foundation of all lasting change. When you know your strengths, values, motivations, and patterns, you can create a growth plan that truly fits you and is far more likely to succeed.

The Importance of Self-Knowledge

Self-knowledge is not just about knowing your likes and dislikes but understanding the deeper aspects of your personality, motivations, and innate tendencies. This understanding:

- Is the first step to true wisdom (as Socrates said)
- Forms the basis for self-improvement as you identify areas for growth that align with your true self
- Helps you accept yourself while still striving for change
- Allows you to recognize patterns in your behavior and thoughts
- Helps you understand others better

Key Insight: Trying to change without self-knowledge is like navigating an unfamiliar city without a map. You might make progress, but you'll likely take many wrong turns along the way.

You're More Than Just Labels

We often introduce ourselves with labels: "I'm a doctor," "I'm a parent," "I'm an artist." While these are part of our identity, they don't tell the whole story. Your true identity is a complex interplay of:

- Genetic attributes
- Acquired beliefs and desires
- Personal experiences
- Core values

Understanding the difference between your social identity (the face you present to the world) and your personal identity (your true self) is crucial. Balancing these identities is key to living authentically and making changes that resonate with who you are.

The Power of Self-Acceptance

Before you can effectively change, you must first accept yourself as you are. This doesn't mean resignation from your flaws, but acknowledging them without judgment.

> *"Beyond a wholesome discipline, be gentle with yourself. You are a child of the universe, no less than the trees and the stars; you have a right to be here."* — **Max Ehrmann, Desiderata.**

Self-acceptance allows you to approach change from a place of self-love rather than self-criticism. It's about recognizing that you are worthy and valuable as you are while still giving yourself permission to grow.

The Paradox of Change

> *"The curious paradox is that when I accept myself just as I am, then I can change."* — **Psychologist Carl Rogers**:

Research shows that people who practice self-acceptance are more likely to make positive changes than those who are harshly self-critical. Self-acceptance reduces fear of failure, creates psychological safety for trying new things, and allows you to see yourself clearly.

Understanding Your Personality Traits

Personality tests can provide valuable insights into your tendencies and motivations. While they shouldn't be seen as definitive, they offer a starting point for self-reflection.

Common Personality Frameworks

The Color Code Test
- Red (Power): Motivated by leadership and productivity

- Blue (Intimacy): Driven by relationships and authenticity
- White (Peace): Seek harmony and independence
- Yellow (Fun): Crave excitement and social connections

Free test: colorcode.com/free-personality-test

Myers-Briggs Type Indicator (MBTI)
- Extraversion (E) Vs. Introversion (I)
- Sensing (S) vs. Intuition (N)
- Thinking (T) vs. Feeling (F)
- Judging (J) vs. Perceiving (P)

Free test: 16personalities.com

The Big Five (OCEAN)
- Openness
- Conscientiousness
- Extraversion
- Agreeableness
- Neuroticism

Free test: truity.com/test/big-five-personality-test

The Holland Career Code
- Realistic
- Investigative
- Artistic
- Social
- Enterprising
- Conventional

Free test: truity.com/test/holland-code-career-test

Warning: Personality tests are tools for self-reflection, not rigid boxes. Most people are a blend of types, and your type may evolve over time. Use the results as insight, not limitation.

Discovering Your Talents

Often, our talents are so natural to us that we don't recognize them as special abilities.

To uncover your talents:
- Practice mindful observation of your daily activities
- Notice what brings you joy and satisfaction
- Pay attention to tasks that come easily to you
- Ask friends and family what they admire about you

Talents can include things like:
- Making people feel at ease
- Solving complex problems
- Organizing information
- Mediating conflicts

Exercise: Talent Identification
- Step 1: Make a list of 10 activities you enjoy.
- Step 2: For each, rate (1–10) how naturally it comes to you.
- Step 3: Note which activities make you lose track of time.
- Step 4: Ask 3–5 people who know you well what they think you're especially good at.
- Step 5: Look for patterns in these responses to identify your natural talents.

Experimenting and Testing

Sometimes, the best way to discover your talents and preferences is through experimentation:

- Try new hobbies or activities
- Take on different roles at work or in volunteer organizations
- Seek feedback from others

The goal is not to be perfect at everything but to find activities that resonate and bring out your best qualities.

Envisioning Your Ideal Life

With a deeper understanding of your personality and talents, envision your ideal life. This is like creating a "bucket list" focused on your everyday existence.

- Imagine no limitations (financial, physical, etc.)
- Consider both big accomplishments and daily routines
- Think about what truly brings you joy and fulfillment
- Don't limit yourself based on what you think is "realistic."

This vision will guide your personal growth journey and help you set goals that align with your true self.

Putting It All Together: Your Personalized Change Plan

Now that you have a deeper understanding of your personality, talents, and ideal life, you can create a personalized plan for change that aligns with who you truly are.

1. Identify the gap between your current life and your ideal life
2. Break down your big goals into smaller, manageable steps
3. Consider how your personality traits might help or hinder your progress
4. Leverage your natural talents to support your goals
5. Develop strategies to work around or improve areas where you struggle

Key Insight: Your plan should be flexible. As you grow and change, your understanding of yourself and your goals may evolve. That's not only okay; it's a sign of progress!

Exercise: Personality-Aligned Goal Setting
- Step 1: Choose a goal you want to achieve.
- Step 2: List your key personality traits and talents.
- Step 3: For each, write how it could help (strength) or hinder (challenge) your goal.
- Step 4: Create specific strategies to leverage strengths and mitigate challenges.
- Step 5: Redesign your approach to align with your natural tendencies.

Example:
- Goal: Establish a regular exercise routine.
- Trait: Introversion.
- Challenge: May avoid group fitness classes.
- Aligned strategy: Create a home workout routine or find solo activities like running or swimming.

Overcoming Personality-Based Challenges
Understanding your personality helps you anticipate and overcome challenges:
- If you're introverted, network in ways that suit you (one-on-one, online)
- If you're impulsive, break goals into smaller, immediate rewards
- If you're a perfectionist, focus on progress over perfection and celebrate small wins

The Role of Self-Talk in Personality and Change

Your self-talk is deeply influenced by your personality. Understanding your personality can help you recognize negative self-talk patterns and develop a more positive, supportive internal dialogue.

- If you're self-critical, practice reframing negative thoughts
- If you catastrophize, challenge yourself to consider positive outcomes
- If you doubt yourself, keep a list of past accomplishments

Embracing Growth While Honoring Your True Self

The goal of understanding your personality isn't to change who you are at your core but to grow into the best version of yourself. This means:

- Embracing your natural strengths and using them more effectively
- Working on weaknesses that hold you back
- Developing new skills and habits that align with your values
- Letting go of societal expectations that don't resonate with your true self

Example: Authentic Change vs. Forced Change

Person A is naturally spontaneous but creates a flexible system with visual reminders and room for improvisation. Person B tries to follow a rigid planning system that feels oppressive and is quickly abandoned. Person A achieves lasting change because their approach aligns with who they truly are.

Chapter Summary

- Self-knowledge forms the foundation for meaningful and lasting change
- True identity goes beyond labels and involves genetics, beliefs, experiences, and values
- Self-acceptance enables change by creating a secure base for growth
- Personality assessments provide insights into your tendencies and strengths
- Talents often go unrecognized because they come easily to us
- Personalizing your change approach increases your chances of success
- Authentic growth honors your core self while developing in areas that matter to you

Reflection Questions

Question 1: What aspects of your personality do you value most, and how do they serve you?

Former Student Responses:
- "I'm naturally empathetic and good at understanding others' feelings."
- "I'm persistent and don't give up easily when facing challenges."
- "I'm creative and can think outside the box to solve problems."
- "I'm organized and detail-oriented, which helps me stay on track."
- "I'm optimistic and can find the positive in difficult situations."
- "I'm analytical and good at breaking down complex problems."
- "I'm adaptable and can adjust to new situations quickly."

Possible Solutions:
- **Empathy**: Leverage this in leadership roles, counseling, or team collaboration; use it to build stronger relationships that support your goals
- **Persistence**: Apply this trait to long-term goals that require sustained effort; break large goals into smaller milestones to maintain motivation
- **Creativity**: Use this for innovative problem-solving in your career; apply creative approaches to overcome obstacles in personal growth
- **Organization**: Build systems and structures that support your goals; help others who struggle with organization, while building your network
- **Optimism**: Use this to maintain motivation during setbacks; share your positive outlook to inspire and attract supportive people
- **Analytical Skills**: Apply systematic approaches to goal-setting and problem-solving; use data and metrics to track progress effectively
- **Adaptability**: Embrace change as an opportunity; adjust your strategies when initial approaches aren't working

Question 2: What beliefs do you hold about yourself that might limit your growth?

Former Student Responses:
- "I believe I'm not smart enough to succeed in competitive fields."
- "I think I'm too old to make significant career changes."
- "I believe I don't have enough willpower to stick with difficult changes."
- "I think I'm not naturally talented enough to excel at anything."

- "I believe I don't deserve success or good things happening to me."
- "I think I'm too introverted to be a good leader."
- "I believe I'm not creative enough to pursue artistic goals."

Possible Solutions:
- **Intelligence Doubts**: Focus on a growth mindset - intelligence can be developed; document your learning achievements; seek evidence of your problem-solving abilities
- **Age Limitations**: Research examples of people who made major changes at your age or older; focus on the advantages your experience brings
- **Willpower Concerns**: Start with tiny habits that require minimal willpower; build confidence through small wins; understand that willpower is like a muscle that strengthens with use
- **Talent Beliefs**: Recognize that skill often matters more than natural talent; focus on deliberate practice and continuous improvement
- **Worthiness Issues**: Practice self-compassion; challenge the origin of these beliefs; seek therapy if needed to address deep-rooted self-worth issues
- **Introversion Limitations**: Reframe introversion as a leadership strength; find leadership styles that match your personality; practice leading in small, comfortable settings first
- **Creativity Doubts**: Understand that creativity can be developed; practice creative exercises; expose yourself to diverse experiences and perspectives

Question 3: Which personality traits present the biggest challenges in your change journey?

Former Student Responses:
- "My perfectionism makes me afraid to start anything unless I can do it perfectly."
- "I'm naturally impatient and want to see results immediately."
- "I'm a people pleaser and struggle to set boundaries or disappoint others."
- "I tend to procrastinate, especially on tasks that feel overwhelming."
- "I'm very self-critical and beat myself up when I make mistakes."
- "I avoid conflict and difficult conversations, even when necessary."
- "I get easily distracted and struggle to maintain focus on long-term goals."

Possible Solutions:

- **Perfectionism**: Practice the "good enough" principle; set "minimum viable" standards; celebrate progress over perfection; use time limits to prevent over-polishing
- **Impatience**: Break goals into smaller milestones with quicker rewards; track daily progress; practice mindfulness to appreciate the journey
- **People-Pleasing**: Practice saying no in low-stakes situations; remember that boundaries help relationships; find supportive people who encourage your growth
- **Procrastination**: Use the "2-minute rule" for starting tasks; break overwhelming projects into tiny steps; address underlying fears that fuel procrastination
- **Self-Criticism**: Practice self-compassion techniques; speak to yourself as you would a good friend; keep a record of accomplishments and positive feedback
- **Conflict Avoidance**: Start with small, low-risk, honest conversations; practice assertiveness techniques; remember that avoiding conflict often creates bigger problems
- **Distractibility**: Use time-blocking and focus techniques; eliminate distractions from your environment; practice single-tasking; consider if ADHD assessment might be helpful

Question 4: What talents or strengths do you possess that you haven't fully leveraged?

Former Student Responses:
- "I'm really good at explaining complex things in simple terms, but I don't use this skill much."
- "People always come to me for advice, but I've never considered coaching or mentoring."
- "I have a knack for organizing events and bringing people together."
- "I'm naturally good at seeing patterns and connections others miss."
- "I have strong intuition about people and situations."
- "I'm excellent at mediating conflicts and finding compromises."
- "I have a talent for making people feel comfortable and welcomed."

Possible Solutions:
- **Teaching/Explaining**: Consider tutoring, training roles, content creation, or public speaking opportunities; use this skill to build your professional reputation
- **Advice-Giving**: Explore formal mentoring programs; consider coaching certification; start a blog or podcast sharing insights

- **Event Organization**: Volunteer to organize workplace or community events; consider event planning as a side business or career change
- **Pattern Recognition**: Apply this to data analysis, strategic planning, or research roles; use it to identify trends in your own behavior and progress
- **Intuition**: Trust your gut feelings more in decision-making; develop this into better emotional intelligence; use it in roles requiring people skills
- **Mediation**: Volunteer for conflict resolution roles; consider training in mediation or negotiation; use this skill to improve team dynamics
- **Hospitality**: Consider roles in customer service, hospitality, or community building; use this talent to expand your network and build relationships

Question 5: How might your ideal life look different if you truly honor your authentic self?

Former Student Responses:
- "I'd probably work in a more creative field instead of staying in finance for security."
- "I'd spend more time in nature and less time in crowded, noisy environments."
- "I'd have deeper, more meaningful relationships instead of trying to please everyone."
- "I'd take more risks and try new things instead of playing it safe all the time."
- "I'd speak up more about things I care about instead of staying quiet."
- "I'd prioritize my health and well-being instead of constantly putting others first."
- "I'd pursue learning and growth opportunities that genuinely interest me."

Possible Solutions:
- **Career Authenticity**: Start transitioning gradually by taking on creative projects within your current role; build creative skills as a side pursuit; network in creative industries
- **Environment Preferences**: Schedule regular nature breaks; choose living and working environments that align with your needs; advocate for outdoor meetings when possible
- **Relationship Depth**: Practice vulnerability in small ways; quality over quantity in friendships; set boundaries with energy-draining relationships
- **Risk-Taking**: Start with small, calculated risks; build confidence through manageable challenges; reframe failure as a learning opportunity

- **Voice and Advocacy**: Practice expressing opinions in low-stakes situations; find causes you care about; join groups aligned with your values
- **Self-Care Priority**: Schedule self-care like any important appointment; practice saying no to requests that compromise your well-being; model healthy boundaries
- **Authentic Learning**: Pursue courses and experiences that genuinely interest you; follow your curiosity; connect learning to your values and goals

Universal Solutions Across All Chapter 5 Questions:
- **Embrace Your Authentic Self**: Use your personality insights to create change strategies that work with your natural tendencies rather than against them.
- **Challenge Limiting Beliefs**: Regularly question beliefs about yourself and seek evidence that contradicts negative self-perceptions.
- **Leverage Your Strengths**: Build your change plan around your natural talents and positive traits to increase your chances of success.
- **Work With Your Challenges**: Instead of fighting your difficult traits, develop strategies to manage them effectively while pursuing your goals.
- **Align Goals With Values**: Ensure your change efforts reflect what truly matters to you, not what others expect or what society deems successful.
- **Practice Self-Acceptance**: Accept yourself as you are while still working toward growth - this paradox actually enables more effective change.
- **Seek Feedback**: Ask trusted friends and family for insights about your strengths and blind spots to gain a more complete self-picture.
- **Experiment and Adjust**: Try different approaches to change based on your personality, and be willing to modify your strategies as you learn what works best for you.

Take Action

- Take at least one personality assessment to gain additional insight
- Ask three people who know you well what they see as your greatest strengths
- Write a description of your ideal life, focusing on how it would feel day-to-day
- Identify one goal and adapt your approach to align with your personality
- Practice self-acceptance by acknowledging both strengths and weaknesses without judgment

"Knowing yourself is the beginning of all wisdom." — **Aristotle.**

In the next chapter, you'll learn how to conduct a personal SWOT analysis (Strengths, Weaknesses, Opportunities, Threats) to gain deeper insights and create strategies for growth that leverage your unique circumstances.

Chapter 6 – SWOT Analysis

Know Yourself, Grow Yourself: Harness the Power of SWOT

Key Insight: A personal SWOT analysis is like a compass for self-discovery. By mapping your Strengths, Weaknesses, Opportunities, and Threats, you gain clarity on where you are and where you can go.

Why Perform a Personal SWOT Analysis?

Before you set out on any journey of change, it's wise to understand your starting point. A personal SWOT analysis helps you:

- Identify your real strengths and how to leverage them
- Get honest about weaknesses that may be holding you back
- Spot opportunities in your environment or network
- Prepare for threats or obstacles that could derail your progress

This tool, borrowed from the business world, is equally powerful when applied to your personal growth. It helps you drill down beneath surface-level goals to uncover root causes and hidden resources.

How to Conduct a Personal SWOT Analysis

Step 1: Draw a large "plus" sign on a blank page, dividing it into four quadrants. Label them: Strengths, Weaknesses, Opportunities, Threats.

Step 2: Use the following prompts for each section:

Strengths
- What am I naturally good at?
- What accomplishments am I most proud of?
- What skills or qualities set me apart from others?
- What resources or support do I already have?

Weaknesses
- What tasks do I avoid or struggle with?
- What skills do I lack that others in my field possess?

- What negative feedback have I received?
- Where do I tend to self-sabotage?

Warning: Be specific and actionable, not self-critical. Instead of "I'm bad with people," write, "I need to develop better active listening skills."

Opportunities
- What trends or changes could I take advantage of?
- Are there people I could connect with for support or mentorship?
- What new skills could I learn?
- What resources or technologies are available to me?

Threats
- What external obstacles or competition do I face?
- Are there economic, social, or personal changes ahead?
- Who or what might undermine my progress?
- What bad habits or distractions could get in the way?

Exercise: Conducting Your Personal SWOT Analysis
- Create your SWOT grid (or download a template online).
- Set a timer for 10 minutes for each quadrant.
- Fill in as many items as you can for each section.
- Look for connections and patterns across the quadrants.

Strengths	Opportunities
- List skills and talents - Note positive traits - Resources you have - Compliments you receive	- New trends - Supportive people - Learning opportunities - Untapped resources
Weaknesses	**Threats**
- Skills you lack - Traits that hold you back - Missing resources - Recurring challenges	- External obstacles - Competition - Negative influences - Distractions

Applying SWOT to Your Baby Steps

Once you've completed your SWOT analysis, relate each component to a specific change you want to make. For example, if your goal is to change your diet:

- **Strength:** Strong willpower when shopping for groceries.
- **Weakness:** Struggle to resist snacks at social events.
- **Opportunity:** A friend is starting a healthy eating challenge.
- **Threat:** Family members who bring junk food into the house.

Using SWOT Results for Personal Growth

After completing your SWOT analysis, put the results into action:

- Leverage your strengths: Use them to overcome weaknesses and seize opportunities.
- Improve your weaknesses: Develop strategies, seek help, or learn new skills.
- Seize opportunities: Create action plans to capitalize on them.
- Mitigate threats: Develop contingency plans and strengthen your resilience.

Key Insight: The goal of a SWOT analysis is not just self-awareness but to create a plan for personal growth and success.

SWOT In Action: Maria's Story

Maria wanted to transition from her corporate job to freelance graphic design. Her SWOT analysis revealed:

Strengths:
- Strong technical design skills
- Existing network of professional contacts
- Excellent time management

Weaknesses:
- Discomfort with self-promotion
- Limited business management experience
- Tendency to undervalue her work

Opportunities:
- Growing demand for remote design work
- Former colleague offering first client referral
- Online courses available for business skills

Threats:
- Competitive freelance marketplace
- Unstable income during the transition
- Health insurance costs

Her Action Plan:
1. Leveraged her network to address the threat of finding clients
2. Used online courses to improve business skills
3. Built a financial buffer for income instability
4. Partnered with a business coach for self-promotion

Within a year, Maria had a thriving freelance business that exceeded her corporate salary.

SWOT Analysis and Previous Chapters

Your SWOT analysis ties together much of what you've learned so far:

- Personality: Your strengths and weaknesses often reflect your natural traits.
- Habits: Good habits are strengths; bad habits are weaknesses or threats.
- Self-Talk: Positive self-talk helps you see strengths and opportunities; negative self-talk magnifies weaknesses and threats.
- Emotional Intelligence: Recognizing and managing emotions is a key strength.

Beyond SWOT: Additional Tools for Personal Growth

While SWOT is powerful, you can deepen your growth by developing. Rate yourself 1–10 in each area above. Scores of 7+ are strengths; 4 or below are areas for growth.

Communication Skills
- Active listening
- Clear expression

- Empathy and understanding

Emotional Intelligence (EQ)
- Self-awareness
- Self-regulation
- Motivation
- Empathy
- Social skills

Positive Thinking
- See opportunities where others see threats
- Turn weaknesses into strengths
- Attract positive people and situations

Assertiveness
- Set clear boundaries
- Express your needs
- Practice confident body language

Managing Stress and Anxiety
- Mindfulness and meditation
- Regular exercise
- Time management
- Seeking help when needed

Putting It All Together: Your Personal Growth Plan
1. Review your SWOT analysis.
2. Set clear, SMART goals based on your findings.
3. Develop action plans for each goal.
4. Leverage strengths, address weaknesses, seize opportunities, and mitigate threats.
5. Use additional tools (communication, EQ, positive thinking) to support your growth.
6. Track your progress and celebrate successes.

Warning: Don't try to work on everything at once. Focus on 1–3 key areas initially, and add more as you make progress.

Chapter Summary

- SWOT analysis helps you identify internal strengths and weaknesses and external opportunities and threats.
- Use your SWOT to create focused, actionable growth plans.
- Leverage your strengths, address your weaknesses, seize opportunities, and mitigate threats.
- Complement SWOT with communication skills, emotional intelligence, positive thinking, assertiveness, and stress management.

Reflection Questions

Question 1: What three strengths do you possess that you haven't fully leveraged?

Former Student Responses:
- "I'm naturally good at explaining complex concepts simply, but I only use this skill occasionally."
- "I have strong analytical abilities that help me solve problems, but I don't apply them systematically to my personal goals."
- "People often tell me I'm a good listener, but I've never considered using this in a professional capacity."
- "I'm naturally organized and can create efficient systems, but I only use this for work, not personal projects."
- "I have a talent for bringing people together and mediating conflicts, but I don't leverage this enough."
- "I'm creative and can think outside the box, but I mostly keep my ideas to myself."
- "I'm persistent and don't give up easily, but I haven't applied this to my biggest life goals."

Possible Solutions:
- **Teaching/Explaining Skills**: Volunteer to train new employees, start a blog or YouTube channel, offer tutoring services, or seek speaking opportunities

- **Analytical Abilities**: Apply systematic problem-solving to personal challenges, use data tracking for health or financial goals, or consider roles requiring strategic thinking
- **Listening Skills**: Explore coaching or counseling training, volunteer for crisis hotlines, or take on mentoring roles
- **Organization Systems**: Create personal productivity systems, help friends organize their spaces, or consider professional organizing as a side business
- **People Skills**: Facilitate team meetings, volunteer for community mediation, or organize social events and networking opportunities
- **Creativity**: Join creative communities, start passion projects, or bring innovative solutions to workplace challenges
- **Persistence**: Apply this trait to long-term goals by breaking them into smaller milestones and celebrating progress along the way

Question 2: Which weakness, if addressed, would create the biggest positive change?

Former Student Responses:
- "My tendency to procrastinate on important tasks until they become urgent and stressful."
- "I avoid difficult conversations, which leads to unresolved conflicts and resentment."
- "I'm terrible at saying no, which leaves me overwhelmed and unable to focus on my priorities."
- "I don't follow through on commitments I make to myself, which undermines my confidence."
- "I'm disorganized and waste time looking for things or missing deadlines."
- "I'm too self-critical and it prevents me from taking risks or trying new things."
- "I don't network or build professional relationships, which limits my career opportunities."

Possible Solutions:
- **Procrastination**: Use the "2-minute rule," break large tasks into smaller steps, set artificial deadlines, and create accountability systems
- **Conflict Avoidance**: Practice having small, low-stakes difficult conversations, learn assertiveness techniques, and reframe conflict as problem-solving

- **Boundary Issues**: Practice saying no to small requests first, create standard responses for common situations, and remember that saying no to one thing means saying yes to your priorities
- **Self-Commitment**: Start with tiny, almost impossible-to-fail commitments, track your follow-through, and gradually increase the stakes
- **Disorganization**: Implement simple systems one area at a time, use digital tools for reminders, and create designated spaces for important items
- **Self-Criticism**: Practice self-compassion techniques, challenge negative thoughts with evidence, and speak to yourself as you would a good friend.
- **Networking Reluctance**: Start with online communities, attend small events, focus on giving value to others rather than asking for help

Question 3: What opportunities exist in your environment that you haven't taken advantage of?

Former Student Responses:
- "My company offers free professional development courses that I've never used."
- "There's a growing demand in my field for people with my skills, but I haven't positioned myself to take advantage."
- "I live near a university that offers community classes and lectures I could attend."
- "My industry has several networking events and conferences I've never attended."
- "There are mentorship programs available through my professional association."
- "The rise of remote work opens up job opportunities I've never considered."
- "My city has entrepreneur meetups and startup incubators I could join."

Possible Solutions:
- **Professional Development**: Schedule specific times for courses, choose programs aligned with your career goals, and apply new skills immediately
- **Market Demand**: Update your LinkedIn profile, create a portfolio showcasing your skills, and actively network in your industry
- **Educational Opportunities**: Audit interesting classes, attend public lectures, and join study groups or book clubs
- **Industry Events**: Start with smaller, local events, prepare conversation starters, and set goals for each event (meet 3 new people, learn about 2 companies)
- **Mentorship**: Research available programs, prepare thoughtful questions, and be ready to offer value in return

- **Remote Work**: Update your resume for remote positions, develop digital collaboration skills, and expand your job search geographically
- **Entrepreneurship**: Attend one meetup per month, start with low-risk side projects, and connect with other aspiring entrepreneurs

Question 4: What threat poses the greatest risk to your growth, and how could you prepare for it?

Former Student Responses:
- "Economic uncertainty could affect my job security and financial stability."
- "My industry is being disrupted by technology and automation."
- "I have health issues that could limit my ability to pursue my goals."
- "My family responsibilities are increasing and taking more of my time and energy."
- "I tend to get distracted by social media and entertainment instead of working on my goals."
- "I'm surrounded by negative people who discourage my growth efforts."
- "I have a tendency to give up when things get difficult."

Possible Solutions:
- **Economic Uncertainty**: Build an emergency fund, develop multiple income streams, continuously update your skills, and maintain a strong professional network
- **Industry Disruption**: Stay informed about technological trends, learn new digital skills, consider how to complement rather than compete with automation
- **Health Challenges**: Work with healthcare providers to optimize your health, adapt goals to your energy levels, and build flexibility into your plans
- **Family Responsibilities**: Communicate your goals with family members, seek support, delegate where possible, and integrate family time with personal growth
- **Digital Distractions**: Use app blockers during focused work time, create phone-free zones, and replace mindless scrolling with purposeful activities
- **Negative Influences**: Limit time with discouraging people, find supportive communities, and practice maintaining your motivation despite criticism
- **Giving Up**: Prepare for setbacks by having comeback plans, celebrate small wins, and remind yourself of your "why" during difficult times

Question 5: How might you combine your strengths with available opportunities to create a unique path forward?

Former Student Responses:
- "I could use my teaching ability and the growing demand for online education to create courses."
- "My analytical skills plus the data revolution could lead to consulting opportunities."
- "My people skills combined with remote work trends could open up virtual team leadership roles."
- "My creativity and the maker movement could lead to a craft business or design services."
- "My organizational skills and the productivity app market could inspire a digital solution."
- "My listening skills and the mental health awareness trend could lead to coaching certification."
- "My persistence and the entrepreneurship boom could help me finally start that business I've been thinking about."

Possible Solutions:
- **Teaching + Online Education**: Research popular course topics, start with free content to build an audience, and gradually develop paid offerings
- **Analysis + Data Trends**: Take courses in data analysis tools, volunteer to analyze data for nonprofits, and build a portfolio of projects
- **People Skills + Remote Work**: Develop virtual leadership skills, seek team lead opportunities, and learn digital collaboration tools
- **Creativity + Maker Movement**: Start with small projects, join maker spaces, and test market demand through craft fairs or online platforms
- **Organization + Productivity**: Create systems for yourself first, document what works, and consider developing apps or consulting services
- **Listening + Mental Health**: Pursue relevant certifications, volunteer with support organizations, and build experience gradually
- **Persistence + Entrepreneurship**: Join entrepreneur groups, start with low-risk ventures, and apply your persistence to consistent daily actions

Universal Solutions Across All Chapter 6 Questions:
- **Conduct Regular SWOT Reviews**: Schedule quarterly assessments to track how your strengths, weaknesses, opportunities, and threats evolve over time.
- **Create Action Plans**: For each insight from your SWOT analysis, develop specific, measurable action steps with deadlines.

- **Leverage Strengths Strategically**: Use your natural talents as the foundation for addressing weaknesses and capitalizing on opportunities.
- **Address High-Impact Weaknesses First**: Focus on the one or two weaknesses that, if improved, would create the most significant positive change in your life.
- **Stay Alert to Opportunities**: Develop the habit of regularly scanning your environment for new possibilities and trends that align with your goals.
- **Prepare for Threats**: Create contingency plans for your biggest risks and build resilience through diversification and skill development.
- **Seek External Perspectives**: Ask trusted friends, mentors, or coaches to provide input on your SWOT analysis for blind spots you might miss.
- **Document Your Progress**: Keep records of how you're leveraging strengths, addressing weaknesses, capitalizing on opportunities, and mitigating threats.
- **Stay Flexible**: Be willing to adjust your strategies as your circumstances change and new information becomes available.

Take Action

- Complete your personal SWOT analysis using the exercise above.
- Identify one strength you can immediately leverage toward a current goal.
- Choose one weakness to improve over the next month.
- Develop a plan to take advantage of one opportunity.
- Create a contingency plan for your most significant threat.

"Know yourself, and you will win all battles." — **Sun Tzu.**

In our final chapter, you'll learn how to put all these elements together and begin your journey toward lasting change, maintaining motivation, overcoming obstacles, and celebrating progress as you transform your life one small step at a time.

Chapter 7 – Your Journey Begins Now

You Don't Have to Be Great to Start—But You Have to Start to Be Great

Key Insight: Every journey—no matter how long or daunting—begins with a single step. The most important action is to begin. Starting creates momentum, and momentum is the engine of transformation.

"Whatever you can do, or dream you can do, begin it. Boldness has genius, power, and magic in it." — **Johann Wolfgang von Goethe.**

You've done the work of self-reflection, set goals, and created a personal growth plan. Now comes the most crucial step: putting your plan into motion. Action is the bridge between intention and achievement. Until you act, your dreams remain only dreams.

Starting is often the hardest part. Our minds are wired to resist change and cling to the familiar. The first step—no matter how small—breaks inertia and creates momentum. Once you start, each subsequent step becomes easier.

Embracing the Process

Personal growth is a journey, not a destination. There will be ups and downs, successes and setbacks. Embrace the entire process as part of your story.

Handling Success and Failure

Both success and failure bring their own lessons and challenges.

- Redefine Failure: The only true failure is quitting. Everything else is a learning opportunity. If you miss a deadline or fall short of a goal, adjust your plan and keep moving forward.
- Celebrate Small Wins: Don't wait for big achievements to celebrate. Acknowledge and reward yourself for small milestones. Celebrating maintains motivation and makes the journey enjoyable.
- Prepare for Success: Success can bring unexpected challenges—new responsibilities, changes in relationships, or even a sense of letdown. Prepare mentally for these possibilities and have strategies in place to handle them.
- Stay Humble: As you achieve your goals, stay grounded. Use your success to help others and set new, more ambitious goals.

Example: The Post-Achievement Dip

Many people experience a sense of letdown after achieving a major goal, sometimes called "post-achievement blues." For example, athletes may feel this after a championship win, or students after graduation.

Prepare for this by identifying what's next, recognizing that much fulfillment comes from the journey itself, and planning a transition period that includes rest and reflection.

Monitoring and Measuring Progress

Tracking your progress is crucial for maintaining motivation and making necessary adjustments. Here's how:

- Keep a Journal: Record both tangible progress and emotional growth.
- Use Metrics: For quantifiable goals (e.g., weight loss, savings), use specific metrics.
- Seek Feedback: Ask trusted friends, family, or mentors for observations on your growth.
- Regular Check-ins: Schedule regular times to review your plan and assess your progress.

A Progress Tracking System

- Choose your tracking method: Digital app, spreadsheet, journal, or accountability partner.
- Determine what you'll track: Outcomes, actions completed, subjective ratings, and insights.
- Set your tracking frequency: Daily, weekly, or monthly.
- Create a reflection protocol: Ask yourself what's working, what's challenging, and what you've learned.
- Schedule review dates: Consistency is key.

Overcoming Obstacles

Obstacles are inevitable. Here are strategies to help you overcome them:

- Anticipate Challenges: Think ahead about potential roadblocks and develop strategies to overcome them.
- Develop Resilience: Each obstacle you overcome builds your capacity to handle future challenges.
- Seek Support: Don't be afraid to ask for help from friends, family, or professionals.
- Stay Flexible: Be willing to adjust your approach if something isn't working.

Warning: Beware the "what-the-hell effect," the tendency to abandon your goals after a minor setback ("I ate one cookie, so I might as well eat the whole box"). Perfection isn't required for progress. One setback doesn't erase your efforts.

The Role of Habits in Change

Lasting change comes through the development of new habits.

- Start Small: Begin with tiny, manageable changes that you can consistently maintain.
- Be Consistent: A small action done daily is more effective than a big effort done occasionally.
- Use Habit Stacking: Attach new habits to existing ones.
- Be Patient: It takes time for new behaviors to become automatic. Focus on the process, not just the outcome.

Maintaining Motivation

Motivation fluctuates. Here's how to keep it high:

- Revisit Your 'Why': Regularly remind yourself why you started. Create a visual reminder of your 'why' to look at daily.
- Visualize Success: Spend time each day visualizing yourself achieving your goals, including the feelings of accomplishment.
- Find Inspiration: Surround yourself with inspiring books, podcasts, or people. Create a collection of quotes or stories that uplift you.
- Use Positive Self-Talk: Replace negative self-talk with positive affirmations. Speak to yourself as you would to a friend.

The Power of Accountability

Accountability can significantly increase your chances of success.

- Share Your Goals: Tell trusted friends or family about your goals. Public commitment increases follow-through.
- Find an Accountability Partner: Partner with someone who has similar goals and check in regularly.
- Join a Group: Group environments create positive peer pressure and shared experiences.
- Consider Professional Help: If you're struggling, seek help from a coach or therapist for objective feedback and strategies.

Embracing Continuous Learning
Personal growth is a lifelong journey.

- Read Widely: Expand your knowledge through books and articles.
- Seek New Experiences: Try new things regularly. Novel experiences create new neural pathways.
- Reflect on Lessons Learned: Take time to reflect on your experiences and extract valuable lessons.
- Stay Curious: Maintain a sense of wonder and ask questions.

Making Changes Stick

- Be Patient: Lasting change takes time. Don't expect overnight transformations.
- Focus on One Change at a Time: Trying to change too much at once can be overwhelming.
- Prepare for Setbacks: Setbacks are normal. Have a plan for how you'll get back on track.
- Celebrate Progress: Acknowledge how far you've come and create meaningful ways to celebrate milestones.

"The journey of a thousand miles begins with one step." — **Lao Tzu.**

Chapter Summary

- Starting is crucial. Taking the first step creates momentum.
- Redefine failure as a learning opportunity.
- Track your progress to maintain motivation.
- Build resilience by anticipating and overcoming challenges.
- Focus on habits for lasting change.
- Maintain motivation by revisiting your 'why' and visualizing success.
- Use accountability to increase your chances of success.
- Embrace continuous learning as a lifelong approach.
- Be patient and persistent as you work to make changes permanent.

Ask Yourself

1. What first step will you take today to begin your journey of change?
2. Which accountability strategy would be most effective for your personality and goals?
3. How will you track your progress and measure success?
4. What potential obstacles might you face, and how will you prepare for them?
5. How will you celebrate milestones along your journey?

Take Action

- Choose one small action you can take today toward your most important goal.
- Set up a simple progress tracking system.
- Identify an accountability partner or group.
- Schedule regular check-ins to review your progress.
- Create a visual reminder of your 'why' to keep you motivated.

"Your journey begins with a choice to get up, step out, and live fully." — **Oprah Winfrey.**

Final Reflection

Question 1: What first step will you take today to begin your journey of change?

Former Student Responses:
- "I want to start exercising, but I'm not sure what to do first."
- "I need to improve my time management, but feel overwhelmed by all the systems out there."
- "I want to build better relationships, but don't know where to start."
- "I've been putting off learning a new skill for my career."
- "I want to eat healthier, but my current habits are so ingrained."
- "I need to work on my self-talk, but it feels too abstract."
- "I want to declutter my life, but don't know which area to tackle first."

Possible Solutions:

- **Exercise Goals**: Put on workout clothes and walk for 5 minutes today, or do 2 push-ups against a wall
- **Time Management**: Choose one task for tomorrow and schedule a specific 15-minute time block for it
- **Relationship Building**: Send one genuine text message to someone you care about, asking how they're doing
- **Skill Development**: Watch one 10-minute tutorial video or read one article about your desired skill
- **Healthy Eating**: Replace one unhealthy snack with a piece of fruit today
- **Self-Talk**: Write down one negative thought you had today and rewrite it in a kinder way
- **Decluttering**: Clear one small surface (like your desk or nightstand) completely

Question 2: Which accountability strategy would be most effective for your personality and goals?

Former Student Responses:
- "I'm introverted and don't like sharing personal goals with many people."
- "I'm competitive and motivated by comparison with others."
- "I tend to let people down and feel guilty about disappointing accountability partners."
- "I work better with professional guidance than peer support."
- "I like technology and apps, but struggle with human accountability."
- "I'm motivated by public commitment but worried about judgment if I fail."
- "I prefer gentle encouragement over tough love approaches."

Possible Solutions:
- **Introverted Personalities**: Find one trusted friend or family member for private check-ins; use anonymous online communities; or keep a daily journal with weekly self-reviews
- **Competitive Types**: Join challenge groups, use apps with leaderboards, or find an accountability partner with a similar competitive drive
- **Guilt-Prone Individuals**: Start with self-accountability through tracking apps; focus on progress reporting rather than commitment-based accountability; work with a professional coach who understands your patterns

- **Professional Guidance Seekers**: Hire a coach, join structured programs, or use professional development courses with built-in accountability
- **Tech-Savvy Individuals**: Use habit-tracking apps, online communities, or digital accountability tools combined with occasional human check-ins
- **Public Commitment Types**: Share goals on social media with progress updates; join public challenges; or commit to friends, but reframe "failure" as a learning experience
- **Gentle Encouragement Preference**: Find supportive, non-judgmental accountability partners; focus on celebration of efforts rather than outcomes; use positive reinforcement systems

Question 3: How will you track your progress and measure success?

Former Student Responses:
- "I've tried tracking before, but I always give up after a few days."
- "I'm not sure what metrics to use for personal development goals."
- "I get obsessed with tracking, and it becomes counterproductive."
- "I prefer simple methods, but don't know what actually works."
- "I want to track both quantitative and qualitative progress."
- "I forgot to track consistently."
- "I don't know how often I should review my progress."

Possible Solutions:
- **Tracking Dropouts**: Use the simplest possible system (one daily checkmark); link tracking to an existing habit (like brushing teeth); or use photo progress instead of detailed logging
- **Metric Confusion**: Focus on input metrics (actions taken) rather than just outcomes; use a simple 1-10 daily rating scale; or track one specific behavior rather than general progress
- **Over-Trackers**: Limit to 3 key metrics maximum; track weekly instead of daily; or use qualitative journaling rather than detailed quantitative data
- **Simplicity Seekers**: Use a basic calendar with checkmarks; try the "don't break the chain" method; or use simple phone apps with minimal features
- **Comprehensive Trackers**: Combine daily quantitative tracking with weekly qualitative reflection; use both objective measures and subjective well-being ratings
- **Forgetful Trackers**: Set phone reminders at consistent times, place tracking tools in visible locations, or use habit stacking (track immediately after another routine)

- **Review Frequency Questions**: Start with weekly 10-minute reviews; schedule monthly deeper assessments; or use daily micro-reviews (2 minutes) with weekly summaries

Question 4: What potential obstacles might you face, and how will you prepare for them?

Former Student Responses:
- "I always start strong but lose motivation after a few weeks."
- "My family doesn't support my goals and sometimes sabotages my efforts."
- "I get overwhelmed when I face setbacks and tend to give up completely."
- "My work schedule is unpredictable and makes consistency difficult."
- "I have perfectionist tendencies that paralyze me when things aren't going perfectly."
- "I struggle with self-discipline and often choose immediate gratification over long-term goals."
- "I tend to take on too much at once and burn out."

Possible Solutions:
- **Motivation Loss**: Create a "why" document to review during low periods; plan rewards for consistency milestones; or find ways to make the process more enjoyable rather than just focusing on outcomes
- **Unsupportive Environment**: Communicate your goals clearly and explain benefits to family; find supportive communities outside your immediate circle; or create boundaries around your goal-related activities
- **Setback Overwhelm**: Develop a specific "comeback plan" before you need it; practice self-compassion techniques; or reframe setbacks as data rather than failures
- **Schedule Unpredictability**: Focus on flexible goals that can adapt to your schedule; create multiple backup plans for different scenarios; or choose goals that require minimal time commitment
- **Perfectionism**: Set "good enough" standards; practice the "2-minute rule" for getting started; or focus on consistency over quality initially
- **Self-Discipline Issues**: Use environmental design to make good choices easier; start with tiny habits that require minimal willpower; or use implementation intentions ("When X happens, I will do Y")
- **Burnout Tendency**: Limit yourself to one major change at a time; build in rest and recovery periods; or start smaller than feels necessary

Question 5: How will you celebrate milestones along your journey?

Former Student Responses:
- "I never celebrate small wins - I always focus on what's next."
- "I don't want to reward myself with things that contradict my goals (like food rewards for fitness goals)."
- "I feel guilty celebrating when I haven't reached my final goal yet."
- "I don't know what kinds of rewards would actually motivate me."
- "I prefer experiences over material rewards."
- "I want celebrations that involve other people."
- "I'm on a tight budget and can't afford expensive rewards."

Possible Solutions:
- **Future-Focused Types**: Schedule celebration time like any other appointment; ask accountability partners to remind you to celebrate; or create a "wins journal" to review regularly
- **Goal-Aligned Celebrations**: Reward fitness progress with new workout gear or a massage; celebrate learning goals with advanced courses; or reward financial goals with a small investment in your future
- **Guilt About Celebrating**: Reframe celebration as fuel for continued progress; remember that acknowledging progress increases motivation; or share celebrations with others who benefit from your growth
- **Motivation Uncertainty**: Experiment with different types of rewards; ask friends what motivates them; or try both immediate small rewards and larger milestone celebrations
- **Experience Preferences**: Plan special outings, try new activities, or visit places you've wanted to explore; attend events or classes related to your interests
- **Social Celebrations**: Share achievements with friends and family, organize group activities, or join communities where you can celebrate others' successes too
- **Budget-Conscious Celebrators**: Use free activities like nature walks or library visits; create homemade treats; or celebrate with time-based rewards like sleeping in or taking a relaxing bath

Universal Solutions Across All Final Reflection Questions:
- **Start Immediately**: Choose the smallest possible first step and take it today - action creates momentum and momentum sustains motivation.

- **Prepare for Obstacles**: Anticipate challenges and have specific strategies ready rather than hoping you'll figure it out when problems arise.
- **Focus on Systems Over Goals**: Build processes and habits that naturally lead to your desired outcomes rather than fixating on end results.
- **Celebrate Progress**: Acknowledge and reward effort and improvement, not just final achievements, to maintain motivation throughout your journey.
- **Stay Flexible**: Be willing to adjust your approach based on what you learn about yourself and what works best for your unique circumstances.
- **Connect with Others**: Find ways to involve supportive people in your journey, whether through accountability, celebration, or shared experiences.
- **Track What Matters**: Monitor the actions you take (inputs) as much as the results you achieve (outputs) for better motivation and course correction.
- **Practice Self-Compassion**: Treat yourself with kindness during setbacks and remember that lasting change is a process, not a single event.

Bibliography

Core Research Foundations & Influential Studies
- Harvard University. Grant Study on Human Flourishing. (Longitudinal research on happiness and personal development).
- Stanford University. Research on Growth Mindset and Achievement (Carol Dweck, Gregory Walton).
- Massachusetts Institute of Technology (MIT). Studies on Habit Formation and Behavioral Change.
- Decades of organizational psychology research on high performance and personal transformation.

Classic and Influential Books
- Arnold Bennett, *How to Live on 24 Hours a Day* (time management and intentional living).
- Dale Carnegie, *How to Win Friends and Influence People* (communication and relationship building).
- Stephen R. Covey, *The 7 Habits of Highly Effective People* (principles of effectiveness and time management).
- Rick Warren, *The Purpose Driven Life* (life purpose, fulfillment, and values).
- Brian Tracy, *Goals!* (goal achievement, visualization, and personal growth).
- James Clear, *Atomic Habits* (habit change and practical strategies for lasting change).

Referenced Popular Works and Tools
- Cal Newport, *Deep Work* (focus and productivity strategies).
- Brené Brown, *Daring Greatly* and *The Gifts of Imperfection* (vulnerability and authenticity).
- Patrick King, *The Like Switch* (social influence and relationship skills).
- Keith Ferrazzi, *Never Eat Alone* (networking and building connections).

Empirical and Practical Psychology
- Daniel Goleman, Emotional Intelligence: Why It Can Matter More Than IQ (EQ, self-awareness, social skills).
- Angela Duckworth, Grit: The Power of Passion and Perseverance (perseverance, motivation).

- T.E. Lawrence, Seven Pillars of Wisdom (vision, persistence, and transformation — referenced thematically).

Additional Reading and Resources
- Charles Duhigg, *The Power of Habit* (habits and behavioral psychology).
- Carol S. Dweck, *Mindset: The New Psychology of Success* (growth mindset theory and practice).
- Annie Dillard, *The Writing Life* (intentional use of time, meaning).
- William Penn, *Some Fruits of Solitude* (on the value of time and intentional living).

PART 2 - GOALS THAT MATTER

"Where there is no vision, the people perish." — **Proverbs 29:18**

Goals That Matter
Purpose-Driven Goal Setting

About Things That Matter
A Self-Improvement Series for Success

Book 2

JC Ryan

About Goals That Matter

Goals Are Dreams With Deadlines.

Just about anyone can improve their lives and see their dreams fulfilled by improving their goal-setting skills. Often, small changes can have a huge impact. You do not need to be a manager, CEO, or business owner to benefit from this book. This book is for every person from all walks of life who wants to reach their goals—managers, employees, entrepreneurs, homemakers, students, and anyone seeking to live with purpose and fulfillment.

You will learn a practical, step-by-step process for turning dreams and hopes into goals and reality. This is not a book about miracles or wishful thinking, but about taking purpose-driven action to determine the things that matter to you and how to achieve them.

By reading this book and implementing the process of visualizing what you want, setting purpose-driven goals that matter, and mapping out your life's course, you can accomplish much more in a short time than most people would in a lifetime. Purpose-driven goal setting will unlock your potential, inspire you, improve your efficiency, give direction to your life, and enhance your confidence and commitment to a fulfilling life.

Ready to begin? Turn the page and start your journey to a life that truly matters.

What Matters To You?

The pace of the world is accelerating, and you might feel the pressure to keep up or even just stay afloat. You may be seeking deeper meaning in your life, striving to make each day more significant. Though it may seem like circumstances control you, you can choose what directs your life—everyone is guided by something.

The word "drive" implies guidance, control, or direction. For example, when you hammer a nail, you guide, control, and direct it into the wood. When you operate a vehicle, you guide, control, and direct it along the road. So, what's driving you?

At this moment, you might be driven by a problem that needs solving, the pressure of deadlines, or immediate demands. Or perhaps you're driven by less visible forces, such as feelings of guilt or resentment, anxieties, a focus on material possessions, or the need for others' approval. Many different situations, values, and emotions can drive your life, and each one can leave you feeling drained. You might be driven by current events, searching for meaning in things that are temporary. You feel the strain of societal divisions and rapidly advancing technology, and you've taken on an emotional burden that wasn't yours to carry.

Even devotion can drive your life, leaving you exhausted and without a true sense of direction. Why? Because it can become about human efforts to reach a higher power, focusing on rules and restrictions, and thought to earn favor. True connection, however, is about that higher power reaching out to humanity.

Many forces can drive your life, but they all tend to lead to the same result: undeveloped potential, unnecessary stress, and a life lacking fulfillment. You need a purpose greater than yourself to direct your life. Nothing can compensate for moving through life without knowing your purpose—not achievement, wealth, recognition, or pleasure. Without purpose, your life will always feel like an activity without meaning and movement without true direction. When your purpose isn't clear, you lack a roadmap to guide your decisions, manage your time, and allocate your resources. You might repeatedly change direction—your career, relationships, or beliefs—hoping that each change will resolve the confusion or fill the emptiness within.

This book is your invitation to discover, clarify, and pursue the things that matter most to you, through the art and science of purpose-driven goal setting.

The Horse in the Granite

The Power of Vision: Seeing What Others Cannot

A man once visited the studio of a sculptor to see him at work. When he arrived, he found an enormous rectangular granite block in the middle of the studio. The sculptor was walking around, staring at the granite block from different angles, making notes and drawing sketches.

The visitor asked, "What are you going to create out of that block?"

"A horse," replied the sculptor.

"How on earth are you going to create a horse out of this piece of granite that does not even remotely resemble a horse?"

The sculptor smiled and said, "The horse is inside the block, I have seen it, and all I have to do is remove every bit that does not look like a horse; then you will see it too."

A few months later, the man went back to see the sculptor, and there, in the middle of the studio, in the place of the granite block, was a perfect horse chiseled out of that seemingly impossible piece of rock he saw before.

In the same way, the sculptor had a dream to create a horse out of the granite block; we also have dreams. But the sculptor went a few steps further than most of us ever do—out of his dream, he created a clear vision of what that horse was going to look like. No one else could see what he was seeing, but once he "saw" that horse, he figured out exactly which parts of granite he had to remove to bring out the horse, then he figured out exactly how he was going to remove it and the tools he was going to use.

We all have dreams like the sculptor had, but as long as we only dream, nothing will come of it. Dreams require more than dreaming. The granite block will remain a block of granite until we remove that which does not resemble a horse.

*"All men dream, but not equally. Those who dream by night in the dusty recesses of their minds awake to the day to find it was all vanity: but the dreamers of the day are dangerous men, for they may act on their dreams with open eyes, to make them possible."— **T.E. Lawrence***

Our lives are much the same as the sculptor's block. We all have dreams of what could be. But dreams alone are not enough. The difference between a life imagined and a life achieved is the willingness to act: to clarify your vision, set meaningful goals, and do the daily work of removing whatever stands between you and your best self.

This book is about that process. It's about moving from hope to vision, from vision to goals, and from goals to action. You'll learn:

- How to create a clear, compelling vision for your life
- How to set goals that truly matter to you—not just what you think you "should" want
- How to plan, prioritize, and commit to your goals
- How to overcome obstacles, stay motivated, and build the habits that make success inevitable
- How to use accountability, reflection, and celebration to sustain your progress

You'll also discover why goal setting is not just for CEOs or athletes but for anyone who wants to live with intention, whether you're a student, a parent, a business owner, or simply someone ready for more.

This is not a book about wishful thinking or "name it and claim it" mantras. It's about practical, purpose-driven action. It's about learning the art and science of goal setting so you can create your own roadmap to a life that is rich with meaning, momentum, and fulfillment.

You have everything you need to begin. The only requirement is the willingness to learn, reflect, and take action. If you follow the process in these pages, you will find yourself doing the things that matter most, experiencing greater confidence, fulfillment, and success—whatever that means for you.

So, what do you see in the granite block of your life? What is the vision waiting to be revealed? Let's begin the work of bringing it to life—one clear, purpose-driven goal at a time.

Chapter 1 – The Foundations of Goal Achievement

The Power of Vision

Every great achievement begins with a vision. Vision is the ability to see, in your mind's eye, a future that does not yet exist—a future that excites you, inspires you, and pulls you forward. It is the "horse in the granite block," the image of possibility that gives shape and direction to your efforts.

Without vision, life becomes a series of disconnected activities. You may find yourself busy but not fulfilled, moving but not progressing. Vision is what separates a life of intention from a life of reaction.

> *"Where there is no vision, the people perish."* — **Proverbs 29:18**

Vision is not just for leaders or dreamers; it's for everyone. Whether you want to improve your health, build a business, deepen your relationships, or grow spiritually, you need a clear picture of where you want to go.

Exercise: Take a moment to close your eyes and imagine your life five years from now if everything went as well as it possibly could. What do you see? How do you feel? Who is with you? What are you doing? Write down your answers. This is the beginning of your vision.

Turn Vision Into Reality

Vision alone is not enough. Many people have dreams, but few turn those dreams into reality. The difference is action, specifically, the action of setting goals.

Goals are the bridge between vision and reality. They transform vague hopes into clear intentions and give you a roadmap to follow. Without goals, vision remains a daydream.

The GPS Metaphor

Imagine driving to a new city without a map or GPS. You might have a sense of where you want to go, but without clear directions, you'll likely get lost or give up. Goals are your GPS—they guide you step by step from where you are to where you want to be.

Goal setting is not just a business skill; it's a life skill. It's learnable and transferable. Anyone can become better at setting and achieving goals, regardless of age, background, or experience.

The Seven Promises of Purpose-Driven Goal Setting

Why bother with goal setting? Research and experience show that people who set and pursue meaningful goals enjoy:

1. **Fulfillment** – A sense of purpose and satisfaction in life.
2. **Self-Esteem** – Confidence grows as you make progress.
3. **Reduced Stress** – Clear goals help you focus on what matters and ignore distractions.
4. **Better Relationships** – You communicate your needs, boundaries, and dreams more clearly.
5. **Happiness** – Achieving goals releases dopamine, the brain's "reward" chemical.
6. **Success** – You are far more likely to accomplish what you set out to do.
7. **Resilience** – Goals help you bounce back from setbacks and keep moving forward.

When you set purpose-driven goals, you unlock your potential and give yourself a reason to get up every morning with energy and hope.

The Five Steps to Goal Achievement (Overview)

This book will guide you through a simple, powerful five-step process for achieving the things that matter most:

Create a Vision - See your desired future clearly. Know what you want and why you want it.

- **Vision is your "why."** It's the emotional fuel that keeps you going when the journey gets tough. Without a compelling vision, goals become chores instead of opportunities.

Set the Goals - Turn your vision into specific, measurable, achievable, relevant, and time-bound (SMART) goals.

- **Goals are your "what."** They define the destination. The more specific and meaningful your goals, the more likely you are to achieve them.

Create the Plan - Map out the steps, resources, and timeline needed to achieve your goals.
- **A goal without a plan is just a wish.** Planning breaks big goals into small, manageable steps and helps you anticipate obstacles.

Commit to the Plan - Make a firm decision to follow through, even when motivation fades.
- **Commitment is your "how."** It's the decision to keep going, even when you don't feel like it. Commitment turns intentions into actions.

Execute the Plan - Take consistent action, adjust as needed, and celebrate your progress.
- **Execution is your "when."** It's about doing the work, day after day, until you cross the finish line. Execution is where dreams become reality.

Each of these steps will be explored in detail in the chapters ahead. For now, let's look at why each is essential.

Why People Without Vision and Goals Drift

Many people drift through life, reacting to circumstances rather than creating them.

Without vision and goals:
- You become vulnerable to distractions and other people's agendas.
- You may achieve things that don't actually matter to you.
- You risk looking back with regret at opportunities missed.

With vision and goals:
- You live proactively, not reactively.
- You attract opportunities and people aligned with your path.
- You persevere through setbacks because you know what you're working toward.

Goal Setting Is for Everyone

You don't need to be a CEO, entrepreneur, or professional athlete to benefit from goal setting.

Homemakers, students, employees, retirees—everyone can use these principles.
Goal setting works for health, relationships, finances, learning, and personal growth.
The process is the same: vision, goals, plan, commitment, execution.

What You Can Expect if You Follow This Process

If you follow the process in this book, you will:

Gain clarity about what you truly want.
Build confidence as you see progress.

Experience more fulfillment and less stress.
Achieve more in less time.
Develop habits that support lifelong growth.

Chapter Summary

Vision is the starting point for all meaningful achievement; it is the vivid, credible picture of your desired future that pulls you forward.

Dreams and hopes inspire, but vision gives direction, and goals provide the steps to make vision a reality.

Goal setting is a learnable and transferable skill—anyone, in any walk of life, can benefit from it.

People who set clear, purpose-driven goals experience greater fulfillment, improved self-esteem, lower stress, better relationships, more happiness, and higher success.

The five essential steps to goal achievement are: create a vision, set the goals, create the plan, commit to the plan, and execute the plan.

Without vision and goals, people drift and become subject to circumstances; with them, you become proactive and resilient.

Goal setting gives you a personal GPS for your life, helping you avoid wasted effort and uncertainty.

The process of purpose-driven goal setting is simple, powerful, and accessible to everyone willing to learn and apply it.

Reflection Questions

Question 1: What is your vision for your life? What excites and inspires you?

Former Student Responses:

"I don't really have a clear vision - I just take things day by day."
"I want to be successful, but I'm not sure what that means for me specifically."
"I have too many ideas and dreams, I can't focus on just one vision."
"My vision feels too big and unrealistic - like owning my own business or traveling the world"
"I used to have dreams, but life got in the way, and now I feel stuck."
"I want to make a difference, but I don't know how or where to start."
"My vision changes depending on my mood or what I see others doing."

Possible Solutions:

Lack of Vision: Start with the visualization exercise - imagine your life 5 years from now if everything went perfectly. Write down what you see, feel, and experience.

Vague Success Definition: Define success on your own terms by identifying what truly matters to you - relationships, freedom, creativity, security, or impact.

Too Many Ideas: Create a "vision parking lot" for all ideas, then identify common themes or choose one area to focus on for the next year.

Unrealistic Dreams: Break big visions into smaller, more believable components. Focus on the feeling and values behind the vision rather than just the outcome.

Lost Dreams: Reconnect with childhood interests or past passions. Ask yourself what you would do if failure weren't possible.

Unclear Impact: Identify problems you care about solving or people you want to help. Start small with local or personal impact.

Changing Vision: Look for underlying values that remain constant even when surface desires change.

Question 2: Where in your life do you feel busy but not fulfilled?

Former Student Responses:

"I'm constantly working but don't feel like I'm making progress toward anything meaningful."

"I spend hours on social media and entertainment, but feel empty afterward."

"I'm always helping others but neglecting my own goals and needs."

"My days are packed with activities, but I can't remember what I accomplished."

"I'm busy with household tasks and responsibilities, but don't feel purposeful."

"I attend lots of meetings and events, but nothing seems to move forward."

"I'm learning lots of things but not applying any of it to real goals."

Possible Solutions:

Meaningless Work: Identify how your current work could connect to larger purposes, or begin planning a transition to more meaningful work

Digital Distraction: Set specific times for social media and entertainment, replace some screen time with goal-oriented activities

People-Pleasing: Practice saying no to requests that don't align with your priorities, schedule time for your own goals first

Scattered Activities: Use time-blocking to focus on fewer, more important activities. Track what you actually accomplish each day.

Routine Without Purpose: Connect daily tasks to larger goals (organizing the home creates a peaceful environment for the family)

- **Unproductive Meetings**: Evaluate which meetings truly serve your goals, suggest more efficient formats, or decline non-essential ones
- **Learning Without Application**: Choose one skill to focus on and immediately apply it to a specific project or goal

Question 3: What would change for you if you had clear goals and a plan to achieve them?

Former Student Responses:

"I think I'd feel more confident and less anxious about the future."
"I'd probably waste less time on things that don't matter."
"I might actually finish projects instead of starting and abandoning them."
"I'd have a better sense of direction and purpose in my daily life."
"I could make decisions more easily because I'd know what I'm working toward."
"I'd feel more motivated to take action instead of just thinking about change."
"I might stop comparing myself to others so much."

Possible Solutions:

- **Increased Confidence**: Start with small, achievable goals to build momentum and prove to yourself that you can follow through
- **Better Time Management**: Use the 80/20 rule to identify high-impact activities that align with your goals
- **Project Completion**: Break large projects into smaller milestones with specific deadlines and accountability measures
- **Daily Purpose**: Connect daily actions to larger goals by asking, "How does this activity serve my vision?"
- **Decision-Making**: Create a simple decision filter based on your top 3 priorities or values
- **Action Motivation**: Focus on the next small step rather than the entire goal, use implementation intentions ("When X happens, I will do Y")
- **Comparison Reduction**: Define success on your own terms and track your personal progress rather than comparing to others

Question 4: What area of your life would benefit most from purpose-driven goal setting?

Former Student Responses:

"My career - I feel stuck and don't know how to advance or change directions."
"My health - I keep starting and stopping exercise and diet plans."
"My finances - I'm living paycheck to paycheck with no clear plan."
"My relationships - I want deeper connections, but don't know how to build them."

"My personal growth - I want to learn and develop, but lack structure."
"My work-life balance - I'm burned out and need better boundaries."
"My creativity - I have artistic interests, but never make time for them."

Possible Solutions:

Career Development: Conduct a skills assessment, research desired roles, set learning goals, and create a networking plan

Health Goals: Start with one small habit (10-minute daily walk), focus on consistency over intensity, track progress visually

Financial Planning: Begin with tracking expenses for one month, then set a small savings goal ($25/week), and automate savings

Relationship Building: Set goals for regular contact with important people, practice active listening, and plan meaningful shared experiences

Personal Growth: Choose one skill or area to focus on, schedule regular learning time, and find ways to apply new knowledge immediately

Work-Life Balance: Set specific boundaries (no emails after 7 PM), schedule personal time like appointments, practice saying no

Creative Pursuits: Schedule creative time like any important appointment, start with 15 minutes daily, and join a creative community for accountability

Universal Solutions Across All Chapter 1 Questions:

Start with Self-Assessment: Use the reflection questions to honestly evaluate where you are now versus where you want to be.

Create a Vision Statement: Write a clear, inspiring description of your ideal life that connects to your deepest values and desires.

Use the SMART Framework: Make goals Specific, Measurable, Achievable, Relevant, and Time-bound to increase the likelihood of success.

Begin with Small Steps: Choose one area to focus on first and break it into manageable actions to avoid overwhelm.

Write Everything Down: Document your vision, goals, and plans to increase commitment and clarity.

Find Accountability: Share your goals with someone you trust or join a supportive community.

Plan for Obstacles: Anticipate challenges and create strategies to overcome them before they arise.

Celebrate Progress: Acknowledge small wins along the way to maintain motivation and momentum.

Take Action

- Write down your vision for one area of your life.
- List three benefits you hope to gain from setting and achieving goals.
- Share your vision with someone you trust.

"The future belongs to those who believe in the beauty of their dreams." — **Eleanor Roosevelt.**

Chapter 2 – Vision: The First Step

The Power of Vision

Every meaningful achievement begins with a vision—a vivid, credible picture of a future you want to create. Vision is more than hope, more than a dream. It is the act of "seeing" your desired future state so clearly that it pulls you forward, even when the path is uncertain.

"Where there is no vision, the people perish." — **Proverbs 29:18**

Vision is the foundation of all goal setting. Without it, your efforts are scattered, your motivation fades, and your actions lack direction. With vision, you become like the sculptor who sees the horse in the granite block, removing everything that doesn't belong until your dream takes shape in reality.

Vision vs. Hope, Dream, and Goal

It's easy to confuse hope, dreams, vision, and goals. Let's clarify:

- **Hope** is a feeling or longing for something better. ("I hope things will improve.")
- **Dream** is an imagined, ideal scenario. ("I dream of owning my own business.")
- **Vision** is a vivid, credible mental picture of a future you want to create. ("I see myself running a thriving café, welcoming customers, and building a community.")
- **Goal** is a specific, measurable result you are committed to achieving. ("I will open my café by June 1st next year.")

Key Insight: Dreams and hopes inspire you. Vision gives you direction. Goals give you traction.

Why Vision Comes Before Goals

Vision is the "why" behind your goals. It's the emotional fuel that keeps you moving when things get tough. Without vision, goals become chores instead of opportunities.

Think about the classic job interview question: "Where do you see yourself in five years?" Organizations value vision because it drives progress. Shouldn't you value it just as much for your own life?

Vision is not just for a career or business. It applies to every area: health, relationships, finances, learning, and personal growth. If you can see it, you can start working toward it.

Creating a Vision

Vision is not something that just appears—it is something you create. It is birthed in you through reflection, imagination, and, sometimes, faith.

Visualization Exercise:

Take a few quiet moments. Close your eyes and imagine your life five years from now if everything went as well as it possibly could.

- Where are you?
- What are you doing?
- Who is with you?
- How do you feel?
- What does your environment look like?

Write down your answers. The clearer your vision, the stronger your motivation will be.

Tip: For many, visioning is a spiritual process. The most powerful visions align with your deepest values and sense of purpose.

Vision as a Roadmap

A vision is your personal GPS. It tells you where you are now and where you want to go. It helps you make decisions, set priorities, and measure progress.

Without a vision, you're likely to drift, repeat old patterns, and settle for less than you're capable of. With vision, you live proactively, not reactively. You attract opportunities and people aligned with your path. You persevere through setbacks because you know what you're working toward.

The Power of Now

You have three timeframes: past, present, and future.

- You can't change the past, but you can learn from it.
- You can't act in the future, but you can prepare for it.
- Only what you do in the present will influence what happens in the future.

"The future depends on what we do in the present." — Mahatma Gandhi

Reflection: How much time do you spend dwelling on the past, worrying about the future, or acting with purpose in the present?

Your motto should be: Visualize the future, learn from the past, and do the things that matter in the present.

The Preparation: Choosing the Right Goals

Choosing the right goals to focus on is a process that requires careful thought. Don't rush it. These are your goals, your life—make sure they matter to you.

- What are you passionate about?
- What inspires you?
- If you could do anything, what would it be?

Talk to friends, family, and mentors. Learn from their experiences, but remember: your most powerful and inspiring goals are the ones you value most.

Self-Assessment: Where Are You Now?

Before you set new goals, take an honest look at your current life.

> Are you where you want to be?
> What's working? What's not?
> What would you change if you could?

Reflection Exercise:

Rate your satisfaction (1–10) in these areas:

> Goal-setting habits
> Time management habits
> Relationships (spouse/partner, family, friends, colleagues, business associates)
> Career path

For each area, ask:

> Why did I give myself this score?
> What would a 10 look like?
> What's one goal I could set to move closer to a 10?

Chapter Summary

- Vision is the foundation of all achievement.
- Dreams and hopes inspire, but vision directs.
- Your vision must be personal, vivid, and motivating.
- A clear vision helps you make decisions, set priorities, and persevere.
- The journey from vision to reality begins with "seeing"—then acting.
- Honest self-assessment is the first step to meaningful change.

Reflection Questions

Based on Chapter 2's reflection questions from "Goals That Matter," here are student responses and corresponding solutions:

Question 1: What is your vision for your life? What excites and inspires you?

Former Student Responses:

"I want to create a thriving café where people feel welcomed and build community connections."

"I dream of traveling the world while working remotely as a digital nomad."

"I envision myself as a published author who inspires others through storytelling."

"I see myself leading a balanced life where I'm successful at work but still have time for my family."

"I want to start a nonprofit organization that helps underprivileged children access education."

"I picture myself financially independent by age 50, able to pursue my passions without money stress."

"I imagine having a healthy, active lifestyle where I can hike mountains well into my 70s."

Possible Solutions:

Café Vision: Start by researching the food service industry, visiting successful cafés to understand their operations, and perhaps working part-time in a café to gain experience

Digital Nomad Dreams: Begin building remote work skills, create a portfolio of work that can be done anywhere, and start with short-term remote work arrangements

Publishing Goals: Start a daily writing habit, join writing groups for feedback, and research the publishing industry while building a platform

Work-Life Balance: Define what "balance" means specifically for you, set boundaries around work hours, and schedule family time like important appointments

- **Nonprofit Vision**: Volunteer with existing organizations to understand the sector, research nonprofit management, and identify specific educational gaps you want to address
- **Financial Independence**: Calculate your target number, create a detailed savings and investment plan, and consider additional income streams
- **Health and Longevity**: Start with small daily habits like walking, gradually build fitness routines, and focus on preventive health measures

Question 2: How satisfied are you with your current habits, relationships, and career?

Former Student Responses:

- **Goal Setting Habits (Rating 3/10)**: "I have lots of ideas but never write them down or follow through systematically."
- **Time Management (Rating 4/10)**: "I'm constantly busy but feel like I'm not making real progress on what matters."
- **Relationships (Rating 6/10)**: "My family relationships are good, but I've lost touch with friends and don't network professionally."
- **Career Path (Rating 5/10)**: "I like my job, but don't see a clear path forward, and I'm not sure if this is what I want long-term."

Possible Solutions:

- **Improving Goal Setting**: Start with the SMART framework, write goals in a dedicated journal, and schedule weekly reviews to track progress
- **Better Time Management**: Use time-blocking techniques, identify your most productive hours, and eliminate or delegate low-priority activities
- **Strengthening Relationships**: Schedule regular check-ins with important people, join professional associations, and make time for social activities
- **Career Development**: Conduct informational interviews in areas of interest, seek mentorship, and create a professional development plan

Question 3: Where are you now versus where you want to be?

Former Student Responses:

"I'm working in accounting but want to transition to sustainable business consulting."

"I'm single and living paycheck to paycheck, but I want to be in a committed relationship and own a home."

"I'm 20 pounds overweight and sedentary, but I want to run a marathon and feel energetic."

"I'm shy and avoid public speaking, but I want to become a confident leader in my field."

"I have no savings and debt, but I want to be financially secure and able to help my parents."

Possible Solutions:

Career Transition: Take courses in sustainability, volunteer with environmental organizations, and network with professionals in the field while maintaining current income

Personal Life Goals: Focus on self-improvement to become the partner you want to attract, create a budget and savings plan, and research homebuying requirements

Health Transformation: Start with a 10-minute daily walk, gradually increase activity, and focus on one healthy eating change per week

Leadership Development: Join Toastmasters or similar groups, volunteer for small leadership roles, and practice speaking in low-stakes environments

Financial Recovery: Create a debt payoff plan, build an emergency fund starting with $25/week, and learn about investing for long-term security

Question 4: What changes do you need to make to align with your vision?

Former Student Responses:

"I need to stop procrastinating and start taking concrete steps toward my business idea."

"I need to improve my communication skills to advance in my career."

"I need to create better work-life boundaries so I can focus on my health and relationships."

"I need to build my confidence and stop letting fear hold me back from opportunities."

"I need to develop better financial habits and stop impulse spending."

Possible Solutions:

Overcoming Procrastination: Break large tasks into 15-minute segments, use the "2-minute rule" for small tasks, and create accountability systems

Communication Skills: Take a public speaking course, practice active listening, and seek feedback from trusted colleagues

Work-Life Boundaries: Set specific work hours, turn off notifications after hours, and communicate boundaries clearly to colleagues

Building Confidence: Start with small challenges, celebrate wins, and work with a coach or therapist if needed

Financial Discipline: Use the 24-hour rule for purchases, automate savings, and track spending to identify patterns

Question 5: What is one meaningful goal you can commit to for the next year?

Former Student Responses:

"Launch my freelance graphic design business and secure three regular clients."
"Complete a certification in project management to advance my career."
"Run my first 5K race and establish a consistent exercise routine."
"Save $10,000 for an emergency fund while paying off credit card debt"
"Strengthen my relationship with my teenage daughter by having weekly one-on-one time."

Possible Solutions:

Freelance Business: Create a business plan, build a portfolio website, and start networking while maintaining your current job.

Professional Certification: Research certification requirements, create a study schedule, and join study groups for accountability.

Fitness Goal: Use a couch-to-5K program, find a running buddy, and register for a race to create commitment

Financial Goal: Set up automatic transfers to savings, use the debt snowball method, and track progress monthly

Relationship Building: Schedule weekly activities, put away devices during this time, and focus on listening and connecting

Universal Solutions Across All Chapter 2 Questions:

Start with Self-Assessment: Use the reflection questions to honestly evaluate where you are now versus where you want to be in each area of life.

Create Specific Visions: Move beyond vague dreams to detailed, vivid pictures of your desired future that include how you'll feel and what you'll experience.

Use the Gap Analysis: Identify the specific differences between your current reality and your vision, then create plans to bridge those gaps.

Focus on One Area First: Rather than trying to change everything at once, choose the area that will have the biggest positive impact on your life.

Make It Personal: Ensure your goals reflect your own values and desires, not what others expect of you or what society deems successful.

Write Everything Down: Document your vision, current state, and goals to increase clarity and commitment.

Seek Support: Share your vision with trusted friends, family, or mentors who can provide encouragement and accountability.

Plan for Obstacles: Anticipate challenges you might face and develop strategies to overcome them before they arise.

Celebrate Progress: Acknowledge small wins along the way to maintain motivation and build momentum toward your larger vision.

Take Action

Write down your vision for one area of your life.
List three benefits you hope to gain from setting and achieving goals.
Share your vision with someone you trust.
Complete the self-assessment exercise and identify one area to focus on first.

"Learn from the past, set vivid, detailed goals for the future, and live in the only moment of time over which you have any control: now." — **Denis Waitley.**

Chapter 3 – Preparation: Choosing the Right Goals

The Things That Matter

Choosing the right goals is not about rushing into action or setting goals just for the sake of it. It's about taking a thoughtful pause to reflect on what truly matters to you. Too often, people set goals based on what they think they "should" want—what society, family, or peers expect—only to find themselves unmotivated or unfulfilled. The most powerful and inspiring goals are those rooted in your own values, passions, and priorities.

It is a waste of time to set goals about things that do not matter to you. Always remember you must determine your own goals; no one else can set your goals for you.

Ask yourself:

   What inspires me?
   What do I love doing?
   If I could do anything, what would it be?
   What can people always rely on me for?

Don't be afraid to talk to others—family, friends, mentors, or people you admire. Ask them how they set goals and what matters most to them. Learn from their experiences, but remember: your goals remain yours, undertaken for your own reasons.

The Power of Personal Motivation

Setting goals to achieve things you aren't passionate about will likely end in failure. Your motivation must always be your personal stake in the goal. If your only reason for pursuing a goal is to impress others, your drive will fade quickly. But if your goal is tied to something you genuinely value, you'll find the energy to persist even when things get tough.

*"There's a lot of power in knowing what you do want, what you're passionate about, and then creating your goals from there. If you don't know what you want, you probably won't be able to attract it." — **Susanne Conrad**.*

Self-Assessment: Where Are You Now?

Before you can set the right goals, you need to know where you are. This honest self-assessment is a crucial step in the self-improvement process and requires a commitment of time and effort. No one else will see this, so be brutally honest.

Below are key areas to reflect on. For each, rate yourself on a scale of 1 to 10, then answer the questions that follow:

My Goal-Setting Habits

    How effective are you at goal setting?
    Why did you give yourself that score?
    What changes (if any) do you think or know you have to make to achieve what you want?
    Do you need to set a new goal for this aspect of your life? If so, write it down.

My Time Management Habits

    How effective are you at managing your time?
    Why did you give yourself that score?
    What changes do you need to make to achieve what you want?
    Do you need to set a new goal for this aspect of your life?

My Relationships

Reflect on your relationships with your spouse/partner, family, friends, work colleagues, and business associates.

    How happy are you with each relationship? (Rate 1–10)
    Why did you give yourself that score?
    What changes do you need to make?
    Do you need to set a new goal for this aspect?

My Career Path

    How happy are you with your career at the moment? (Rate 1–10)
    Why did you give yourself that score?
    What changes do you need to make?
    Do you need to set a new goal for this aspect?

Tip: Remember, career goals do not have to be about climbing the corporate ladder or becoming wealthy. It's just as valid to want stability, fulfillment, or more time for other areas of your life.

The Importance of Honest Reflection

Working through these questions and answering them honestly will help you understand where you are at the moment and how your current life differs from what you hope or dream it could be. This is not a scientific test but a personal conversation with yourself. The more thought you put into this, the greater the rewards in accomplishing more in your life, doing things you enjoy, achieving your goals, and feeling fulfilled.

"Luck is what happens when preparation meets opportunity." — **Seneca**

Learning from Others

Don't hesitate to ask for help or perspective from family, friends, or professionals. Sometimes, others can see our strengths and blind spots more clearly than we can. Their insights can help you clarify what matters most and set more meaningful goals.

Practical Exercise: The Self-Assessment Inventory

1. Set aside quiet, uninterrupted time.
2. For each area above, write your score and honest answers.
3. Identify at least one area where you want to set a new goal.
4. Write down why this goal matters to you—your personal "why."

The Value of Preparation

Preparation is not about perfection; it's about clarity. By understanding where you are and what matters most, you set yourself up for success. You avoid the trap of setting too many goals or the wrong goals and instead focus your energy on what will truly move your life forward.

Chapter Summary

The most powerful goals are those rooted in your own values and passions.
Honest self-assessment is essential before setting new goals.
Rate yourself in key areas: goal setting, time management, relationships, and career.
Preparation and clarity now will save you time, energy, and frustration later.
Learn from others, but make your goals your own.

Reflection Questions

Question 1: What are the most important areas of your life where you want to see improvement?

Former Student Responses:

"I want to improve my work-life balance - I'm constantly stressed and never have time for myself or my family."

"My financial situation is a mess - I live paycheck to paycheck with no savings or clear plan."

"I need to get healthier - I'm out of shape, eat poorly, and have no energy."

"My relationships feel superficial - I want deeper connections with friends and family."

"I feel stuck in my career with no clear direction or growth opportunities."

"I want to develop myself personally - learn new skills and become more confident."

"My home and personal organization are chaotic - I waste time looking for things and feel overwhelmed."

Possible Solutions:

Work-Life Balance: Set specific work hours and stick to them, schedule personal time like important meetings, and practice saying no to non-essential commitments

Financial Health: Start tracking expenses for one month, automate savings of even $25/week, read one financial article per week, create a simple debt payoff plan

Physical Health: Begin with 10-minute daily walks, replace one unhealthy snack with fruit, drink one extra glass of water daily, and schedule annual health checkups

Relationships: Schedule regular one-on-one time with important people, practice active listening, and share something meaningful about yourself weekly

Career Development: Identify three skills needed for advancement, network with one new person monthly, update resume quarterly, and research career paths

Personal Growth: Read for 15 minutes daily, take one online course, join a learning community, practice a new skill consistently

Organization: Declutter one area per week, create designated spaces for important items, use simple planning systems, and establish daily tidying routines

Question 2: How do you typically prioritize your goals when you have multiple areas that need attention?

Former Student Responses:

"I try to work on everything at once and end up making no real progress anywhere."

"I focus on whatever feels most urgent at the moment, which means I'm always putting out fires."

"I tend to work on the easiest goals first and avoid the more challenging ones."

"I don't really have a system - I just hope I'll somehow get to everything eventually."

"I get overwhelmed by having too many goals and often give up entirely."

"I prioritize based on what others expect of me rather than what I actually want."

"I start with good intentions but lose focus when life gets busy."

Possible Solutions:

Everything at Once: Choose one primary area to focus on for 90 days, limit yourself to 3 major goals maximum, use the "one thing" approach

Urgency-Driven: Distinguish between urgent and important using the Eisenhower Matrix, schedule time for important non-urgent activities, create systems to prevent crises

Easy First: Identify which goal would have the biggest positive impact on other areas, tackle one challenging goal alongside easier ones for balance

No System: Use simple prioritization methods like ranking goals 1-10 in importance, consider which goals align with your core values, ask "What would I regret not pursuing?"

Overwhelm: Start with just one goal, break large goals into tiny steps, and celebrate small wins to build momentum

External Pressure: Clarify your own values and priorities, practice setting boundaries, remember that you can't please everyone

Lost Focus: Write goals down and review weekly, create visual reminders, build accountability systems, and connect daily actions to larger purposes

Question 3: What specific, measurable outcomes do you want to achieve in the next 6-12 months?

Former Student Responses:

"I want to lose weight and get in shape, but I'm not sure what's realistic."
"I'd like to save money for emergencies, maybe a few thousand dollars."
"I want to advance in my career somehow - get promoted or find a better job."
"I'd like to improve my relationships, but I don't know how to measure that."
"I want to learn new skills, particularly in technology or communication."
"I'd like to be more organized and productive with my time."
"I want to start a side business or creative project."

Possible Solutions:

Weight/Fitness: Set specific targets like "lose 15 pounds by June" or "walk 10,000 steps daily for 3 months," focus on process goals like "exercise 4 times per week."

Financial Goals: "Save $3,000 in 12 months" ($250/month), "Build emergency fund equal to 3 months' expenses," "Pay off $2,000 credit card debt by December"

Career Advancement: "Complete certification in [specific skill] by August," "Apply for 5 internal positions in next 6 months," "Increase salary by 10% within one year"

Relationship Improvement: "Have weekly one-on-one time with spouse," "Call parents every Sunday for 6 months," "Host monthly dinner with friends"

Skill Development: "Complete online course in [specific skill] by March," "Practice public speaking at 6 events this year," "Learn to use 3 new software programs"

Organization/Productivity: "Maintain a clean desk for 30 consecutive days," "Complete daily planning routine for 90 days," "Reduce email checking to 3 times daily."

Side Business/Creative: "Launch website by April," "Create and sell first product by September," "Complete first draft of book by year-end"

Question 4: How do your current goals align with your deeper values and long-term vision?

Former Student Responses:

"I'm not sure I've ever really thought about my deeper values - I just set goals based on what seems important."

"My goals feel disconnected from what I actually care about most."

"I set goals based on what I think I should want, not what I actually want."

"I have a vague sense of my values, but haven't connected them to specific goals."

"My goals are mostly reactive - trying to fix problems rather than building toward something positive."

"I feel pressure to pursue goals that look impressive to others."

"I'm not sure what my long-term vision even is."

Possible Solutions:

Unclear Values: Complete a values assessment exercise, reflect on peak life experiences to identify what mattered most, ask "What would I stand for even if it cost me something?"

Disconnected Goals: Review current goals and ask "Why does this matter to me?" for each one, eliminate goals that don't connect to your core values

Should vs. Want: Distinguish between external expectations and internal desires, practice asking "What do I actually want?" rather than "What should I want?"

Vague Connection: Write out your top 5 values, then map each goal to at least one value, and adjust goals that don't align

Reactive Goals: Balance problem-solving goals with vision-building goals, spend time imagining your ideal future, set goals that move you toward something positive

External Pressure: Practice defining success on your own terms, limit sharing goals with people who impose their expectations, and focus on internal validation.

No Long-term Vision: Use visualization exercises to imagine your life in 5-10 years, identify themes and patterns in what excites you, start with a shorter-term vision, and expand

Question 5: What obstacles or challenges do you anticipate in pursuing these goals?

Former Student Responses:

"I always start strong but lose motivation after a few weeks."
"I don't have enough time with work and family responsibilities."
"I lack the knowledge or skills needed to achieve what I want."
"I'm worried about failing and looking foolish to others."
"I tend to get distracted by new opportunities or urgent demands."
"I don't have the financial resources to pursue some of my goals."
"My family or friends might not understand or support my goals."

Possible Solutions:

Motivation Loss: Create systems that don't rely on motivation, track progress visually, connect with accountability partners, revisit your "why" regularly

Time Constraints: Audit how you currently spend time, identify time-wasters to eliminate, use time-blocking for goal activities, start with just 15 minutes daily

Knowledge/Skills Gap: Identify specific skills needed, create a learning plan with deadlines, find mentors or courses, start with free resources like YouTube or library books

Fear of Failure: Reframe failure as learning, start with low-risk experiments, focus on effort rather than outcome, share goals with supportive people only

Distraction/Focus: Use single-tasking techniques, create distraction-free environments, practice saying no to non-essential opportunities, review priorities weekly

Financial Constraints: Look for low-cost alternatives, start with goals that require minimal investment, consider earning extra income specifically for goals

Lack of Support: Find like-minded communities online or locally, communicate the benefits of your goals to family, and seek support outside your immediate circle when needed

Universal Solutions Across All Chapter 3 Questions:

Start with Self-Assessment: Use honest reflection to understand where you are now and what truly matters to you.

Focus on Alignment: Ensure your goals reflect your authentic values and desires, not external expectations.

Use the SMART Framework: Make goals Specific, Measurable, Achievable, Relevant, and Time-bound for maximum effectiveness.

Plan for Obstacles: Anticipate challenges and create specific strategies to overcome them before they arise.

Build Support Systems: Connect with people who encourage your growth and can provide accountability.

Track Progress: Use simple systems to monitor advancement and celebrate milestones along the way.

Stay Flexible: Be willing to adjust goals as you learn and grow, while maintaining commitment to your core vision.

Balance Challenge and Realism: Set goals that stretch you without being overwhelming or impossible to achieve.

Take Action

- Complete the self-assessment inventory for each key area of your life.
- Identify one area where you want to set a new, meaningful goal.
- Write down your "why" for this goal.
- Share your intention with a trusted friend or mentor.

"Whether you think you can, or you think you can't—you're right." — ***Henry Ford***

Chapter 4 – Setting Goals That Matter

Vision as the Primer for Goal Setting

A vision is a vivid picture of your desired future. But vision alone is not enough. To bring your vision to life, you must set clear, actionable goals. Goals are the "how" that bridges the gap between where you are now and where you want to be. If your vision is to own a business, your goals might include learning new skills, registering your company, raising capital, and hiring staff. Each of these is a concrete step toward realizing your vision.

Start with your current situation:

> Where are you now?
> Where will you be in one, two, five, or ten years if you keep doing what you're doing?
> Are you on track to realize your vision?
> Do you need to make changes?

Be brutally honest. The clearer you are about your goals and what you want to achieve, the more likely you are to succeed.

The Science of Goal Setting

Researchers Edwin A. Locke and Gary P. Latham discovered that setting clear and specific goals produces four powerful results:

1. **Focus:** You spend your time and energy on what matters.
2. **Effort:** You're motivated to put in more work to achieve your goals.
3. **Persistence:** You stay committed, even when things get tough.
4. **Learning:** You grow as you work toward your goals.

Specificity is key. Vague goals like "get healthier" or "be successful" are hard to measure and even harder to achieve. Instead, define your goals in concrete terms: "Lose 10kg by December," "Save $5,000 this year," or "Read 12 books in 12 months."

The Power of Specificity

A goal is a result or achievement toward which effort is directed. It is the finish line, the target, the purpose. The more specific your goal, the easier it is to plan, track, and achieve.

> Vague: "I want to lose weight."

Specific: "I will lose 10kg by December 1st by walking 30 minutes daily and tracking my meals."

Vague: "I want to improve my career."

Specific: "I will complete an online certification in digital marketing by June 30th and apply for three new jobs by August."

Exercise: Write down one area of your life you want to improve. Now, rewrite your goal to make it as specific as possible. Ask: How will I know when I've achieved it? What will success look like?

The Preparation: Start Where You Are

Before you set new goals, take stock of your current reality. What have you achieved so far? Are you on track to realize your vision? What needs to change?

Self-Assessment Questions:

What is working well in your life right now?
What is not working?
What have you accomplished that you're proud of?
What do you want to change most?

This honest assessment will help you set realistic, motivating goals that match your vision and current circumstances.

Setting SMART Goals

SMART is a proven framework for goal setting:

- **Specific:** What exactly do you want to achieve?
- **Measurable:** How will you track progress and know when you've succeeded?
- **Achievable:** Is your goal realistic, given your resources and constraints?
- **Relevant:** Does this goal matter to you and align with your vision?
- **Time-bound:** What is your deadline?

Example: "I will save $5,000 for an emergency fund by setting aside $200 from each paycheck and tracking my progress monthly. My deadline is December 31st."

Aligning Goals with Your Values

The goals that matter most are those that align with your deepest values and priorities. If you set goals to please others or to meet external expectations, your motivation will fade. But when your goals reflect what you truly care about, you'll find the energy to persist through challenges.

Ask yourself:

> Why is this goal important to me?
> How does it connect to my vision and values?
> What will achieving this goal allow me to do or become?

The Power of Written Goals

Writing down your goals increases your commitment and clarity. Studies show that people who write their goals are significantly more likely to achieve them than those who don't. Take the time to write your goals in a journal, planner, or digital document. Review them regularly and update them as needed.

Goal Setting in All Areas of Life

Goal setting isn't just for your career or finances. It applies to every area of your life:

- Health and fitness
- Relationships
- Personal growth and learning
- Spirituality
- Hobbies and recreation
- Community and service

For each area, ask: What is one meaningful goal I can set for the next year?

Chapter Summary

> Vision is the primer for goal setting; goals are the steps that bring your vision to life.
> Specific, written goals focus your energy, increase motivation, and drive persistence.
> Use the SMART framework to clarify your goals.
> Align your goals with your values for lasting motivation.
> Write down your goals and review them regularly.
> Set goals in all areas of your life for balanced growth.

Reflection Questions

Question 1: What is one area of your life where you need a more specific goal?

Former Student Responses:

"I want to 'get healthier' but I don't know what that actually means or how to measure it."

"I keep saying I want to 'advance my career' but I haven't defined what advancement looks like."

"I want to 'improve my relationships' but that's too vague to take action on."

"I say I want to 'be more organized' but I don't have specific targets."

"I want to 'save money' but I haven't set an actual amount or timeline."

"I want to 'learn new skills' but I haven't identified which skills or how I'll learn them."

"I want to 'be more productive' but I don't know how to measure productivity."

Possible Solutions:

Health Goals: Transform "get healthier" into "lose 15 pounds by June 30th by walking 10,000 steps daily and eating 5 servings of vegetables per day"

Career Advancement: Change "advance my career" to "complete a project management certification by September and apply for 3 senior positions by year-end"

Relationship Improvement: Specify "have weekly one-on-one dinner with my spouse and call my parents every Sunday for the next 6 months"

Organization: Define "declutter and organize my home office by March 15th and maintain a clean desk for 30 consecutive days."

Financial Goals: Set "save $5,000 for emergency fund by December 31st by automatically transferring $200 from each paycheck"

Skill Development: Choose "complete an online course in data analysis by August and practice Excel skills 30 minutes daily"

Productivity: Establish "complete my top 3 priority tasks before checking email each day for the next 90 days"

Question 2: How does your current goal align with your vision and values?

Former Student Responses:

"I'm not sure my goals actually reflect what I care about most - they seem more like what I think I should want."

"My goals are mostly about fixing problems rather than building toward something positive."

"I set goals based on what looks impressive to others, not what truly matters to me."

"I haven't really thought about how my daily goals connect to my bigger life vision."

"My goals feel disconnected from my core values - I'm pursuing things that don't really fulfill me."

"I have goals in different areas, but they don't seem to work together toward a common purpose."

"I'm not even sure what my values are, so I don't know if my goals align with them."

Possible Solutions:

Values Clarification: Complete a values assessment to identify your top 5 core values, then map each goal to at least one value

Vision Connection: Write a one-page description of your ideal life in 5 years, then ensure each goal moves you toward that vision

Internal vs. External Motivation: Ask "Am I pursuing this because I want it, or because others expect it?" Adjust goals to reflect authentic desires

Purpose Integration: Create an overarching life mission statement and ensure all goals support this larger purpose

Fulfillment Check: Rate each goal 1-10 on how excited and fulfilled it makes you feel; reconsider goals below 7

Holistic Approach: Review all your goals together to ensure they complement rather than compete with each other

Regular Alignment Reviews: Schedule monthly check-ins to assess whether your goals still align with your evolving values and vision

Question 3: What is your biggest obstacle to setting or achieving meaningful goals?

Former Student Responses:

"I get overwhelmed by having too many goals and end up not making progress on any of them."

"I start strong but lose motivation after a few weeks when I don't see immediate results."

"I'm afraid of setting big goals because I might fail and disappoint myself or others."

"I don't have enough time with work and family responsibilities to focus on personal goals."

"I lack the knowledge or skills needed to achieve what I want."

"I get distracted by new opportunities and lose focus on my original goals."

"I don't believe I deserve to achieve big things or that I'm capable of success."

Possible Solutions:

Overwhelm Management: Limit yourself to 3 major goals maximum; use the "Rule of 3" - focus on one goal per major life area (health, career, relationships)

Motivation Maintenance: Create a "why" document explaining your deeper reasons; schedule weekly vision reviews; track progress visually; celebrate small wins

Fear of Failure: Reframe failure as learning; start with smaller, low-risk goals to build confidence; focus on effort and progress rather than perfect outcomes

Time Constraints: Audit current time usage; identify 30 minutes daily for goal activities; use time-blocking; eliminate or delegate low-priority activities

Knowledge Gaps: Identify specific skills needed; create learning plans with deadlines; find mentors; start with free resources like YouTube or library books

Distraction Issues: Use the "shiny object syndrome" antidote - write down new ideas but don't act on them immediately; review priorities weekly; practice saying no

Self-Worth Issues: Work with a therapist or coach; practice self-compassion; start with small achievements to build confidence; challenge limiting beliefs with evidence

Question 4: How will you track your progress and celebrate milestones?

Former Student Responses:

"I've tried tracking before, but I always forget or give up after a few days."

"I don't know what metrics to use for goals that aren't easily measurable."

"I feel like celebrating small wins is premature - I should wait until I achieve the whole goal."

"I get obsessed with tracking, and it becomes more important than actually making progress."

"I don't have a good system for remembering to check my progress regularly."

"I'm not sure how often I should review my goals - daily, weekly, monthly?"

"I don't know what kinds of celebrations would actually motivate me."

Possible Solutions:

Tracking Consistency: Use the simplest possible system (calendar checkmarks, phone app, or photo progress); link tracking to existing habits like morning coffee

Measuring Intangibles: Use 1-10 rating scales for subjective goals; track input metrics (actions taken) rather than just outcomes; keep a qualitative journal.

Celebration Mindset: Understand that celebrating progress creates momentum for continued success; small celebrations reinforce positive behaviors

Balanced Tracking: Limit tracking to 3 key metrics maximum; focus on trends rather than daily fluctuations; remember tracking serves progress, not vice versa

Review Systems: Set phone reminders for weekly 10-minute reviews; schedule monthly deeper assessments; use Sunday planning sessions.

Review Frequency: Daily micro-check-ins (2 minutes), weekly progress reviews (10 minutes), monthly goal assessments (30 minutes)

Meaningful Rewards: Choose celebrations that align with your goals (fitness goal = new workout gear); plan both immediate and milestone rewards; include social sharing with supportive people

Question 5: Who can support you or hold you accountable as you pursue your goals?

Former Student Responses:

"I prefer to keep my goals private because I'm embarrassed if I don't achieve them."

"My family and friends don't really understand my goals or why they matter to me."

"I've had accountability partners before, but we both just stopped checking in with each other."

"I don't want to burden others with my personal goals and progress."

"I'm not sure what kind of support I actually need - encouragement, advice, or tough love?"

"I worry that sharing my goals will create pressure that makes me less likely to succeed."

"I don't know anyone who has similar goals or would understand my journey."

Possible Solutions:

Privacy Concerns: Start by sharing with one trusted person; remember that accountability increases success rates dramatically; reframe "failure" as a learning experience

Unsupportive Environment: Find online communities related to your goals; join local groups or classes; seek professional coaching or mentoring

Accountability Breakdown: Create structured check-in schedules; use apps or tools for accountability; establish clear expectations and consequences upfront

Burden Beliefs: Recognize that most people enjoy helping others succeed; offer reciprocal support; frame requests as opportunities for others to contribute

Support Type Clarity: Identify whether you need informational support (advice), emotional support (encouragement), or accountability support (check-ins)

Pressure Sensitivity: Choose supportive rather than judgmental accountability partners; focus on progress reporting rather than performance pressure

Community Building: Use social media groups, local meetups, professional associations, or online forums to find like-minded individuals

Universal Solutions Across All Chapter 4 Questions:

Use the SMART Framework: Make every goal Specific, Measurable, Achievable, Relevant, and Time-bound to increase clarity and success likelihood.

Align Goals with Values: Ensure your goals reflect your authentic desires and core values rather than external expectations or societal pressures.

Start Small and Build: Begin with goals that stretch you without overwhelming you; success builds confidence for tackling bigger challenges.

Create Support Systems: Actively seek accountability partners, mentors, or communities that understand and encourage your growth journey.

Track Progress Consistently: Use simple, sustainable systems to monitor advancement and celebrate milestones along the way.

Plan for Obstacles: Anticipate challenges and create specific strategies to overcome them before they derail your progress.

Regular Review and Adjustment: Schedule consistent times to assess progress, realign goals with evolving priorities, and make necessary course corrections.

Celebrate Progress: Acknowledge and reward effort and improvement, not just final achievements, to maintain motivation throughout your journey.

Take Action

Choose one area of your life and set a SMART goal for the next three months.
Write your goal down and share it with someone you trust.
Set a reminder to review your goal weekly and track your progress.
Celebrate your first milestone, no matter how small.

"Setting goals is the first step in turning the invisible into the visible." — **Tony Robbins.**

Chapter 5 – Planning for Success

Why Planning Bridges Vision and Reality

You have a vision, and you've set your goals. Now comes the step that separates dreamers from doers: **planning**.

A vision without a plan is just a wish. Goals without a plan are simply hopes. Planning is the bridge that connects your intentions to actual results. Just as a GPS needs both a starting point and a destination to plot a route, you need a plan to move from where you are to where you want to be.

"A goal without a plan is just a wish." – **Antoine de Saint-Exupéry**

The Power of a Written Plan

When you write your plan down, you:

- Clarify your steps and priorities.
- Break overwhelming goals into manageable actions.
- Increase your commitment and accountability.
- Make it easier to track progress and adjust as needed.

Key Insight: A written plan is a contract with yourself. It's a sign that you're serious about your goals.

Turning Goals Into Action Steps

For every goal, ask:
What must I do to achieve this goal?
What are the steps and actions that will get me there?
In what order should I do them?
What resources or support will I need?

Example:
If your goal is to run a marathon:

1. Research a training plan.
2. Buy proper running shoes.
3. Start with three short runs per week.

4. Register for the marathon.
5. Increase distance gradually.
6. Complete a half-marathon as a milestone.

Prioritizing and Sequencing

Not all steps are equally important or urgent.

- Identify which actions must come first.
- Decide which steps can be done in parallel and which must be sequential.
- Put your steps in logical order.

Tip: Work backward from your goal deadline to set interim targets and milestones.

Setting Milestones and Deadlines

Milestones are checkpoints that keep you motivated and on track.

Assign a realistic deadline to each step.
Celebrate each milestone as you reach it.

Planning Template

Step	Action Item	Deadline	Resources Needed	Who/What Can Help?	Status
1					
2					
3					

What Resources and Support Do You Need?

What skills, knowledge, or tools are required?
Who can help you? (Mentors, friends, professionals)
What obstacles might you face, and how will you prepare for them?

If you realize you need to improve your time management, make it a priority to learn those skills. (See Book 3 in this series, *Time That Matters*)

Scheduling and Sticking to Your Plan

Block time in your calendar for your most important actions.

Build routines that make progress automatic.
Review your schedule weekly and adjust as needed.

Consistency beats intensity. It's better to take small, regular steps than to make big, sporadic efforts.

Planning Templates and Examples

Use the templates in the appendix to map out your plan.

Break big goals into small, actionable steps.
Assign deadlines and resources.
Track your progress and celebrate each milestone.

Anticipating Obstacles and Adjusting

Every plan meets resistance.

List potential obstacles for each step.
Write a "Plan B" or workaround for each.
Expect setbacks, but don't let them stop you.

Be flexible. No plan survives first contact with reality unchanged. Adjust as you go.

Chapter Summary

Planning bridges the gap between goal-setting and goal-getting.
Break big goals into actionable steps, prioritize, and assign deadlines.
Identify resources, support, and potential obstacles.
Be flexible—review and adjust your plan as needed.
Use accountability and routines to maintain momentum.

Reflection Questions

Question 1: What specific, measurable outcomes do you want to achieve in the next 6-12 months?

Former Student Responses:

"I want to get promoted to a senior position and increase my salary by at least 15%"
"I want to save $10,000 for a down payment on a house by next December."
"I want to lose 25 pounds and run a 5K race by my birthday in 8 months."
"I want to complete my master's degree program and graduate with honors."

"I want to launch my freelance consulting business and secure 5 regular clients."
"I want to improve my relationship with my teenage daughter by having weekly one-on-one time."
"I want to read 24 books this year and start a book club in my community."

Possible Solutions:

Career Advancement: Create a professional development plan, identify required skills, seek mentorship, document achievements, and schedule regular check-ins with supervisors

Financial Goals: Set up automatic transfers to savings, track expenses monthly, identify additional income sources, and create a realistic timeline with milestones

Health and Fitness: Use a structured training program like Couch-to-5K, track daily food intake, schedule regular weigh-ins, and find an accountability partner

Education: Create a study schedule, join study groups, utilize the professor's office hours, and break large assignments into smaller tasks

Business Launch: Develop a business plan, build a professional network, create a portfolio, and start with part-time clients while maintaining current income

Relationship Building: Schedule weekly activities in advance, put away devices during this time, and focus on active listening and shared interests

Personal Growth: Set a reading schedule, join online book communities, and start small with local friends before expanding to community-wide

Question 2: How will you break down these larger goals into smaller, actionable steps?

Former Student Responses:

"I know I need to break things down, but I'm not sure how small the steps should be."
"I tend to create plans that look good on paper but are too overwhelming in practice."
"I get stuck trying to figure out the perfect sequence of steps."
"I break things down but then get distracted by other priorities."
"I'm good at planning but struggle with following through on the small daily actions."
"I make my action steps too vague, like 'work on business plan'"
"I underestimate how long things will take and get discouraged."

Possible Solutions:

Step Size Guidance: Make steps small enough to complete in 15-30 minutes; if a step takes longer, break it down further

Practical Planning: Test your plan by doing the first few steps before committing to the entire sequence; adjust based on reality

Sequence Flexibility: Start with obvious first steps and let the path become clearer as you progress; perfect planning isn't required

Priority Management: Use time-blocking to protect time for goal-related activities; say no to non-essential commitments

Daily Action: Focus on one small action per day rather than trying to do everything; consistency beats intensity

Specific Actions: Replace vague steps like "work on business plan" with specific tasks like "write executive summary section."

Realistic Timing: Add buffer time to estimates; track how long tasks actually take to improve future planning

Question 3: What resources, skills, or support do you need to succeed?

Former Student Responses:

"I need to learn new technical skills, but don't know where to start."
"I need more time in my schedule, but can't figure out where to find it."
"I need financial resources to invest in my goals, but I have a tight budget."
"I need emotional support from people who understand what I'm trying to achieve."
"I need better organizational systems to keep track of everything."
"I need to overcome my fear of networking and asking for help."
"I need accountability because I tend to let myself off the hook too easily."

Possible Solutions:

Skill Development: Start with free resources like YouTube and library books; take one online course at a time; find free workshops or webinars

Time Management: Conduct a time audit to identify where time is currently spent; eliminate or delegate low-priority activities; wake up 30 minutes earlier

Financial Resources: Look for low-cost alternatives; start with goals requiring minimal investment; consider earning extra income specifically for goals

Emotional Support: Join online communities related to your goals; find one accountability partner; share goals with supportive friends or family

Organization Systems: Start with simple tools like calendars and notebooks; use free apps before investing in premium versions; focus on one system at a time

Networking Confidence: Start with online networking; attend small, local events; prepare conversation starters; focus on helping others rather than asking for help

Accountability: Schedule regular check-ins with a trusted friend; join a mastermind group; hire a coach if budget allows; use apps with social features

Question 4: How will you maintain motivation when progress feels slow or obstacles arise?

Former Student Responses:

"I usually start strong but lose steam after a few weeks when I don't see immediate results."

"I get discouraged when I face setbacks and tend to give up completely."

"I compare myself to others and feel like I'm not making progress fast enough."

"I lose motivation when life gets busy and my goals feel less urgent."

"I struggle with perfectionism and get demotivated when things don't go exactly as planned."

"I don't know how to celebrate small wins - I always focus on what's left to do."

"I need external validation to stay motivated, but don't always get it."

Possible Solutions:

Sustaining Momentum: Track daily actions rather than just outcomes; create visual progress charts; set smaller milestones with quicker rewards

Setback Recovery: Develop a specific "comeback plan" before you need it; practice self-compassion; reframe setbacks as learning opportunities

Comparison Management: Focus on your own progress over time; limit social media exposure; remember that everyone's journey is different

Priority Maintenance: Connect daily actions to your deeper "why"; schedule goal time like important appointments; review your vision regularly

Perfectionism Management: Set "good enough" standards; celebrate progress over perfection; focus on consistency rather than flawless execution

Celebration Practice: Plan specific rewards for milestones; share achievements with supportive people; keep a "wins journal" to review regularly

Internal Motivation: Develop self-validation skills; focus on effort and growth rather than external recognition; connect with your personal values

Question 5: What potential obstacles do you anticipate, and how will you prepare for them?

Former Student Responses:

"I always get derailed when work gets busy or family emergencies come up."

"I tend to procrastinate on the most important tasks and focus on easier, less impactful activities."

"I worry that people close to me won't understand or support my goals."

"I'm concerned about not having enough money to pursue some of my goals."

"I struggle with self-doubt and impostor syndrome, especially when trying new things."

"I get overwhelmed when I have multiple goals and don't know which to prioritize."

"I have a history of starting projects but not finishing them."

Possible Solutions:

- **Life Disruptions**: Build flexibility into your plans; have backup options for busy periods; focus on minimum viable progress during challenging times
- **Procrastination**: Use the "2-minute rule" for getting started; tackle the most important task first each day; break overwhelming tasks into tiny steps
- **Lack of Support**: Communicate your goals clearly to family; find supportive communities outside your immediate circle; prepare responses to criticism
- **Financial Constraints**: Start with low-cost or free approaches; look for scholarships or payment plans; consider earning extra income for goal funding
- **Self-Doubt**: Keep evidence of past successes; practice positive self-talk; start with smaller challenges to build confidence
- **Multiple Goals**: Limit yourself to 1-3 major goals at a time; use the "Rule of 3" - one goal per major life area; review priorities monthly
- **Follow-Through Issues**: Start with extremely small commitments; track completion rates; celebrate finishing small projects before tackling larger ones

Universal Solutions Across All Chapter 5 Questions:

Create Detailed Action Plans: Break every goal into specific, time-bound steps that are small enough to feel manageable and clear enough to execute without confusion.

Build Support Systems: Actively cultivate relationships with people who understand and encourage your goals, whether through existing relationships or new communities.

Plan for Obstacles: Anticipate likely challenges and create specific strategies to overcome them before they derail your progress.

Focus on Process Over Outcome: Track and celebrate the actions you take consistently rather than just the end results you achieve.

Maintain Flexibility: Be willing to adjust your approach, timeline, or even goals as you learn what works best for your situation.

Develop Internal Motivation: Connect your goals to your deeper values and vision so you can maintain momentum even without external validation.

Practice Self-Compassion: Treat setbacks as learning opportunities rather than failures, and speak to yourself with the same kindness you'd show a good friend.

Start Small and Build: Begin with goals and actions that stretch you without overwhelming you, then gradually increase the challenge as you build confidence and momentum.

Take Action

Choose one of your top goals and create a detailed action plan using the template above.
Set deadlines and identify milestones for the next month.
Share your plan with a friend, mentor, or accountability partner.
Schedule your first progress review in your calendar.

"The best way to get started is to quit talking and begin doing." – **Walt Disney.**

Chapter 6 – Executing Your Plan

Why Action Trumps Perfection

It's easy to fall into the trap of endless planning and preparation, waiting for the "perfect" moment to act. But the truth is, **action always beats inaction—even if it's imperfect**. The world rewards those who do, not just those who plan.

*"You don't have to be great to start, but you have to start to be great." – **Zig Ziglar.***

You can have the best vision, the most detailed goals, and the most beautiful plan, but unless you take action, nothing will change. Most people have some sort of vision of what they want to be, but out of those who have a vision, only a few will turn their vision into goals, and out of those with goals, few will turn them into plans. Out of those with plans, very few ever take action.

The 80/20 Rule: Focus on High-Impact Actions

The Pareto Principle, or 80/20 Rule, tells us that **80% of your results come from 20% of your efforts**. Identify the few key activities that move you closest to your goal and prioritize them.

> What are the 1–3 most important actions you can take today that will have the biggest impact on your goal?
> Focus on these first, every day.

Don't get lost in busy work or minor details. Instead, ask yourself: What is the one thing I can do right now that will make everything else easier or unnecessary?

Overcoming Inertia and Procrastination

Inertia keeps you stuck; procrastination delays your dreams. The antidote is to take one small step—any step—right now.

- **Break big tasks down** into tiny, manageable pieces.
- **Use the "2-minute rule.** If a task takes less than two minutes, do it now.
- **Set a timer for 10–15 minutes** and commit to working on your goal until it rings.

The hardest part is often just getting started. Once you begin, momentum takes over.

The Power of Now and Present-Moment Action

The only time you can act is **now**. Don't wait for motivation; let action create motivation. Every time you act, you build momentum.

> Ask: What can I do in the next 10 minutes to move forward?
> Remind yourself: Progress, not perfection.
>> *"The future depends on what we do in the present." – Mahatma Gandhi*

Quick Wins and Momentum

Quick wins build confidence and create a sense of progress.

> Start with the easiest or most rewarding task.
> Celebrate each completed step, no matter how small.
> Each win fuels your momentum for the next step.

Every small action you take is a vote for the person you want to become. The more votes you cast, the more your identity shifts and your confidence grows.

Why Most People Fail to Execute

Studies show that 80% of people never set goals for themselves. Of the 20% who do, 75% fail to achieve their goals, mainly because they never take action. Out of 100 people, only five will take action and achieve their goals.

If you want to be one of that 5%, you must act. Don't let fear, perfectionism, or overthinking hold you back.

> *"An average person with average talent, ambition, and education can outstrip the most brilliant genius in our society—if that person has clear, focused goals." – Brian Tracy.*

The Importance of Consistency

Consistency beats intensity every time. It's better to take small, regular steps than to make big, sporadic efforts.

> Schedule time for your most important actions.
> Build routines that make execution automatic.
> Track your progress and adjust as needed.

Chapter Summary

Action trumps perfection. Don't wait for the perfect plan—start now.
Focus on high-impact actions (the 80/20 rule).
Overcome inertia and procrastination by taking the smallest possible step.
Act in the present moment. The only time you can change your future is now.
Quick wins create momentum. Celebrate every step forward.
Consistency and commitment are the keys to turning plans into reality.

Reflection Questions

Question 1: What is the single most important action you can take today to move closer to your goal?

Former Student Responses:

"I know I should start working on my business plan, but I keep putting it off because it feels overwhelming."

"I need to have a difficult conversation with my manager about my career development, but I'm avoiding it."

"I should start exercising, but I can't decide between joining a gym or working out at home."

"I need to update my resume and LinkedIn profile, but I don't know where to start."

"I should call that potential mentor I met at the networking event, but I'm nervous about reaching out."

"I need to research graduate programs, but there are so many options, I feel paralyzed."

"I should start tracking my expenses to get my finances in order, but I'm afraid of what I'll find."

Possible Solutions:

Overwhelming Business Plan: Break it into one small task - spend 15 minutes today writing just the executive summary outline, or researching one competitor

Difficult Career Conversation: Schedule a 15-minute informal chat with your manager about "exploring growth opportunities" rather than a formal career discussion

Exercise Paralysis: Start with what requires no decision - take a 10-minute walk around your neighborhood today

Resume Updates: Open your current resume and update just one section today - your contact information or most recent job description

Networking Anxiety: Send a simple LinkedIn message thanking them for their time and asking one specific question about their career path

Graduate School Research: Pick one program today and spend 20 minutes reading about its admission requirements

Financial Fear: Track just today's expenses in a simple notebook or phone app - start with one day of data

Question 2: Where are you spending time on low-impact activities that could be better used elsewhere?

Former Student Responses:

"I spend hours scrolling through social media without even realizing it."

"I watch TV shows I don't even enjoy just because they're on."

"I attend meetings that don't really require my input or benefit me."

"I spend too much time on email, checking it constantly throughout the day."

"I get caught up in office gossip and conversations that don't add value."

"I'm a perfectionist-edit work that's already good enough."

"I spend time on household tasks that could be delegated or simplified."

Possible Solutions:

Social Media Time: Use app timers to limit daily usage, or designate specific times for checking (like 15 minutes after lunch)

Mindless TV: Replace one show per week with goal-related activities, or use TV time for multitasking (folding laundry, light exercise)

Unnecessary Meetings: Politely decline optional meetings or suggest shorter durations; prepare specific agenda items to make required meetings more efficient

Email Overload: Check email only 3 times daily (morning, lunch, end of day) and turn off notifications between checks

Office Distractions: Set boundaries by saying "I need to focus on this project right now" and redirect conversations to break times

Over-Perfecting: Set time limits for tasks and stick to them; use the "good enough" principle for non-critical work.

Household Inefficiency: Batch similar tasks together, delegate age-appropriate chores to family members, or hire help for tasks you dislike

Question 3: What small, quick win can you achieve right now to build momentum?

Former Student Responses:

"I could clean and organize my workspace so I feel more motivated to work on my goals."

"I could write down my top 3 goals and post them where I'll see them daily."

"I could schedule my first workout session for this week."
"I could reach out to one person in my network with a friendly check-in message."
"I could read one article about my industry or area of interest."
"I could update one section of my LinkedIn profile."
"I could save $20 by bringing lunch to work instead of buying it today."

Possible Solutions:

Workspace Organization: Spend 10 minutes clearing your desk and setting up a dedicated space for goal-related work

Goal Visibility: Write your top 3 goals on sticky notes and place them on your bathroom mirror, computer monitor, or car dashboard

Exercise Commitment: Open your calendar right now and block 30 minutes for a workout, even if it's just a walk

Network Connection: Send one text or email to someone you haven't spoken to in a while, asking how they're doing

Learning Action: Bookmark one relevant article to read during your next break, or listen to a 10-minute podcast episode

Profile Update: Add one recent accomplishment or skill to your LinkedIn profile today

Financial Win: Calculate how much you'll save this week by making one small spending change and transferring that amount to savings

Question 4: How can you make action a daily habit, not a once-in-a-while event?

Former Student Responses:

"I start strong but lose momentum after a few days when life gets busy."
"I only work on my goals when I feel motivated, which isn't very often."
"I try to do too much at once and then burn out quickly."
"I forget about my goals until something reminds me, then I feel guilty."
"I don't have a consistent routine, so goal work gets pushed aside."
"I wait for big blocks of free time that never seem to come."
"I get distracted by urgent tasks and never get to the important goal work."

Possible Solutions:

Momentum Loss: Start with just 5-10 minutes daily rather than hour-long sessions; consistency beats intensity

Motivation Dependence: Schedule goal work at the same time daily, regardless of how you feel; action creates motivation, not vice versa.

Burnout Prevention: Focus on one small daily action per goal rather than trying to make progress on everything at once

Forgetfulness: Set daily phone reminders or link goal work to existing habits (after morning coffee, before checking email)

Routine Absence: Choose one specific time slot daily (early morning, lunch break, evening) and protect it for goal work

Time Perfectionism: Use "micro-sessions" of 10-15 minutes instead of waiting for perfect conditions

Urgent vs. Important: Do your most important goal-related task first thing each morning before checking email or messages

Question 5: What is holding you back from starting, and what steps can you take to overcome it?

Former Student Responses:

"I'm afraid I'll fail and look foolish, so I keep researching and planning instead of acting."

"I don't feel qualified or experienced enough to pursue my goals yet."

"I'm worried about what others will think if I change direction in my life."

"I don't have enough money saved up to take risks with my career."

"I'm overwhelmed by how much I need to learn and don't know where to start."

"I'm comfortable with my current situation, even though I'm not happy with it."

"I keep waiting for the 'right time' when everything will be perfect."

Possible Solutions:

Fear of Failure: Reframe failure as learning; start with low-risk experiments; remember that not trying is the only real failure

Imposter Syndrome: Focus on learning and growing rather than being perfect; everyone starts as a beginner; competence comes through practice

Social Pressure: Remember that most people are focused on their own lives; surround yourself with supportive people; your happiness matters more than others' opinions

Financial Constraints: Start with goals that require minimal investment; build skills while maintaining current income; create a transition fund gradually

Information Overload: Choose one specific skill to focus on first; use the "just-in-time" learning approach; start with free resources

Comfort Zone Addiction: Acknowledge that growth requires discomfort; start with tiny steps outside your comfort zone; focus on the pain of staying the same

Perfect Timing Myth: Recognize that there's never a perfect time; start with what you have where you are; adjust as you go rather than waiting for ideal conditions

Universal Solutions Across All Chapter 6 Questions:

Apply the 80/20 Rule: Focus on the 20% of actions that will produce 80% of your results rather than getting caught up in busy work.

Use the Two-Minute Rule: If something takes less than two minutes and moves you toward your goal, do it immediately rather than adding it to your to-do list.

Start Before You're Ready: Take action with incomplete information rather than waiting for perfect conditions or complete knowledge.

Build Momentum Through Small Wins: Focus on consistency and small daily actions rather than sporadic large efforts.

Eliminate Low-Value Activities: Regularly audit how you spend your time and eliminate or reduce activities that don't align with your goals.

Create Implementation Intentions: Use "if-then" planning to make action more automatic ("If it's 7 AM, then I will work on my goal for 15 minutes").

Focus on Process Over Outcome: Measure success by the actions you take consistently rather than just the results you achieve.

Overcome Analysis Paralysis: Set time limits for planning and research, then commit to taking action even if your plan isn't perfect.

Take Action

Identify your top three high-impact actions for your current goal.
Commit to working on your most important task for at least 10 minutes today.
Celebrate a quick win by completing a small task and acknowledging your progress.
Review your plan and make sure you're focusing on the 20% of actions that will yield 80% of your results.

Chapter 7 – Your Journey Begins Now

"You don't have to be great to start, but you have to start to be great." – Zig Ziglar.

It's time to shift from planning and preparation to action. You've done the hard work of self-reflection, goal-setting, and creating a personal development plan. Now comes the most crucial step: putting your plan into motion.

The Power of Starting

Remember the words often attributed to Goethe:

"Whatever you can do, or dream you can do, begin it. Boldness has genius, power, and magic in it!"

Until you commit to action, there's always an opportunity to shy away from your goals. It's through action that we prove our commitment—not just to others, but to ourselves. Every journey, no matter how long or challenging, begins with a single step. By taking that first step, you set in motion a chain of events that can lead to extraordinary outcomes.

Key Insight: Starting is often the hardest part of any change process. Our brains are wired to resist change and stay in familiar territory. When you take decisive action—even a small step—you overcome this initial resistance and create momentum that makes subsequent actions easier.

Embracing the Process

Personal growth is a process, not a destination. There will be ups and downs, successes and setbacks. Embrace them all as part of your unique story.

Handling Success and Failure

Both success and failure bring their own challenges. Here's how to prepare for both:

Redefine Failure
- The only true failure is quitting.
- Everything else is a learning opportunity.
- If you miss a deadline or fall short of a goal, adjust your plan and keep moving forward.

Celebrate Small Wins
> Don't wait for the big achievements to celebrate.
> Acknowledge and reward yourself for small milestones along the way.
> Building in celebrations maintains motivation and makes the journey enjoyable.

Prepare for Success
> Success can bring unexpected challenges, like unwanted attention or changes in relationships.
> Prepare mentally for these possibilities.
> Have strategies in place to handle them.

Stay Humble
> As you achieve your goals, remember to stay grounded.
> Use your success as motivation to help others.
> Set new, more ambitious goals.

The Post-Achievement Dip

Many people experience a sense of letdown after achieving a major goal—sometimes called "the blues" or "post-achievement depression." For example, athletes often experience this after winning championships, and students may feel it after graduation.

This happens because:
> The driving purpose that organizes your activities is suddenly gone.
> The regular routine and community associated with the goal disappear.
> The anticipated happiness from achievement rarely matches expectations.

Preparing for this phenomenon
> Before achieving your goal, identify what's next.
> Recognize that the journey itself provided much of the fulfillment.
> Plan a transition period that includes rest and reflection before jumping into the next challenge.

Monitoring and Measuring Progress

Tracking your progress is crucial for maintaining motivation and making necessary adjustments to your plan. Here are some effective ways to do this:

- **Keep a Journal:** Regular journaling can help you track both tangible progress and emotional growth.
- **Use Metrics:** For goals that can be quantified, like weight loss or savings, use specific metrics to track progress.
- **Seek Feedback:** Ask trusted friends, family, or mentors for their observations on your growth.

- **Regular Check-ins:** Schedule regular times to review your plan and assess your progress.

Progress isn't always linear. Sometimes, you'll take two steps forward and one step back. This is normal and part of the growth process.

<u>A Progress Tracking System</u>

1. **Choose your tracking method(s):**
    Digital app or spreadsheet
    Physical journal or planner
    Visual chart or board
    Accountability partner check-ins
2. **Determine what you'll track:**
    Measurable outcomes (weight, savings, etc.)
    Actions completed (workouts, meditation sessions)
    Subjective ratings (energy levels, happiness)
    Insights and learnings
3. **Set your tracking frequency:**
    Daily for habits and actions
    Weekly for measurable outcomes
    Monthly for a bigger-picture review
4. **Create a reflection protocol:**
    What's working well?
    What challenges am I facing?
    What adjustments do I need to make?
    What have I learned?
5. **Schedule regular review dates in your calendar.**
    The best tracking system is one you'll actually use consistently, so choose what works for your personality and lifestyle.

Overcoming Obstacles

As you work towards your goals, you'll inevitably face obstacles. Here are strategies to help you overcome them:

Anticipate Challenges
   Think ahead about potential roadblocks.
   Develop strategies to overcome them before they arise.
   Create "if-then" plans for common obstacles.

Develop Resilience
    Resilience is like a muscle—the more you use it, the stronger it becomes.
    Each obstacle you overcome builds your capacity to handle future challenges.
    Focus on what you can control rather than what you can't.

Seek Support
    Don't be afraid to ask for help when you need it.
    Whether it's from friends, family, or a professional coach, support can make a significant difference.
    Different challenges may require different types of support.

Stay Flexible
    Be willing to adjust your approach if something isn't working.
    Flexibility is key to long-term success.
    Sometimes, the path to your goal isn't a straight line.

Warning: When obstacles arise, beware of the "what-the-hell effect"—the tendency to completely abandon your goals after a small setback. Remember that perfection isn't required for progress, and one setback doesn't erase all your previous efforts.

The Role of Habits in Change

Lasting change often comes through the development of new habits. Here's how to make habits work for you:

Start Small
    Begin with tiny, manageable changes that you can consistently maintain.
    Make the habit so small it's almost impossible to fail (e.g., one push-up).
    Focus on consistency rather than intensity.

Be Consistent
    Consistency is more important than intensity when forming new habits.
    A small action done daily is more effective than a big effort done occasionally.
    Track your "streak" of consecutive days to build momentum.

Use Habit Stacking
    Attach new habits to existing ones to make them easier to remember and implement.
    Use the formula: "After I [current habit], I will [new habit]."
    Build chains of positive habits throughout your day.

Be Patient
    It takes time for new behaviors to become automatic.
    Give yourself at least 21 days, and often longer, for a new habit to take root.
    Focus on the process rather than the outcome.

Maintaining Motivation

Motivation can wax and wane throughout your journey. Here are strategies to keep your motivation high:

Revisit Your 'Why'
  Regularly remind yourself why you started this journey in the first place.
  Create a visual reminder of your 'why' to look at daily.
  Connect your immediate actions to your larger purpose.

Visualize Success
  Spend time each day visualizing yourself achieving your goals.
  Make your visualization detailed and multisensory.
  Include the feeling of accomplishment in your visualization.

Find Inspiration
  Surround yourself with inspiring books, podcasts, or people who motivate you.
  Create a collection of quotes or stories that uplift you.
  Seek out role models who have achieved what you aspire to.

Use Positive Self-Talk
  Replace negative self-talk with positive affirmations.
  Speak to yourself as you would to a good friend facing similar challenges.
  Remember, your thoughts shape your reality.

The Power of Accountability

Accountability can significantly increase your chances of success. Consider these accountability strategies:

Share Your Goals
  Tell trusted friends or family members about your goals.
  Their support can be invaluable.
  Public commitment increases follow-through.

Find an Accountability Partner
  - Partner with someone who has similar goals.
  - Check in with each other regularly.
  - Celebrate successes and troubleshoot challenges together.

Join a Group
  Whether it's a local meetup or an online community, joining a group of like-minded individuals can provide support and motivation.

Group environments create positive peer pressure.
Shared experiences make the journey less lonely.

Consider Professional Help
If you're struggling, don't hesitate to seek help from a coach, therapist, or other professional.
They can provide objective feedback and specialized strategies.
Sometimes, an outside perspective is exactly what you need.

Embracing Continuous Learning

Personal growth is a lifelong journey. Cultivate a mindset of continuous learning:

Read Widely
Expand your knowledge through books, articles, and other resources.
Explore topics both directly related to your goals and in completely different areas.
Different perspectives can spark new insights.

Seek New Experiences
Step out of your comfort zone and try new things regularly.
Novel experiences create new neural pathways in your brain.
Even small changes to your routine can stimulate creativity and growth.

Reflect on Lessons Learned
Take time to reflect on your experiences and extract valuable lessons.
Ask yourself what worked, what didn't, and why.
Keep a "lessons learned" journal to track your insights.

Stay Curious
Maintain a sense of wonder about the world.
Ask questions and seek answers.
Curiosity keeps your mind active and engaged.

Making Changes Stick

As you implement changes in your life, focus on making them permanent:

Be Patient
Lasting change takes time.
Don't expect overnight transformations.
Trust the process and keep going.

Focus on One Change at a Time
Trying to change too much at once can be overwhelming.

Focus on one area until it becomes habitual before moving to the next.
Success in one area builds confidence for tackling others.

Prepare for Setbacks

Setbacks are normal and expected.
Have a plan for how you'll get back on track when they occur.
View setbacks as learning opportunities rather than failures.

Celebrate Progress

Acknowledge how far you've come, not just how far you have to go.
Create meaningful ways to celebrate milestones.
Share your achievements with your support network.

The Journey Continues

As we conclude this book, remember that this is not the end but rather the beginning of your personal growth journey. Every day presents new opportunities for growth, learning, and self-improvement.

You have within you the power to create the life you desire. You've done the hard work of self-reflection, goal-setting, and planning. Now, it's time to take action.

Remember the words of Lao Tzu: *"The journey of a thousand miles begins with one step."*

Your journey begins now, with the very next action you take after closing this book.

Will it be easy? Not always. Will it be worth it? Absolutely.

So, take a deep breath, summon your courage, and take that first step. The future you dream of is waiting for you to create it.

Chapter Summary

Starting is crucial—taking the first step creates momentum for your entire journey.
Redefine failure as a learning opportunity rather than a reason to quit.
Track your progress to maintain motivation and make necessary adjustments.
Build resilience by anticipating challenges and developing strategies to overcome them.
Focus on habits to create lasting change through small, consistent actions.
Maintain motivation by regularly revisiting your 'why' and visualizing success.
Use accountability to significantly increase your chances of success.

Embrace continuous learning as a lifelong approach to personal growth.
Be patient and persistent as you work to make changes permanent.

Reflection Questions

Question 1: What first step will you take today to begin your journey of change?

Former Student Responses:

"I want to start working on my business plan, but I keep putting it off because it feels overwhelming."

"I need to have a difficult conversation with my manager about my career development, but I'm avoiding it."

"I should start exercising, but I can't decide between joining a gym or working out at home."

"I need to update my resume and LinkedIn profile, but I don't know where to start."

"I should call that potential mentor I met at the networking event, but I'm nervous about reaching out."

"I need to research graduate programs, but there are so many options, I feel paralyzed."

"I should start tracking my expenses to get my finances in order, but I'm afraid of what I'll find."

Possible Solutions:

Overwhelming Business Plan: Break it into one small task - spend 15 minutes today writing just the executive summary outline, or researching one competitor

Difficult Career Conversation: Schedule a 15-minute informal chat with your manager about "exploring growth opportunities" rather than a formal career discussion

Exercise Paralysis: Start with what requires no decision - take a 10-minute walk around your neighborhood today

Resume Updates: Open your current resume and update just one section today - your contact information or most recent job description

Networking Anxiety: Send a simple LinkedIn message thanking them for their time and asking one specific question about their career path

Graduate School Research: Pick one program today and spend 20 minutes reading about its admission requirements

Financial Fear: Track just today's expenses in a simple notebook or phone app - start with one day of data

Question 2: Which accountability strategy would be most effective for your personality and goals?

Former Student Responses:

"I'm introverted and don't like sharing personal goals with many people."
"I'm competitive and motivated by comparison with others."
"I tend to let people down and feel guilty about disappointing accountability partners."
"I work better with professional guidance than peer support."
"I like technology and apps, but struggle with human accountability."
"I'm motivated by public commitment but worried about judgment if I fail."
"I prefer gentle encouragement over tough love approaches."

Possible Solutions:

Introverted Personalities: Find one trusted friend or family member for private check-ins; use anonymous online communities; or keep a daily journal with weekly self-reviews

Competitive Types: Join challenge groups, use apps with leaderboards, or find an accountability partner with a similar competitive drive

Guilt-Prone Individuals: Start with self-accountability through tracking apps; focus on progress reporting rather than commitment-based accountability; work with a professional coach who understands your patterns

Professional Guidance Seekers: Hire a coach, join structured programs, or use professional development courses with built-in accountability

Tech-Savvy Individuals: Use habit-tracking apps, online communities, or digital accountability tools combined with occasional human check-ins

Public Commitment Types: Share goals on social media with progress updates; join public challenges; or commit to friends, but reframe "failure" as a learning experience

Gentle Encouragement Preference: Find supportive, non-judgmental accountability partners; focus on celebration of efforts rather than outcomes; use positive reinforcement systems

Question 3: How will you track your progress and measure success?

Former Student Responses:

"I've tried tracking before, but I always give up after a few days."
"I'm not sure what metrics to use for personal development goals."
"I get obsessed with tracking, and it becomes counterproductive."
"I prefer simple methods, but don't know what actually works."
"I want to track both quantitative and qualitative progress."

"I forgot to track consistently."

"I don't know how often I should review my progress."

Possible Solutions:

Tracking Dropouts: Use the simplest possible system (one daily checkmark); link tracking to an existing habit (like brushing teeth); or use photo progress instead of detailed logging

Metric Confusion: Focus on input metrics (actions taken) rather than just outcomes; use a simple 1-10 daily rating scale; or track one specific behavior rather than general progress

Over-Trackers: Limit to 3 key metrics maximum; track weekly instead of daily; or use qualitative journaling rather than detailed quantitative data

Simplicity Seekers: Use a basic calendar with checkmarks; try the "don't break the chain" method; or use simple phone apps with minimal features

Comprehensive Trackers: Combine daily quantitative tracking with weekly qualitative reflection; use both objective measures and subjective well-being ratings

Forgetful Trackers: Set phone reminders at consistent times, place tracking tools in visible locations, or use habit stacking (track immediately after another routine)

Review Frequency Questions: Start with weekly 10-minute reviews; schedule monthly deeper assessments; or use daily micro-reviews (2 minutes) with weekly summaries

Question 4: What potential obstacles might you face, and how will you prepare for them?

Former Student Responses:

"I always start strong but lose motivation after a few weeks."

"My family doesn't support my goals and sometimes sabotages my efforts."

"I get overwhelmed when I face setbacks and tend to give up completely."

"My work schedule is unpredictable and makes consistency difficult."

"I have perfectionist tendencies that paralyze me when things aren't going perfectly."

"I struggle with self-discipline and often choose immediate gratification over long-term goals."

"I tend to take on too much at once and burn out."

Possible Solutions:

Motivation Loss: Create a "why" document to review during low periods; plan rewards for consistency milestones; or find ways to make the process more enjoyable rather than just focusing on outcomes

Unsupportive Environment: Communicate your goals clearly and explain benefits to family; find supportive communities outside your immediate circle; or create boundaries around your goal-related activities

Setback Overwhelm: Develop a specific "comeback plan" before you need it; practice self-compassion techniques; or reframe setbacks as data rather than failures

Schedule Unpredictability: Focus on flexible goals that can adapt to your schedule; create multiple backup plans for different scenarios; or choose goals that require minimal time commitment

Perfectionism: Set "good enough" standards; practice the "2-minute rule" for getting started; or focus on consistency over quality initially

Self-Discipline Issues: Use environmental design to make good choices easier; start with tiny habits that require minimal willpower; or use implementation intentions ("When X happens, I will do Y")

Burnout Tendency: Limit yourself to one major change at a time; build in rest and recovery periods; or start smaller than feels necessary

Question 5: How will you celebrate milestones along your journey?

Former Student Responses:

"I never celebrate small wins - I always focus on what's next."

"I don't want to reward myself with things that contradict my goals (like food rewards for fitness goals)."

"I feel guilty celebrating when I haven't reached my final goal yet."

"I don't know what kinds of rewards would actually motivate me."

"I prefer experiences over material rewards."

"I want celebrations that involve other people."

"I'm on a tight budget and can't afford expensive rewards."

Possible Solutions:

Future-Focused Types: Schedule celebration time like any other appointment; ask accountability partners to remind you to celebrate; or create a "wins journal" to review regularly

Goal-Aligned Celebrations: Reward fitness progress with new workout gear or a massage; celebrate learning goals with advanced courses; or reward financial goals with a small investment in your future

Guilt About Celebrating: Reframe celebration as fuel for continued progress; remember that acknowledging progress increases motivation; or share celebrations with others who benefit from your growth

Motivation Uncertainty: Experiment with different types of rewards; ask friends what motivates them; or try both immediate small rewards and larger milestone celebrations

Experience Preferences: Plan special outings, try new activities, or visit places you've wanted to explore; attend events or classes related to your interests

Social Celebrations: Share achievements with friends and family, organize group activities, or join communities where you can celebrate others' successes too

Budget-Conscious Celebrators: Use free activities like nature walks or library visits; create homemade treats; or celebrate with time-based rewards like sleeping in or taking a relaxing bath

Universal Solutions Across All Chapter 7 Questions:

Start Immediately: Choose the smallest possible first step and take it today - action creates momentum and momentum sustains motivation.

Prepare for Obstacles: Anticipate challenges and have specific strategies ready rather than hoping you'll figure it out when problems arise.

Focus on Systems Over Goals: Build processes and habits that naturally lead to your desired outcomes rather than fixating on end results.

Celebrate Progress: Acknowledge and reward effort and improvement, not just final achievements, to maintain motivation throughout your journey.

Stay Flexible: Be willing to adjust your approach based on what you learn about yourself and what works best for your unique circumstances.

Connect with Others: Find ways to involve supportive people in your journey, whether through accountability, celebration, or shared experiences.

Track What Matters: Monitor the actions you take (inputs) as much as the results you achieve (outputs) for better motivation and course correction.

Practice Self-Compassion: Treat yourself with kindness during setbacks and remember that lasting change is a process, not a single event.

Embrace the Journey: Remember that the process of pursuing goals is often as valuable as achieving them - focus on who you're becoming, not just what you're accomplishing.

Take Action

Choose one small action you can take today toward your most important goal.
Set up a simple progress-tracking system that works for you.
Identify an accountability partner or group to support your journey.
Schedule regular check-ins to review your progress and adjust your plan.
Create a visual reminder of your 'why' to keep you motivated.

"Your journey begins with a choice to get up, step out, and live fully." – **Oprah Winfrey.**

Chapter 8 – Reflect, Refine, and Celebrate

The Power of Reflection

Achieving meaningful goals isn't just about relentless forward motion—it's about pausing, looking back, and learning from your journey. Reflection is the secret ingredient that transforms experience into wisdom. It helps you recognize what's working and what isn't and how you can adjust your course for even greater success.

> *"We do not learn from experience... we learn from reflecting on experience."* – **John Dewey.**

Regular review and reflection are essential to keep your goals alive and relevant. Without them, you risk drifting off course, losing motivation, or missing out on opportunities for growth.

Building a Practice of Review

Just as pilots check their instruments and flight paths regularly, you must check in with your goals and progress. Schedule a weekly or monthly review—put it in your calendar as a non-negotiable appointment with yourself.

During your review, ask:

- What progress have I made toward my goals?
- What challenges did I face, and how did I respond?
- What did I learn about myself this week/month?
- Which actions had the biggest impact?
- Where did I get off track, and what can I do differently?

Write your answers in a journal, planner, or digital document. Over time, these reflections will become a powerful record of your growth and resilience.

Refining Goals as Your Vision Evolves

Life is dynamic. As you grow, your vision and circumstances may change. Don't be afraid to refine your goals or even let go of those that no longer serve you. Flexibility is not a sign of failure—it's a sign of wisdom and self-awareness.

How to Refine Your Goals:

Revisit your vision: Does it still inspire you?
Review your goals: Are they still relevant and meaningful?
Adjust timelines, milestones, or action steps as needed.
Set new goals as your vision expands or shifts.

Remember, the purpose of goal setting is not to lock yourself into a rigid path but to give you direction and momentum. Allow yourself to grow and adapt.

The Role of Gratitude and Celebration

Gratitude is a powerful force for sustaining motivation and happiness. When you focus on what you've accomplished rather than what's left to do, you build confidence and positive momentum.

- List three things you're grateful for each week related to your progress.
- Celebrate milestones—no matter how small. Treat yourself to something meaningful, share your success with a friend, or simply take a moment to savor your achievement.
- Recognize and appreciate your effort, not just your results.

Celebration isn't just about rewards—it's about reinforcing the habits and mindset that lead to lasting change.

Keeping Your Goals Alive and Relevant

Don't let your goals become "out of sight, out of mind." Make them visible and present in your daily life:

- Post your goals somewhere you'll see them often.
- Use reminders, vision boards, or affirmations.
- Share your goals and progress with your accountability partner or support group.
- Revisit your "why" regularly to keep your motivation strong.

If you find your enthusiasm fading, return to your vision and ask: Why did I set this goal? What will achieving it mean for my life and those around me?

The Goal Review Ritual

1. Schedule a weekly or monthly review session.
2. Bring your goal list, action plan, and journal.
3. Reflect on the past period: What did you accomplish? What did you learn?

4. Update your action steps and timelines as needed.
5. Write down at least one thing you're grateful for and one thing you're proud of.
6. Plan a small celebration for your next milestone.

Chapter Summary

Regular review and reflection turn experience into wisdom and keep you on course.
Flexible goal setting allows you to adapt as your vision and circumstances change.
Gratitude and celebration sustain motivation and reinforce positive habits.
Keeping your goals visible and relevant is essential for long-term success.

Reflection Questions

Question 1: How often do you review your goals and progress?

Former Student Responses:

"I set goals at the beginning of the year but rarely look at them again until December."
"I check in sporadically when I remember, maybe once every few months."
"I review my goals when something goes wrong or I feel off track."
"I don't have a formal review process - I just hope I'm making progress."
"I get overwhelmed by the idea of reviewing because I'm afraid I'll see I'm behind."
"I review my work goals regularly, but never my personal ones."
"I used to review weekly but got out of the habit when life got busy."

Possible Solutions:

- **Annual-Only Reviewers**: Schedule monthly 30-minute review sessions in your calendar; set phone reminders; start with quarterly reviews if monthly feels overwhelming
- **Sporadic Checkers**: Create a simple weekly ritual - Sunday evening for 15 minutes; link review time to an existing habit like weekend planning
- **Crisis-Driven Reviews**: Implement preventive reviews to catch issues early; schedule reviews regardless of how things are going
- **No Formal Process**: Use the Goal Review Ritual from the chapter; create a simple template with just 3-4 questions to answer each week
- **Review Avoidance**: Remember that reviews help you course-correct, not judge yourself; focus on learning and adjusting rather than performance evaluation

Work vs. Personal Split: Integrate personal goal review into your existing work planning process; treat personal goals with the same importance as professional ones

Lost Habit: Restart with just 5 minutes weekly; use accountability partners to help rebuild the habit; be patient with yourself as you reestablish the routine

Question 2: What have you learned from your recent successes and setbacks?

Former Student Responses:

"I realize I'm better at achieving goals when I have external accountability."

"I've learned that I consistently underestimate how long things will take."

"My biggest successes came when I focused on one goal at a time instead of trying to do everything."

"I discovered that I lose motivation when I don't see progress quickly enough."

"I learned that my perfectionism actually prevents me from making progress."

"I found that I'm more successful when I have a clear routine and structure."

"I realized that I give up too easily when I face the first obstacle."

Possible Solutions:

Accountability Insight: Find an accountability partner, join a goal-setting group, or hire a coach; share your goals publicly; schedule regular check-ins with someone you trust

Time Estimation Issues: Track how long tasks actually take; add a 25-50% buffer time to estimates; break large tasks into smaller, more predictable chunks

Focus Benefits: Use the "Rule of 3" - maximum three major goals at once; complete one goal before starting another; create a "parking lot" for future goals

Quick Progress Needs: Set smaller milestones with shorter timeframes; track daily actions rather than just outcomes; celebrate small wins regularly

Perfectionism Problems: Set "good enough" standards; use time limits for tasks; practice the "2-minute rule" for getting started imperfectly

Structure Success: Create consistent routines around goal work; use time-blocking; establish non-negotiable appointments with yourself

Obstacle Avoidance: Develop a "comeback plan" before you need it; reframe obstacles as learning opportunities; practice resilience-building exercises

Question 3: Are there any goals you need to refine, replace, or let go of?

Former Student Responses:

"I have a goal to learn three languages, but I realize that's too ambitious right now."

"My career goal doesn't align with my values anymore - I've grown and changed."

"I set a fitness goal based on what I thought I should want, not what I actually want."

"Some of my goals were set to impress others rather than fulfill myself."
"I have goals that made sense two years ago but don't fit my current life situation."
"I'm holding onto goals that no longer excite me but feel guilty about letting them go."
"I realize some of my goals conflict with each other, and I need to choose."

Possible Solutions:

Over-Ambitious Goals: Scale back to one language; focus on conversational level rather than fluency; set a foundation goal first

Values Misalignment: Reassess your core values; rewrite career goals to match your current priorities; consider transition goals if change is needed

External Motivation: Replace "should" goals with "want" goals; ask "Why does this matter to me?" for each goal; eliminate goals that don't generate genuine excitement

Impression Management: Focus on internal validation rather than external approval; share goals only with supportive people; define success on your own terms

Outdated Goals: Conduct a goal audit every six months; update goals to reflect current circumstances; don't feel guilty about changing direction

Guilt About Letting Go: Remember that letting go of irrelevant goals frees energy for meaningful ones; practice self-compassion; view goal evolution as growth

Conflicting Goals: Prioritize based on your core values; sequence goals rather than pursuing simultaneously; seek creative solutions that address multiple goals

Question 4: How do you celebrate your progress and express gratitude for your journey?

Former Student Responses:

"I don't really celebrate - I just move on to the next thing on my list."
"I feel guilty celebrating small wins when I haven't reached the final goal yet."
"I don't know what kinds of celebrations would actually motivate me."
"I celebrate by buying things, but that doesn't align with my financial goals."
"I prefer to celebrate with other people, but I'm embarrassed to share my goals."
"I forget to celebrate because I'm always focused on what's left to do."
"I don't feel like I've accomplished enough to warrant celebration."

Possible Solutions:

No Celebration Habit: Schedule celebration time like any other appointment; create a "wins journal" to review regularly; ask accountability partners to remind you to celebrate

- **Guilt About Celebrating**: Reframe celebration as fuel for continued progress; remember that acknowledging progress increases motivation; celebrate the effort, not just outcomes
- **Celebration Uncertainty**: Experiment with different types of rewards; try both immediate small rewards and larger milestone celebrations; ask friends what motivates them
- **Misaligned Rewards**: Choose celebrations that support your goals (fitness goal = new workout gear); use experience-based rewards; celebrate with time-based treats
- **Social Celebration Needs**: Find supportive communities where you can share wins; celebrate others' successes to create a positive culture; start small with one trusted person
- **Future-Focused Mindset**: Practice gratitude by listing three things you accomplished each week; use visual progress tracking; celebrate process improvements, not just outcomes
- **Achievement Minimization**: Keep a record of all progress, no matter how small; compare yourself to where you started, not where you want to be; practice self-compassion

Question 5: What new goal or milestone are you most excited to pursue next?

Former Student Responses:

"I want to write a book, but I'm not sure where to start or if I'm qualified."
"I'm excited about starting my own business, but I'm scared of the financial risk."
"I want to run a marathon, but I've never been a runner before."
"I'd like to learn a new skill that could advance my career."
"I want to improve my relationships and be more present with my family."
"I'm interested in giving back to my community, but don't know how."
"I want to travel more and experience different cultures."

Possible Solutions:

- **Writing Goal**: Start with a daily writing habit of 15 minutes; join a writing group; begin with shorter pieces like blog posts; focus on sharing your unique perspective
- **Business Dreams**: Start as a side business while maintaining current income; create a detailed business plan; seek mentorship from successful entrepreneurs; start small and test your concept
- **Marathon Aspiration**: Use a structured program like Couch-to-5K first; join a running group; set intermediate goals like a 5K, then 10K; focus on consistency over speed

- **Skill Development**: Identify specific skills needed for your career goals; start with free online resources; set aside dedicated learning time; apply new skills immediately
- **Relationship Improvement**: Schedule regular one-on-one time with family members; practice active listening; put away devices during family time; plan meaningful shared experiences
- **Community Service**: Research local organizations; start with small volunteer commitments; use your existing skills to help others; connect service to your values
- **Travel Goals**: Start with local exploration; create a travel savings fund; research destinations that align with your interests; plan one meaningful trip rather than many superficial ones

Universal Solutions Across All Chapter 8 Questions:

Establish Regular Review Rituals: Create consistent times for reflection that become non-negotiable appointments with yourself.

Practice Flexible Goal Setting: Allow your goals to evolve as you grow and learn, viewing changes as wisdom rather than failure.

Build Celebration into Your Process: Make acknowledgment and gratitude regular practices that fuel continued motivation and progress.

Focus on Learning Over Judgment: Use reviews to gather information and insights rather than to evaluate your worth or performance.

Align Goals with Current Values: Regularly assess whether your goals still reflect who you are becoming, not just who you were when you set them.

Create Accountability Systems: Share your review process with others who can support your reflection and celebration practices.

Document Your Journey: Keep records of your progress, insights, and growth to see patterns and appreciate how far you've come.

Practice Self-Compassion: Treat yourself with kindness during reviews, celebrating progress while gently noting areas for improvement.

Stay Connected to Your Why: Regularly revisit the deeper reasons behind your goals to maintain motivation and ensure continued relevance.

Take Action

Schedule your next review session and commit to making it a regular habit.
Update your goals and action plan based on your latest insights.
Identify one way to celebrate your next milestone.
Share your progress and gratitude with someone who supports you.

*"Success is a journey, not a destination. The doing is often more important than the outcome." – **Arthur Ashe.***

Reflection and Action

Final Reflection

Congratulations on reaching the end of your journey through *Goals That Matter: Purpose Driven Goal Setting*. You have explored your dreams, clarified your vision, set meaningful goals, created actionable plans, and learned how to overcome obstacles and sustain momentum. Now, it's time to pause, reflect, and commit to the next steps that will turn your intentions into reality.

Take a quiet moment to consider the following questions. Write your answers in a journal, your workbook, or wherever you will see them again. These reflections are not just for today—they are guideposts to revisit as you continue your journey.

Reflection Questions:

Question 1: What is the most important goal you are committed to achieving in the next 12 months? Why does it matter to you?

Former Student Responses:

- "I want to launch my freelance consulting business because I'm tired of working for someone else and want financial freedom."
- "I want to lose 30 pounds and run a half-marathon because my health is declining and I want to be around for my kids."
- "I want to save $15,000 for a house down payment because I'm tired of renting and want stability for my family."
- "I want to complete my master's degree because it will open up career advancement opportunities."
- "I want to repair my relationship with my teenage daughter because we've grown distant, and I miss our connection."
- "I want to write and publish my first book because I have stories to tell and want to leave a legacy."
- "I want to transition to a career in nonprofit work because I want my work to have more meaning and impact."

Possible Solutions:

Business Launch: Start with one client while maintaining current income; create a detailed business plan with monthly milestones; build a professional network through industry events

Health Goals: Begin with a structured program like Couch-to-5K; track daily food intake; find an accountability partner or join a running group

Financial Savings: Set up automatic transfers of $1,250 monthly; track expenses to identify areas to cut; consider a side hustle for extra income

Education: Create a study schedule with specific deadlines; join study groups; utilize the professor's office hours for support

Relationship Repair: Schedule weekly one-on-one time; practice active listening; consider family counseling if needed

Writing Project: Commit to writing 500 words daily; join a writers' group; set monthly chapter completion goals

Career Transition: Volunteer with nonprofits to gain experience; network with professionals in the field; create a transition timeline while maintaining current income

Question 2: What is the first small step you can take today to move toward this goal?

Former Student Responses:

"I know I should start, but I keep putting it off because it feels overwhelming."
"I have so many ideas about where to begin that I get paralyzed by choice."
"I'm waiting for the perfect time when I have more money/time/energy"
"I'm afraid of failing, so I keep researching instead of acting."
"I don't know if I'm qualified enough to start yet."
"I want to have everything planned out perfectly before I begin."
"I'm worried about what others will think if I don't succeed."

Possible Solutions:

Overwhelm: Break the goal into the smallest possible first step - spend 15 minutes today on one specific action.

Analysis Paralysis: Set a timer for 10 minutes and choose one action to take immediately, regardless of whether it's "perfect."

Perfect Timing Myth: Start with what you have right now - even 5 minutes of progress is better than waiting

Fear of Failure: Reframe the first step as an experiment rather than a commitment; focus on learning rather than succeeding

Imposter Syndrome: Remember that everyone starts as a beginner; competence comes through practice, not preparation

Perfectionism: Use the "good enough" principle - take action with 70% of the information rather than waiting for 100%

Fear of Judgment: Start small and private; share your goal only with supportive people initially

Question 3: Which of the three pillars—goal setting, time management, or social wealth—needs the most attention in your life right now?

Former Student Responses:

"Goal setting - I have vague dreams but no clear, specific goals with deadlines"

"Time management - I'm constantly busy but never seem to make progress on what matters most"

"Social wealth - I don't have supportive people in my life who understand my goals."

"All three - I feel like I'm failing at everything and don't know where to start."

"Goal setting - I set goals, but they're not aligned with what I actually want."

"Time management - I waste too much time on social media and low-priority activities."

"Social wealth - I'm surrounded by negative people who discourage my growth."

Possible Solutions:

Goal Setting Focus: Use the SMART framework to turn one vague dream into a specific, measurable goal with a deadline

Time Management Priority: Conduct a time audit for one week, then eliminate or delegate your biggest time-wasters

Social Wealth Development: Join one community (online or offline) related to your goals; find one accountability partner

Feeling Overwhelmed: Choose just one pillar to focus on for the next 90 days; master it before moving to the next.

Misaligned Goals: Revisit your core values and ensure your goals reflect what you actually want, not what you think you should want

Digital Distractions: Use app timers to limit social media; replace one hour of scrolling with goal-focused activity daily

Negative Environment: Set boundaries with discouraging people; actively seek out positive, growth-minded individuals

Question 4: Who can support you or hold you accountable as you pursue your goal? How will you invite them into your journey?

Former Student Responses:

"I prefer to keep my goals private because I'm embarrassed if I don't achieve them."
"I don't know anyone who would understand or support my goals."
"I've tried accountability partners before, but we both just stopped checking in."
"I don't want to burden others with my personal goals."
"I'm not sure what kind of support I actually need."
"My family and friends don't really believe in my goals."
"I worry that sharing my goals will create pressure that makes me less likely to succeed."

Possible Solutions:

Privacy Concerns: Start by sharing with just one trusted person; remember that accountability dramatically increases success rates

Lack of Support Network: Join online communities, local meetups, or professional groups related to your goals

Failed Accountability: Create structured check-ins with clear expectations; use apps or tools to maintain consistency

Burden Beliefs: Reframe requests for support as opportunities for others to contribute; offer reciprocal accountability

Unclear Support Needs: Identify whether you need informational support (advice), emotional support (encouragement), or accountability support (check-ins)

Unsupportive Environment: Find new supportive relationships while setting boundaries with discouraging people

Pressure Sensitivity: Choose supportive rather than judgmental accountability partners; focus on progress reporting rather than performance pressure

Question 5: How will you track your progress, celebrate your milestones, and stay motivated when challenges arise?

Former Student Responses:

"I've tried tracking before, but I always give up after a few days."
"I don't know what metrics to use for my type of goal."
"I feel like celebrating small wins is premature - I should wait until I achieve the whole goal."
"I get obsessed with tracking, and it becomes more important than actually making progress."
"I don't know how often I should review my progress."
"I forgot to track consistently."
"I don't know what kinds of celebrations would actually motivate me."

Possible Solutions:

Tracking Dropouts: Use the simplest possible system (daily checkmarks on a calendar); link tracking to an existing habit

Metric Confusion: Focus on input metrics (actions taken) rather than just outcomes; use a simple 1-10 daily rating scale

Celebration Resistance: Understand that celebrating progress creates momentum; small rewards reinforce positive behaviors

Over-Tracking: Limit to 3 key metrics maximum; focus on trends rather than daily fluctuations.

Review Frequency: Start with weekly 10-minute reviews; schedule monthly deeper assessments

Tracking Forgetfulness: Set phone reminders at consistent times; place tracking tools in visible locations

Motivation Uncertainty: Experiment with different types of rewards; choose celebrations that align with your goals

Question 6: What have you learned about yourself through this process that will help you succeed, not just in this goal, but in future ones as well?

Former Student Responses:

"I realize I'm better at achieving goals when I have external accountability."
"I've learned that I consistently underestimate how long things will take."
"I discovered that I lose motivation when I don't see progress quickly enough."
"I found that I'm more successful when I focus on one goal at a time."
"I learned that my perfectionism actually prevents me from making progress."
"I realized I need to connect my goals to my deeper values to stay motivated."
"I discovered that I give up too easily when I face the first obstacle."

Possible Solutions:

Accountability Insight: Build accountability into all future goals; find partners, groups, or coaches who can support your journey

Time Estimation Learning: Add 25-50% buffer time to all future estimates; track actual completion times to improve planning

Quick Progress Needs: Set smaller milestones with shorter timeframes; track daily actions rather than just long-term outcomes

Focus Benefits: Apply the "Rule of 3" to future goal-setting - maximum three major goals at once

Perfectionism Awareness: Set "good enough" standards for future goals; practice the "2-minute rule" for getting started imperfectly

- **Values Connection**: Always connect future goals to your core values and deeper "why" for sustained motivation
- **Resilience Building**: Develop specific "comeback plans" for future goals; practice viewing obstacles as learning opportunities rather than failures

Universal Solutions Across All Final Reflection Questions:

Start Immediately: Choose the smallest possible first step and take it today - action creates momentum that sustains motivation.

Build Support Systems: Actively cultivate relationships with people who understand and encourage your goals, whether through existing relationships or new communities.

Track What Matters: Monitor the actions you take (inputs) as much as the results you achieve (outputs) for better motivation and course correction.

Celebrate Progress: Acknowledge and reward effort and improvement, not just final achievements, to maintain motivation throughout your journey.

Learn from Experience: Use each goal-setting experience to understand your patterns, strengths, and areas for improvement.

Stay Connected to Your Why: Regularly revisit the deeper reasons behind your goals to maintain motivation and ensure continued relevance.

Practice Self-Compassion: Treat yourself with kindness during setbacks and remember that lasting change is a process, not a single event.

Embrace the Journey: Remember that the process of pursuing goals is often as valuable as achieving them - focus on who you're becoming, not just what you're accomplishing.

Take Action

The difference between a wish and a goal is action. Don't wait for the perfect moment—begin now, even if your first step is small.

- **Write down your top goal and your "why."** Post it where you'll see it daily.
- **Break your goal into actionable steps.** Use the templates in the appendix to map out your plan.
- **Schedule your first action step.** Block time for it in your calendar today.
- **Share your goal and plan with someone you trust.** Ask them to check in with you regularly.

- **Set up a simple tracking system.** Use a journal, app, or spreadsheet to record your progress.
- **Celebrate your first milestone.** Plan a small reward for yourself as soon as you complete it.
- **Commit to a regular review.** Set a reminder to reflect on your progress each week or month.
- **Practice self-compassion.** When you face setbacks, be gentle with yourself and recommit to your path.

Remember, you have everything you need within you to achieve the things that matter most. This is not the end of your story; it's the beginning of a new chapter. Keep learning, keep growing, and keep moving forward, one purposeful step at a time.

Final Encouragement

Remember, the journey to achieving your goals is ongoing. Use these tools, revisit your vision, and keep taking small, consistent steps. Every action you take brings you closer to the life you want to create.

> *"Success is the sum of small efforts, repeated day in and day out."* **– Robert Collier.**

Thank you for allowing this book to be part of your journey. Keep moving forward—one goal, one step, one day at a time.

Now—go do the things that matter.

Appendices & Resources

Goal-Setting Worksheets and Templates

SMART Goals Worksheet

Goal Area	Specific Goal	Measurable Outcome	Achievable Steps	Relevant "Why"	Time-Bound Deadline
Example: Health	Lose 10kg	Weekly weigh-in	Walk 30 min/day	To feel energetic for my kids	6 months

1. Identify the area of your life you want to improve.
2. Write your goal in specific terms.
3. Define how you'll measure progress.
4. List the steps you'll take.
5. Connect your goal to your deeper motivation.
6. Set a clear deadline.

Action Plan Template

Step	Action Item	Deadline	Resources Needed	Who/What Can Help?	Status
1					
2					
3					

- Break your goal into small, actionable steps.
- Assign deadlines and identify what you'll need.
- Track your status and update as you progress.

Weekly Progress Tracker

Week	Goal/Action	Progress Made	Challenges	Next Steps

1				
2				
3				

At the end of each week, review what you accomplished, what got in the way, and what you'll do next.

Your Vision Board

How to Create a Vision Board

1. Collect images, words, and symbols that represent your goals and dreams.
2. Arrange them on a board, poster, or digital canvas.
3. Place your vision board somewhere you'll see it daily.
4. Update it as your vision evolves.

Example Layout

- Top left: Career & Finances
- Top right: Health & Fitness
- Bottom left: Relationships & Community
- Bottom right: Personal Growth & Spirituality

Goal Alignment Checklist

Before committing to a goal, ask:

- Is this goal specific and measurable?
- Does it inspire and excite me?
- Is it realistic, given my resources and constraints?
- Does it align with my core values and vision?
- Do I know why I want to achieve it?
- Have I written it down and shared it with someone I trust?

Recommended Reading and Digital Tools

We need to get an affiliate link and then put it in the hyperlinks below. Maybe we could use the Booklinker universal hyperlink?

Books

Atomic Habits by James Clear
(https://www.amazon.com/Atomic-Habits-Proven-Build-Break-ebook/dp/B01N5AX61W)

Goals! by Brian Tracy
(https://www.amazon.com/Goals-Third-Everything-WantFaster-Possible-ebook/dp/B0D36ZMXXF)

The 7 Habits of Highly Effective People by Stephen Covey
(https://www.amazon.com/Habits-Highly-Effective-People-Powerful-ebook/dp/B07WF972WK)

Drive by Daniel H. Pink
(https://www.amazon.com/Drive-Surprising-Truth-About-Motivates-ebook/dp/B0033TI4BW)

Mindset by Carol S. Dweck
(https://www.amazon.com/Mindset-Updated-Changing-Fulfil-Potential-ebook/dp/B01M036N60)

Apps & Tools

Habitica (habit tracking)
Todoist (task management)
Trello (project planning)
Google Calendar (scheduling)
Coach.me (goal tracking & coaching)

App Name	Purpose	Main Link
Habitica	Habit tracking	https://habitica.com
Todoist	Task management	https://todoist.com
Trello	Project planning	https://trello.com
Google Calendar	Scheduling	https://calendar.google.com
Coach.me	Goal tracking & coaching	https://www.coach.me
(CoachMe Fitness)	Fitness coaching	https://coachmefitness.app

Self-Assessment: Goal Setting, Time Management, and Relationship Habits

Rate yourself (1–10) in each area below
Goal Setting: How clear and actionable are your current goals?
Time Management: How well do you use your time to move toward your goals?
Social Wealth: How strong is your network of supportive people?
Self-Talk: How positive and encouraging is your internal dialogue?
Resilience: How well do you bounce back from setbacks?

Reflection
What's working well?
Where do you want to improve?
What's one action you can take this week to move forward in each area?

Simple Goal Setting Guide

1. **Clarify Your Vision:** What do you want your life to look like in one, five, or ten years?
2. **Set SMART Goals:** Make your goals specific, measurable, achievable, relevant, and time-bound.
3. **Create an Action Plan:** Break your goals into small, manageable steps.
4. **Commit and Track:** Write your goals down, share them, and track your progress.
5. **Review and Refine:** Regularly reflect, adjust, and celebrate your progress.

Bibliography

Primary Source

Allen, James. *As A Man Thinketh*. 1903. Reprint, New York: Dover Publications, 1999.

Neuroscience and Brain Research

Davidson, Richard J., et al. "Alterations in Brain and Immune Function Produced by Mindfulness Meditation." *Psychosomatic Medicine* 65, no. 4 (2003): 564-570.

Dietrich, Arne. "Neurocognitive Mechanisms Underlying the Experience of Flow." *Consciousness and Cognition* 13, no. 4 (2004): 746-761.

Doidge, Norman. *The Brain That Changes Itself: Stories of Personal Triumph from the Frontiers of Brain Science*. New York: Penguin Books, 2007.

Lazar, Sara W., et al. "Meditation Experience Is Associated with Increased Cortical Thickness." *NeuroReport* 16, no. 17 (2005): 1893-1897.

Ochsner, Kevin N., et al. "Rethinking Feelings: An fMRI Study of the Cognitive Regulation of Emotion." *Journal of Cognitive Neuroscience* 14, no. 8 (2002): 1215-1229.

Siegel, Daniel J. *The Developing Mind: How Relationships and the Brain Interact to Shape Who We Are*. 2nd ed. New York: Guilford Press, 2012.

Simons, Daniel J., and Christopher F. Chabris. "Gorillas in Our Midst: Sustained Inattentional Blindness for Dynamic Events." *Perception* 28, no. 9 (1999): 1059-1074.

Emotional Intelligence and Regulation

Barrett, Lisa Feldman. *How Emotions Are Made: The Secret Life of the Brain*. Boston: Houghton Mifflin Harcourt, 2017.

Beck, Aaron T. *Cognitive Therapy and the Emotional Disorders*. New York: International Universities Press, 1976.

Damasio, Antonio. *Descartes' Error: Emotion, Reason, and the Human Brain*. New York: Putnam, 1994.

Ekman, Paul. *Emotions Revealed: Recognizing Faces and Feelings to Improve Communication and Emotional Life*. New York: Times Books, 2003.

Goleman, Daniel. *Emotional Intelligence: Why It Matters More Than IQ.* New York: Bantam Books, 1995.

Gross, James J. "Emotion Regulation: Affective, Cognitive, and Social Consequences." *Psychophysiology* 39, no. 3 (2002): 281-291.

Neff, Kristin D. "Self-Compassion: An Alternative Conceptualization of a Healthy Attitude Toward Oneself." *Self and Identity* 2, no. 2 (2003): 85-101.

Pert, Candace B. *Molecules of Emotion: The Science Behind Mind-Body Medicine.* New York: Scribner, 1997.

Positive Psychology and Resilience

Fredrickson, Barbara L. "The Role of Positive Emotions in Positive Psychology: The Broaden-and-Build Theory of Positive Emotions." *American Psychologist* 56, no. 3 (2001): 218-226.

Kabat-Zinn, Jon. "An Outpatient Program in Behavioral Medicine for Chronic Pain Patients Based on the Practice of Mindfulness Meditation." *General Hospital Psychiatry* 4, no. 1 (1982): 33-47.

Maddi, Salvatore R. "The Story of Hardiness: Twenty Years of Theorizing, Research, and Practice." *Consulting Psychology Journal* 54, no. 3 (2002): 173-185.

Tedeschi, Richard G., and Lawrence G. Calhoun. "Posttraumatic Growth: Conceptual Foundations and Empirical Evidence." *Psychological Inquiry* 15, no. 1 (2004): 1-18.

Waldinger, Robert J., and Marc S. Schulz. "What's Love Got to Do with It? Social Functioning, Perceived Health, and Daily Happiness in Married Octogenarians." *Psychology and Aging* 25, no. 2 (2010): 422-431.

Cognitive Psychology and Decision-Making

Csikszentmihalyi, Mihaly. *Flow: The Psychology of Optimal Experience.* New York: Harper & Row, 1990.

Kahneman, Daniel. *Thinking, Fast and Slow.* New York: Farrar, Straus and Giroux, 2011.

Narrative Psychology and Meaning-Making

Frankl, Viktor E. *Man's Search for Meaning.* Boston: Beacon Press, 1946.

McAdams, Dan P. "The Psychology of Life Stories." *Review of General Psychology* 5, no. 2 (2001): 100-122.

Park, Crystal L. "Making Sense of the Meaning Literature: An Integrative Review of Meaning Making and Its Effects on Adjustment to Stressful Life Events." *Psychological Bulletin* 136, no. 2 (2010): 257-301.

White, Michael, and David Epston. *Narrative Means to Therapeutic Ends*. New York: Norton, 1990.

Habit Formation and Behavioral Change

Duhigg, Charles. *The Power of Habit: Why We Do What We Do in Life and Business*. New York: Random House, 2012.

Fogg, BJ. "A Behavior Model for Persuasive Design." *Proceedings of the 4th International Conference on Persuasive Technology*. ACM, 2009.

Lally, Phillippa, et al. "How Are Habits Formed: Modelling Habit Formation in the Real World." *European Journal of Social Psychology* 40, no. 6 (2010): 998-1009.

Classical References

Henley, William Ernest. "Invictus." 1875.

Lao Tzu. *Tao Te Ching*. Translated by Stephen Mitchell. New York: Harper & Row, 1988.

Contemporary Applications

Clear, James. *Atomic Habits: An Easy & Proven Way to Build Good Habits & Break Bad Ones*. New York: Avery, 2018.

Covey, Stephen R. *The 7 Habits of Highly Effective People*. New York: Free Press, 1989.

Dweck, Carol S. *Mindset: The New Psychology of Success*. New York: Random House, 2006.

Note: This bibliography represents the foundational research and sources that inform the practical applications presented in *Thoughts That Matter*. While James Allen's original insights were based on philosophical observation rather than scientific study, modern neuroscience and psychology have validated many of his core principles through rigorous empirical research. The citations provided offer readers opportunities for deeper exploration of the scientific foundations underlying Allen's timeless wisdom.

PART 3 - TIME THAT MATTERS

To everyone who wants to spend more time on what truly matters, and less on what doesn't.

"It is not that we have a short space of time, but that we waste much of it. Life is long enough, and it has been given in sufficiently generous measure to allow the accomplishment of the very greatest things if the whole of it is well invested." — **Lucius Annaeus Seneca**

Time That Matters
TIME MANAGEMENT HABITS OF SUCCESSFUL PEOPLE

About Things That Matter
A SELF-IMPROVEMENT SERIES FOR SUCCESS

Book 3

JC Ryan

About Time That Matters

This book will challenge your beliefs and habits. By the end, you'll have the tools to manage your time and ensure you're doing what matters most.

- **Time management starts with a commitment to change.** Planning is key, but so is guarding your schedule from distractions and the expectations of others.
- **Mastering time management improves your quality of life:** Less stress, more productivity, stronger relationships, and a sense of fulfillment.
- **Tracking time isn't enough:** True time management is about making changes, using your time efficiently for what matters.

Time is the great equalizer. No matter who you are, where you live, or what you do, you have the same 24 hours in each day as everyone else. Yet, some people seem to achieve so much more, live with less stress, and find fulfillment in both work and life. What's their secret? It's not magic, talent, or luck. It's time management, mastering the art of doing the things that matter, when they matter, and making every minute count.

This book is your invitation to discover, clarify, and pursue the things that matter most to you by learning the time management habits of successful people. You'll find practical tools, timeless concepts, and proven strategies to help you take control of your schedule, reduce stress, and create space for what truly matters.

You don't need to be a CEO, entrepreneur, or productivity guru to benefit from these principles. Whether you're a student, parent, business owner, or simply someone who wants more out of life, this book is for you.

Buckle up. Your beliefs and thinking are about to be challenged. All I ask is that you keep an open mind. By the end of this book, you will have all the tools you require to better manage your time and ensure you are doing the things that matter.

This book is not a course in the latest shiny electronic time management system. You can be as efficient with pen and paper as with an app. The most important things you need to succeed with time management are your brain, your motivation, and your habits.

This book is not about doing double the work in half the time or how to save time and use that to do more work. Rather, it is to show you how to plan and fit the things that matter into your schedule and to establish and maintain a healthy balance between your personal and work life.

If you apply what you learn and are willing to change your habits, you will become better at it, and over time, you will reap enormous benefits.

Ready to begin? Turn the page and start your journey to a life that truly matters..

Life Is Like A Jar

There is a story about a professor of philosophy who gave a demonstration to his students to illustrate the concept of the things that matter in life. He used a large glass jar and started to fill it with golf balls.

When he filled the jar with golf balls, he asked the students if the jar was full. They agreed that it was full. Then he picked up a box of small marbles and poured them into the jar as well, and they rolled into the open spaces between the golf balls. He then asked the students again if the jar was full. They all agreed it was.

Then he picked up a bag of sand and poured it into the jar. As with the marbles, the sand filled up the rest of the visible spaces. He asked the students again if they agreed that the jar was full. They all agreed the jar was full.

He then took out two pints of beer and poured them into the jar as well, effectively filling the empty space between the grains of sand. The students agreed again that the jar was full now, and indeed it was. But what was he trying to teach them?

"Your life is like a jar," the professor said. You decide what you want to fill it with. The golf balls are the first and most important things that matter: your faith, family, health, happiness, dreams, and aspirations. The marbles are the second most important things, after the house, car, and material possessions. The sand is everything else, the small stuff.

"The lesson to be learned is: To fit all the golf balls, marbles, and sand into the jar, they must be added in a specific sequence. If you fill it with sand first, there will not be sufficient space for the golf balls and marbles. If you fill it with the marbles first, there will be no space for golf balls or sand.

"It is the same for your life, if you spend your time on the small stuff, there is no room for the things that matter. If you spend your time and effort on the things that matter first, there will always be room for the small stuff as well.

"In other words, set your priorities."

"Professor, I get the meaning of the golf balls, marbles, and sand, but what's with the beer?" One student wanted to know.

The professor smiled and said, "If you do things in the right order, no matter how full your life may seem, there'll always be space for a couple of beers with friends."

- *Key Insight*

- *If you fill your life with the small stuff first, there's no room for what matters most. But if you prioritize the big things, everything else will fit.*

You are invited to join us on an expedition to discover the things that matter by mastering the art and science of time management. This book will challenge your beliefs and habits, but by the end, you'll have the tools to manage your time and ensure you're doing what matters most.

Unlike the other books in the *About Things That Matter* series, *Time That Matters* focuses on the practical, daily application of your values and goals. It's not just about being more productive; it's about making room for what truly matters, reducing stress, and living with intention.

Everyone. Whether you're a manager, entrepreneur, parent, student, or anyone who wants to reclaim their time and focus, this book is for you. You don't need to be a productivity expert, just someone who wants more from each day.

If you've read *Change That Matters* and *Goals That Matter*, you'll find familiar principles here, but always with a time management lens and new practical tools. If you're starting here, you'll get everything you need to begin making meaningful, lasting changes in your daily life.

You will learn:
- How to identify and prioritize what matters most
- The core principles and commandments of effective time management
- How to build habits, routines, and systems that stick
- The best tools and techniques for modern time management (digital and analog)
- How to conquer procrastination, overwhelm, and stress
- How to create a personal plan for time mastery that fits your unique life

Ready to begin?

Turn the page and start your journey to a life that truly matters—one hour, one day, one choice at a time.

Chapter 1 – Why Time Matters More Than Ever

What Really Matters

The classic jar story told in classrooms and boardrooms alike perfectly illustrates why time management is about so much more than just squeezing more into your day and working longer hours.

***Reflection**. What is the ratio of golf balls to marbles to sand and beer in the jar of your life?*

Why Time Management Is Essential for a Life That Matters

Time is the great equalizer. No matter who you are, you get the same 24 hours in a day as everyone else. Yet some people seem to accomplish more, experience less stress, and find greater fulfillment. What's their secret? It's not about working harder. It's about working on what matters most.

Time management isn't just about productivity; it's about purpose.

It's about ensuring your precious hours and minutes are invested in the things that give your life meaning, not just in the endless demands and distractions of modern life.

The Accelerating Pace of Life—and the Challenge of Focus

The world is moving faster than ever. Technology, information, and expectations crowd our days. Many of us feel perpetually busy, but not truly productive. We're pulled in a thousand directions, and it's easy to lose sight of what's truly important.

Poor time management isn't just missed deadlines or forgotten appointments.

It's missed moments with family, neglected health, abandoned dreams, and a creeping sense that life is slipping by.

Where This Book Fits in the Series

If you've read *Change That Matters* or *Goals That Matter*, you already know the importance of clarifying your values and setting meaningful goals. This book builds on those foundations, but with a new focus.

You'll find a few familiar concepts here, but always with a practical, time-focused lens. If you're starting here, you'll get everything you need to begin making meaningful, lasting changes in your daily life.

Who This Book Is For

This book is for everyone: students, parents, entrepreneurs, professionals, retirees—anyone who wants to reclaim their time and live with intention. You don't need to be a productivity expert; you just need to want more from each day.

This isn't a book about doing more for the sake of more. It's not about becoming a robot or filling every minute with work.
It's about making space for what matters, reducing stress, and living a life that feels rich and meaningful.

You won't find rigid systems or one-size-fits-all solutions here. Instead, you'll learn principles, tools, and strategies you can adapt to your unique life and goals.

If you follow the processes in these pages, you'll discover how to:

- Identify and prioritize what matters most
- Build habits, routines, and systems that stick
- Use the best tools and techniques for modern time management
- Conquer procrastination, overwhelm, and stress
- Create a personal plan for time mastery that fits your unique life

You'll experience less stress, more fulfillment, and the confidence that comes from knowing you're making the most of your days.

10 Bold Guarantees

If you apply what you learn here, you can expect:
1. More time for the things that matter most
2. Greater clarity about your priorities
3. Less stress and overwhelm
4. More consistent progress toward your goals
5. Stronger relationships
6. Improved health and well-being
7. Increased productivity and satisfaction
8. Better work-life balance
9. Greater confidence and self-esteem
10. A sense of fulfillment and purpose in your daily life

Author's Perspective

Believe me, I lived by these principles. I've seen the chaos that comes from letting time slip away, and I've seen the transformation that happens when you take control. I hope that you'll find, as I have, that mastering your time is the gateway to mastering your life.

The Evolution of Time Management

Time management isn't new. From sundials to smartphones, humans have always sought ways to make the most of their days. But the challenge has never been greater, or the rewards more profound.

Today, time management is about more than efficiency. It's about aligning your time with your values, your goals, and your vision for a life that truly matters.

Time Management as a Pillar of the Trio of Success

In the *About Things That Matter* series, we talk about the three pillars of a successful, fulfilling life:

1. Clear goals and a plan to achieve them
2. Effective time management
3. Strong relationships and social wealth

This book is your deep dive into the second pillar. Master it, and you'll have the foundation you need to build anything you desire.

Chapter Summary

- The "jar story" shows why time management is about putting the big things first.
- Time is the great equalizer; how you use it determines your results.
- This book builds on the foundations of *Change That Matters* and *Goals That Matter*, but with a laser focus on daily time mastery.
- You'll learn practical tools and principles to reclaim your time, reduce stress, and create a life that matters.
- Mastering time is the gateway to fulfillment, balance, and lasting success.

Reflection Questions

Question 1: What are the "golf balls" in your life—the things that matter most?

Former Student Responses:

"I'm not really sure what matters most to me - I just go through the motions each day."
"My family is important, but I spend most of my time at work or on my phone."

"I know health and relationships matter, but I prioritize work deadlines and urgent tasks."

"I want to say my faith and personal growth matter most, but I rarely make time for them."

"Everything feels important - work, family, friends, hobbies - I can't choose priorities."

"I used to know what mattered, but life got busy and I lost sight of my values."

"I think I should care about certain things, but I'm not sure they're actually important to me."

Possible Solutions:

Values Clarification: Complete a values assessment exercise to identify your core principles and what truly drives you

Life Audit: Track how you actually spend your time for a week and compare it to what you say matters most

Death Bed Test: Ask yourself, "What would I regret not prioritizing if I only had one year to live?"

Energy Assessment: Notice which activities energize you versus drain you - often our "golf balls" are energy-giving

Childhood Dreams Review: Reconnect with what excited you before external pressures shaped your priorities

Role Definition: Identify your key life roles (parent, partner, professional, friend) and what success looks like in each

External vs. Internal Motivation: Distinguish between what you think you should value versus what genuinely matters to you.

Question 2: Where is your time currently going? Are you making space for what matters, or is your jar full of sand?

Former Student Responses:

"I spend way too much time on social media and watching TV without even realizing it."

"My days are packed with meetings and emails, but I don't feel like I accomplish anything meaningful."

"I'm constantly putting out fires at work and never have time for planning or important projects."

"I say family is my priority, but I spend more time on work and household tasks than with them."

"I waste time on things that don't matter because the important stuff feels overwhelming."

"I'm always busy but can't remember what I actually did at the end of the day."

"I know I should exercise and take care of myself, but I never seem to find the time."

Possible Solutions:

Time Audit: Track your activities in 15-30 minute blocks for one week to see where time actually goes

Digital Detox: Use app timers to limit social media and entertainment consumption

Batch Processing: Group similar tasks (emails, phone calls, errands) to reduce context switching

Calendar Blocking: Schedule your "golf balls" first, then fit other activities around them

The 80/20 Rule: Identify which 20% of your activities produce 80% of your meaningful results

Evening Planning: Spend 10 minutes each evening planning the next day's priorities

Elimination Practice: Identify three low-value activities to reduce or eliminate this week

Question 3: What would your life look like if you managed your time with intention and purpose?

Former Student Responses:

"I'd probably feel less stressed and more in control of my days."

"I might actually make progress on my long-term goals instead of just surviving each day."

"I'd have better relationships because I'd be more present and available."

"I could pursue hobbies and interests that I've been putting off for years."

"I'd feel more fulfilled because I'd be living according to my values."

"I might sleep better knowing I spent my day on meaningful activities."

"I'd have more energy because I wouldn't waste it on things that don't matter."

Possible Solutions:

Vision Creation: Write a detailed description of your ideal day, week, and month

Goal Alignment: Ensure your daily activities support your long-term objectives

Energy Management: Schedule demanding tasks during your peak energy hours

Boundary Setting: Learn to say no to requests that don't align with your priorities

Routine Development: Create morning and evening routines that support your goals

Progress Tracking: Use simple metrics to measure advancement toward what matters

Regular Reviews: Schedule weekly and monthly check-ins to assess alignment between time use and values

Question 4: Which area—goals, time, or relationships—needs your attention most right now?

Former Student Responses:
   Goals: "I have vague dreams but no clear, specific goals with deadlines."
   Time: "I'm constantly busy but never seem to make progress on what matters most"
   Relationships: "I've been so focused on work that I've neglected my family and friends."
   All Three: "I feel like I'm failing at everything and don't know where to start."
   Goals: "I set goals, but they're not realistic or aligned with what I actually want."
   Time: "I waste too much time on social media and low-priority activities."
   Relationships: "I'm surrounded by people but feel lonely and disconnected."

Possible Solutions:
   Goals Focus: Use the SMART framework to turn vague dreams into specific, measurable objectives
   Time Management Priority: Conduct a time audit and eliminate your biggest time-wasters
   Relationship Investment: Schedule regular one-on-one time with important people in your life
   Integrated Approach: Choose one area to focus on for 90 days, knowing that improvement in one area often benefits the others
   Systems Thinking: Recognize how goals, time, and relationships interconnect and support each other.
   Professional Help: Consider coaching or counseling if you feel overwhelmed in multiple areas
   Community Support: Join groups focused on personal development to address all three areas simultaneously

Question 5: What's one step you can take today to begin taking control of your time?

Former Student Responses:
   "I could start by tracking how I actually spend my time instead of guessing."
   "I should put my phone in another room when I'm trying to focus."
   "I could write down my top three priorities for tomorrow before I go to bed."
   "I need to schedule time for exercise instead of hoping I'll find time later."
   "I could say no to one commitment that doesn't align with my goals."
   "I should block out time for my most important project first thing in the morning."
   "I could delete social media apps from my phone to reduce mindless scrolling."

Possible Solutions:
   Immediate Action: Choose the smallest possible step and do it within the next hour
   Environment Design: Remove distractions and create cues for positive behaviors

Calendar Integration: Block time for your most important activity tomorrow

Accountability: Tell someone about your commitment and ask them to check in with you

Habit Stacking: Attach your new time management behavior to an existing routine

Technology Tools: Set up apps or systems that support your time management goals

Reflection Practice: End each day by asking, "Did I spend my time on what matters most?"

Universal Solutions Across All Chapter 1 Questions:

Start with Awareness: Most time management problems begin with a lack of awareness about how time is actually being spent versus how we think it's being spent.

Clarify Your Values: Without clear priorities, any time management system will fail because you won't know what to optimize for.

Begin Small: Choose one simple change to implement consistently rather than trying to overhaul your entire life at once.

Use Visual Tools: Whether digital or paper, make your priorities and schedule visible to reinforce good decisions.

Build Support Systems: Share your time management goals with others who can provide accountability and encouragement.

Regular Review: Schedule weekly check-ins to assess progress and adjust your approach based on what you learn.

Focus on Progress: Celebrate small improvements rather than demanding perfection from yourself.

Align Actions with Values: Ensure your daily activities support your long-term vision and most important relationships.

Take Action

- List your top 5 priorities—the "golf balls" in your life.
- Track your time for one day and notice where it really goes.
- Identify one time waster ("sand") you can reduce or eliminate this week.
- Share your commitment to better time management with a friend or accountability partner.

"Don't count every hour in the day. Make every hour in the day count." – **Anonymous.**

Looking Ahead: In the next chapter, we'll explore the core principles and commandments of time management, so you can build a strong foundation for lasting change.

Chapter 2 – Critical Concepts and Commandments

Before you can master your time, you must understand the core concepts that underpin all effective time management. These are not just tips or tricks—they are the fundamental truths and rules that shape how you use your time, every day. Embrace them, and you will lay a solid foundation for lasting change.

7 Fundamental Time Management Concepts

1. Time Cannot Be Managed—Only Your Actions Can

Time flows forward relentlessly, like sand slipping through an hourglass—no matter what you do, you can't slow it down, speed it up, or store it for later. The truth is, you cannot manage time itself; you can only manage your own actions and choices within it.

Every person receives the same 24 hours each day. What separates those who thrive from those who struggle is not their ability to control the passage of time, but their ability to decide what they do with it.

Effective time management is really self-management: it's about making conscious, intentional choices about how you spend each moment, focusing on what matters most, and taking responsibility for your actions. When you accept that you can't control time, but you can control yourself, you unlock the power to shape your days and, ultimately, your life.

Key Insight. Think of time management as "self-management." The real question is: What am I doing with the time I have?

2. All Are Equal in the Eyes of Time

No matter your status, wealth, or background, every person on earth receives the same 24 hours in a day. Time is the great equalizer; it does not discriminate or play favorites. The difference between people who thrive and those who struggle isn't how much time they have, but how they choose to use it. Whether you're a CEO, a student, a parent, or an entrepreneur, you face the same daily limit. What sets high achievers apart is not privilege or luck, but the conscious, intentional choices they make about where to invest their hours and attention. When you truly grasp that everyone gets the same amount, you realize that your power lies not in wishing for more time, but in making the most of the time you have.

Reflection: How do the most successful people you know use their time differently?

3. Time Is Like Money—Budget It

Just as you wouldn't spend your money carelessly and expect financial security, you can't spend your time thoughtlessly and expect to achieve what matters most. Time, like money, is a limited resource: once it's gone, you can't get it back. That's why it's essential to budget your time with the same intention and discipline you'd use for your finances. When you invest your hours wisely, allocating them to your highest priorities, protecting them from waste, and tracking where they go, you'll reap the rewards in every area of life. Those who treat time as precious and plan how they use it consistently find more fulfillment, less stress, and greater progress toward their goals.

> *Practical Tip:* Track your time for a week, just like you would track your expenses. Where is it really going?

4. The Secret Is To Schedule What Matters

The real secret of effective time management isn't just making to-do lists; it's about scheduling what you have to do. If something truly matters to you, it must have a specific place in your calendar, not just a spot on your to-do list.

A to-do list is simply a wish list until you decide when and where each task will happen. By assigning your most important activities to actual time slots, you ensure they get the attention they deserve and are protected from distractions and less meaningful demands.

Scheduling transforms intention into action and helps you honor your priorities, making it far more likely you'll follow through and achieve what matters most. If it's not on your calendar, it's not a real commitment.

> *Action Step:* Before adding a new task, ask: "Where will this fit in my schedule?" If there's no room, reprioritize or say no.

5. The 80/20 Rule (Pareto Principle)

The Pareto Principle, also known as the 80/20 Rule, is one of the most powerful concepts in time management. It states that 20% of your activities produce 80% of your results. In other words, a small fraction of what you do each day is responsible for the majority of your progress and success. The key to effective time management isn't trying to do everything—it's about identifying and focusing on the "vital few" tasks that truly matter, while minimizing, delegating, or eliminating the "trivial many" that consume time but add little value.

For example, if you look at your workweek, you may find that just a handful of projects or client relationships generate most of your achievements or income. Similarly, in your personal life, a few habits or routines are likely responsible for most of your well-being and happiness. By regularly reviewing your activities and asking, "Which 20% of my actions are driving 80% of my results?" you can prioritize these high-impact tasks and protect time for them in your schedule. The rest—emails, meetings, minor chores—should be streamlined, delegated, or dropped whenever possible. Mastering the

80/20 Rule means working smarter, not harder, and ensuring your energy is always invested where it will make the greatest difference.

Exercise: List your top 10 regular tasks. Which two deliver the most value? How can you spend more time on those?

6. You Have More Time Than You Think

Time audit: Find hidden hours.

Most people underestimate how much time they actually have available each day. The real issue isn't a lack of hours, but how those hours are spent—often lost to hidden pockets of distraction, inefficiency, or low-value tasks.

By conducting a simple time audit, tracking your activities in 15- or 30-minute blocks for a week, you'll almost always discover "hidden hours" that can be reclaimed for what matters most.

You may be surprised to find how much time slips away to things like social media, unnecessary meetings, or mindless multitasking. The truth is, you likely have more time than you think; the opportunity lies in becoming aware of where it goes and making intentional choices to invest it in your priorities. When you shift your focus from the quantity of time to the quality of how it's used, you unlock the potential to achieve more with the hours you already have.

Challenge: Audit your daily routines. Where can you reclaim wasted minutes and invest them in what matters?

7. Always Know What You're Doing With Your Time

Awareness: "What am I doing, and why?"

At any given moment, you should be able to answer that question. This level of awareness is the foundation of effective time management. Clarity is power. Only when you are conscious of how you're spending your time and the reasons behind your actions can you ensure your efforts are aligned with your true goals and priorities.

Regularly reviewing your schedule and checking your activities against your objectives helps prevent drifting into distraction or busyness for its own sake. Instead of running on autopilot, you become intentional, making choices that move you closer to what matters most.

By cultivating this habit of mindful awareness, you transform your time from something that happens to you into a resource you actively direct toward a meaningful life.

Reflection: At the end of each day, ask: "Did I spend my time on what matters most?"

8 Commandments Of Effective Time Management

1. Kick the Robbers Out

Time robbers are those sneaky distractions and low-value activities that steal your hours and leave you wondering where the day went. These include unplanned phone calls, endless email threads, mindless social media scrolling, unnecessary meetings, and TV or digital distractions. Left unchecked, these "robbers" can consume a significant portion of your day, leaving little time for what truly matters.

To reclaim your time, start by identifying your biggest time wasters. Be honest—track your activities for a few days and notice where your attention drifts. Once you've spotted the culprits, take action: schedule specific times for calls, emails, and social media, and stick to those boundaries. Turn off notifications, batch similar tasks together, and set clear agendas for meetings. By proactively guarding your time from robbers, you create space for focused, meaningful work and personal priorities.

Some of the biggest time wasters:

- Unplanned phone calls
- Endless emails
- Social media scrolling
- Unnecessary meetings
- TV and digital distractions

Action: Schedule specific times for calls, email, and social media. Stick to your plan.

2. Priority Determines What Matters

Not all tasks are created equal. The most effective time managers know that urgency is not the same as importance. It's easy to get caught up in what's screaming for attention: emails, messages, and minor requests, while neglecting the tasks that truly move you toward your goals. Stephen Covey's Time Management Matrix is a powerful tool for distinguishing between what is urgent and what is important. In the next chapter, you will learn more about this powerful time management tool.

To use this principle, regularly ask yourself: "If I could only do one thing today, what would matter most?" Focus your energy on those high-impact, important tasks—even if they aren't urgent. Schedule time for them before anything else. By consciously choosing your priorities, you ensure your time is invested in what matters, not just what's loudest.

Tip: Ask: "If I could only do one thing today, what would matter most?"

3. Learn the Magic Word: "No"

One of the most powerful tools in time management is the ability to say "no." You can't do it all, and every "yes" to something unimportant is a "no" to something that matters. Learning to say "no" to requests, invitations, and tasks that don't align with your priorities is essential for protecting your time and energy.

Practice this skill by pausing before you agree to anything new. Check your calendar and commitments. If it doesn't fit, politely decline or negotiate a later time. Remember, saying "no" isn't rude—it's responsible. When you guard your time fiercely, you make room for your highest priorities and avoid overcommitment and burnout.

Practice: Before agreeing to anything new, pause and check your calendar. If it doesn't fit, say no or negotiate.

4. Juggling Is an Illusion (The Multitasking Myth)

Despite what many believe, multitasking is a myth. The human brain cannot truly focus on more than one complex task at a time. When you try to juggle multiple things, you end up switching rapidly between them, which wastes time, increases mistakes, and leaves you feeling frazzled.

Instead, focus on one thing at a time. Batch similar tasks together—like answering emails or making phone calls—and give them your full attention. You'll work faster, produce higher-quality results, and experience less stress. Remember: single-tasking is the real secret to productivity.

Try This: Batch similar tasks together (like emails or calls) and give them your full attention.

5. Take the "I" Out of It (Delegate and Teamwork)

You don't have to do everything yourself. Effective time managers know when to delegate, outsource, or share tasks with others. Instead of asking, "How will I do this?" ask, "How should this be done—and by whom?" Delegation isn't about shirking responsibility; it's about ensuring tasks are handled by the right person, freeing you to focus on your highest-value activities.

When you delegate, you empower others, build teamwork, and prevent overload. Whether at work or at home, look for opportunities to share the load. The result is more time, less stress, and better outcomes for everyone involved.

Benefit: Delegation frees you to focus on your highest-value activities.

6. Do the Right Thing Right the First Time

Rushed or sloppy work often leads to mistakes, rework, and wasted time. The commandment here is simple: slow down, focus, and aim for excellence the first time. Quality matters more than speed, especially for tasks that are important or complex.

Before starting any task, ask the 4WH questions: What needs to be done? Why is it important? Who is responsible? When is it due? How will it be accomplished? By clarifying these details and committing to doing the job right, you save time and energy in the long run.

Reminder: Use this checklist before starting anything new. It helps prevent confusion, duplication of effort, and missed deadlines. Applying the 4WH strategy turns vague intentions into concrete, actionable plans.

- **What** must be done?
- **Why** is it important?
- **Who** will do it?
- **When** must it be done?
- **How** will it be accomplished?

7. You Have to Plan It All

Failing to plan is planning to fail. The most powerful tool in time management is your calendar. Plan your day, week, and month in advance, and review your schedule regularly. This proactive approach allows you to prioritize, block time for what matters, and prepare for the unexpected.

Action: Set aside dedicated time each week for planning. Review your goals, schedule your top priorities, and adjust as needed. When you plan ahead, you reduce stress, avoid last-minute scrambles, and ensure your time is invested where it counts most.

Chapter Summary

- Mastering time starts with mastering your choices and actions.
- Everyone gets the same 24 hours—how you use them is what counts.
- Budget your time like money, schedule what matters, and use the 80/20 rule.
- Know your time robbers, set priorities, and learn to say "no."
- Focus on one thing at a time, delegate, and plan everything.
- Use visuals like the Covey Matrix and a weekly planner to keep your priorities clear.

Reflection Questions

Question 1: Which of these 7 concepts or 8 commandments do you struggle with most?

Former Student Responses:

"I struggle with saying 'no' - I feel guilty turning people down even when I'm overwhelmed."

"The 80/20 rule is hard for me because everything feels equally important."

"I can't stop multitasking even though I know it's ineffective."

"I have trouble scheduling what matters because urgent things always take over."

"I don't know how to delegate because I think I can do everything better myself."

"Planning feels like a waste of time when my schedule changes constantly."

"I understand time robbers exist, but I can't identify mine clearly."

Possible Solutions:

- **Saying No Difficulty**: Practice with low-stakes situations first; create standard responses like "Let me check my calendar and get back to you"; remember that saying no to one thing means saying yes to your priorities
- **80/20 Rule Confusion**: Track your activities for a week and identify which ones produce the most meaningful results; ask "Which tasks, if eliminated, would barely affect my goals?"
- **Multitasking Habit**: Start with single-tasking for just 15 minutes at a time; turn off notifications during focused work; batch similar tasks together
- **Scheduling Challenges**: Block time for important tasks first thing in the morning; treat important activities like unmovable appointments; use time-blocking in your calendar
- **Delegation Resistance**: Start by delegating small, low-risk tasks; provide clear instructions and deadlines; remember that delegation frees you for higher-value work
- **Planning Skepticism**: Start with just 10 minutes of daily planning; focus on planning your top 3 priorities rather than every detail; adjust plans as needed rather than abandoning planning altogether
- **Time Robber Blindness**: Use a time audit to track activities in 15-minute blocks; notice when you feel most distracted or unproductive; ask others what they observe about your time use

Question 2: What are your biggest time robbers—and how can you reduce or eliminate them?

Former Student Responses:

"Social media scrolling - I lose hours without realizing it."

"Unnecessary meetings that could be emails or quick calls."

"Constantly checking and responding to emails throughout the day."

"Getting caught up in office gossip and non-work conversations."

"Perfectionism - I spend too much time polishing things that are already good enough."

"Saying yes to every request, even ones that don't align with my goals."

"Procrastination - I waste time avoiding important tasks."

Possible Solutions:

- **Social Media Addiction**: Use app timers to limit daily usage; remove apps from your phone and only check on computer; schedule specific times for social media (like 15 minutes after lunch)

- **Meeting Overload**: Decline optional meetings; suggest shorter durations (25 minutes instead of 30); ask for agendas in advance; propose alternatives like quick calls or emails
- **Email Overwhelm**: Check email only 2-3 times daily at scheduled times; turn off email notifications; use the 2-minute rule (respond immediately if it takes less than 2 minutes, otherwise schedule time for it)
- **Social Distractions**: Set boundaries by saying, "I need to focus on this project right now"; move to a quieter workspace; use headphones as a signal you're not available for chat
- **Perfectionism**: Set time limits for tasks and stick to them; use the "good enough" principle for non-critical work; ask "Will anyone notice if I spend more time on this?"
- **Over-Commitment**: Practice saying "Let me check my priorities and get back to you"; create criteria for what you'll say yes to; remember that every yes to something unimportant is a no to something important
- **Procrastination**: Use the 2-minute rule for starting tasks; break large projects into small, manageable steps; work in focused 25-minute blocks (Pomodoro Technique)

Question 3: How can you shift from a "to-do list" mindset to a scheduling mindset?

Former Student Responses:
"I make long to-do lists but never seem to get through them."
"I write things down but don't assign specific times to work on them."
"My calendar is full of meetings but empty of time for my important projects."
"I feel like scheduling is too rigid - what if something urgent comes up?"
"I don't know how long tasks actually take, so I can't schedule accurately."
"I schedule things, but then ignore my schedule when other things come up."
"I think scheduling personal tasks feels too formal or business-like."

Possible Solutions:
- **Endless To-Do Lists**: Limit daily to-do lists to 3-5 items maximum; move tasks from your list directly into calendar time blocks; treat your calendar as the real to-do list
- **No Time Assignment**: For each task on your list, immediately ask, "When will I do this?" and block that time in your calendar; if you can't find time, the task isn't really a priority
- **Meeting-Heavy Calendars**: Block time for important projects first, then schedule meetings around them; protect at least 2-3 hours daily for focused work; treat project time as seriously as meeting time.

- **Rigidity Concerns**: Build buffer time into your schedule for unexpected issues; view your schedule as a flexible guide, not a rigid rule; reschedule rather than abandon planned activities
- **Time Estimation Problems**: Track how long tasks actually take for a week; add a 25% buffer time to your estimates; start with shorter time blocks and extend if needed
- **Schedule Abandonment**: Put your calendar somewhere visible; set reminders for scheduled activities; review your calendar first thing each morning and last thing each evening
- **Formality Resistance**: Start with just scheduling one important personal task daily; use casual language in your calendar ("work on novel" instead of "creative writing project"); remember that scheduling shows respect for your goals

Question 4: Where are you multitasking, and what could you batch or delegate instead?

Former Student Responses:
- "I try to answer emails while on conference calls."
- "I eat lunch while working on reports and checking my phone."
- "I help my kids with homework while cooking dinner and planning tomorrow's schedule."
- "I listen to podcasts while doing important work that requires concentration."
- "I switch between multiple projects throughout the day instead of focusing on one."
- "I check social media while watching TV and having conversations with family."
- "I try to clean the house while on work calls."

Possible Solutions:
- **Email During Meetings**: Batch email responses into 2-3 dedicated time blocks daily; give full attention to meetings or decline if they're not valuable; take notes during meetings instead of multitasking
- **Lunch Multitasking**: Designate lunch as a true break - eat mindfully, take a walk, or have a real conversation; batch report work into focused blocks; check phone only at designated times
- **Family Time Multitasking**: Delegate age-appropriate tasks to children; batch meal prep on weekends; schedule planning time separately from family time; be fully present during homework help
- **Podcast + Concentration**: Save podcasts for commuting, exercising, or doing routine tasks; work in silence or with instrumental music during complex tasks; recognize that learning requires focused attention

Project Switching: Use time-blocking to dedicate specific hours to each project; complete one project phase before moving to another; group similar tasks together (all writing, all phone calls, etc.)

Entertainment Multitasking: Choose one activity at a time - either watch TV, check social media, or have conversations; put devices away during family time; practice single-tasking as a form of mindfulness

Cleaning + Calls: Batch household tasks into dedicated time blocks; use hands-free time for casual calls only; delegate cleaning tasks to family members; hire help if budget allows

Question 5: What's one change you can make this week to align your time with your true priorities?

Former Student Responses:

"I could wake up 30 minutes earlier to have quiet time for planning and reflection."

"I could block out 2 hours every morning for my most important project before checking email."

"I could say no to one commitment that doesn't align with my goals."

"I could schedule weekly one-on-one time with my family members."

"I could batch all my errands into one afternoon instead of spreading them throughout the week."

"I could turn off notifications during my focused work time."

"I could delegate one task that someone else could do adequately."

Possible Solutions:

Early Morning Priority Time: Start with just 15 minutes earlier this week; use this time for your most important goal; prepare everything the night before to make mornings smoother

Morning Focus Blocks: Put your phone in another room; close email and social media tabs; let colleagues know you're not available during these hours; start with 1 hour if 2 feels overwhelming

Strategic No: Identify one current commitment that drains energy without providing value; practice saying "I need to focus on my priorities right now"; suggest alternatives or refer them to someone else

Family Time Scheduling: Put family time in your calendar like any important appointment; turn off work devices during this time; let each family member choose the activity sometimes

Errand Batching: List all errands and group them by location; choose one day/time per week for all errands; combine errands with other activities when possible

Notification Management: Turn off all non-essential notifications; check messages at designated times only; use "Do Not Disturb" modes during focused work

Delegation Practice: Choose a task that's 80% as good when done by someone else; provide clear instructions and deadlines; resist the urge to redo delegated work

Universal Solutions Across All Chapter 2 Questions:

Start Small: Choose one commandment or concept to focus on for the next week rather than trying to implement everything at once.

Track Your Progress: Use a simple method to monitor how well you're applying these principles - even a daily rating from 1-10.

Build Awareness: The first step to change is noticing your current patterns without judgment.

Create Systems: Use tools like calendars, timers, and templates to make good time management habits automatic.

Practice Self-Compassion: Remember that changing ingrained habits takes time - celebrate small improvements.

Seek Support: Share your time management goals with others who can provide accountability and encouragement.

Regular Review: Schedule weekly check-ins to assess what's working and what needs adjustment.

Focus on Progress, Not Perfection: Aim for consistent improvement rather than flawless execution of every principle.

Take Action

- Identify your top three time robbers and make a plan to address them.
- Review your schedule and ensure your most important tasks are blocked out first.
- Practice saying "no" at least once this week to something that doesn't fit your priorities.
- Use the 4WH strategy for your next big task or project.
- Set aside 30 minutes for weekly planning and reflection.

"The key is not to prioritize what's on your schedule, but to schedule your priorities." –
Stephen R. Covey.

Looking Ahead: In the next chapter, we'll explore how to harness change, set priorities, and build habits that make time management second nature.

Chapter 3 - What's Causing Unnecessary Crises

To identify which activities in your life are causing unnecessary crises, you need to develop self-awareness about your routines, analyze your patterns, and apply structured reflection. Here's a step-by-step approach based on the principles from *About Things That Matter* and *Goals That Matter*:

Conduct a Time and Activity Audit

Track your daily activities for a week. Write down what you do in 15–30 minute blocks. Be honest and thorough.

- At the end of the week, review your log and highlight situations that resulted in stress, last-minute rushes, missed deadlines, or emotional upheaval.
- Ask: When did I feel most overwhelmed or "in crisis mode"? What preceded those moments?

Identify Patterns and Triggers

Look for recurring activities or behaviors that precede a crisis.

Common crisis-causing activities include:
- Procrastinating on important tasks until the last minute
- Saying "yes" to too many commitments
- Not planning ahead for deadlines or responsibilities
- Neglecting to communicate or clarify expectations with others
- Ignoring small problems until they become urgent

Ask yourself:
- What do these situations have in common?
- Are there specific times of day, people, or places that trigger a crisis?

Apply the "Five Whys" Technique

For each crisis, ask "Why did this happen?" five times to get to the root cause.

Example:
- Why was I late submitting my report?
  → Because I started it the night before.

- Why did I start it so late?
  → Because I prioritized other tasks.

- Why did I prioritize other tasks?
  → Because I didn't schedule dedicated time for the report.

- Why didn't I schedule time?
  → Because I didn't review my deadlines at the start of the week.

- Why didn't I review my deadlines?
  - → Because I haven't built a weekly planning habit.

Look for Emotional and Environmental Triggers

Sometimes, unnecessary crises are caused by:

- Avoidance of uncomfortable tasks (emotional trigger)
- Disorganized workspaces or lack of systems (environmental trigger)
- People or situations that repeatedly disrupt your plans

Reflect and Take Action

After identifying the activities and patterns that lead to unnecessary crises:

- Decide which ones you can eliminate, delegate, or address earlier.
- Build habits that prevent crisis (weekly planning, daily reviews, setting reminders).
- Learn to say "no" to commitments that consistently lead to overload or chaos.

Ask for Feedback

Sometimes, others see our crisis patterns more clearly than we do. Ask a trusted friend, colleague, or family member:

- "What do you notice about when I seem most stressed or in crisis mode?"
- "Are there things I do (or don't do) that seem to create last-minute emergencies?"

In Summary

To identify activities causing unnecessary crises:

- Track your time and review for patterns of stress or chaos.
- Use the Covey Matrix to spot tasks that become urgent due to neglect.
- Apply the "Five Whys" to uncover root causes.
- Reflect on emotional and environmental triggers.
- Take action to eliminate, delegate, or schedule these activities earlier.

By bringing awareness and structure to your routines, you can shift from living in crisis mode to living with intention and calm.

Reflection Questions

Question 1: What is your biggest time management challenge right now?

Former Student Responses:

- "I constantly feel like I'm putting out fires instead of working on important projects."
- "I get distracted by social media and emails throughout the day."
- "I have too many commitments and can't seem to say no to anything."
- "I procrastinate on big tasks until they become urgent and stressful."
- "I don't have a consistent routine - every day feels chaotic."

- "I spend too much time in meetings that don't seem productive."
- "I feel overwhelmed by my to-do list and don't know where to start."

Possible Solutions:
- **Crisis Management**: Use the Covey Matrix to identify Quadrant II activities (important but not urgent) and schedule time for them weekly to prevent future crises
- **Digital Distractions**: Set specific times for checking email and social media; use app blockers during focused work periods; turn off non-essential notifications
- **Over-Commitment**: Practice the "pause and check" method before saying yes; create criteria for what aligns with your priorities; schedule buffer time between commitments
- **Procrastination**: Use the 2-minute rule for small tasks; break large projects into 15-minute segments; apply the Pomodoro Technique for sustained focus
- **Lack of Routine**: Start with one consistent morning routine; use time-blocking to create structure; establish regular weekly planning sessions
- **Meeting Overload**: Decline optional meetings; suggest shorter durations; ask for agendas in advance; propose alternatives like quick calls or emails
- **Overwhelm**: Limit daily to-do lists to 3-5 items; use the 80/20 rule to identify high-impact activities; delegate or eliminate low-priority tasks.

Question 2: What did your time audit reveal about your current routines?

Former Student Responses:
- "I spend way more time on social media than I realized - almost 3 hours a day"
- "I'm constantly switching between tasks and never get into deep focus."
- "Most of my time goes to urgent but unimportant activities."
- "I waste a lot of time looking for things because I'm disorganized."
- "I don't have any time blocked for my most important goals."
- "I'm always available to others but never protect time for myself."
- "I underestimate how long tasks take and always run behind schedule."

Possible Solutions:

- **Excessive Social Media**: Use app timers to limit daily usage to 30 minutes; schedule specific times for checking (like 15 minutes after lunch); remove apps from phone and only check on computer

- **Task Switching**: Use time-blocking to dedicate specific hours to similar activities; batch email responses into 2-3 daily sessions; create "do not disturb" periods for deep work

- **Urgent vs. Important**: Apply the Covey Matrix daily; schedule Quadrant II activities first; learn to distinguish between what feels urgent and what's actually important.

- **Disorganization**: Implement the "everything has a home" principle; spend 10 minutes each evening organizing for tomorrow; use digital tools to reduce paper clutter

- **No Goal Time**: Block time for your top priority first thing each morning; treat goal work like unmovable appointments; protect this time from other requests

- **Always Available**: Set boundaries by communicating your availability; use "office hours" for non-urgent requests; practice saying, "I'm in a focus block right now, can we talk at 3 PM?"

- **Time Estimation**: Track how long tasks actually take for a week; add 25% buffer time to estimates; break large tasks into smaller, more predictable chunks

Question 3: Which Quadrant II (important but not urgent) activity will you schedule this week?

Former Student Responses:

- "I want to start exercising regularly, but I never seem to find the time."
- "I need to plan my career development and update my skills."
- "I should spend more quality time with my family without distractions."
- "I want to work on my side business idea, but keep putting it off."
- "I need to organize my finances and create a budget."
- "I should start that online course I bought months ago."
- "I want to begin writing the book I've been thinking about."

Possible Solutions:
- **Exercise**: Schedule 30 minutes three times this week at specific times; start with walking or simple bodyweight exercises; treat it like a doctor's appointment
- **Career Development**: Block 2 hours this weekend to research industry trends; schedule 30 minutes daily to work on one new skill; reach out to one professional contact weekly
- **Family Time**: Schedule device-free family dinners; plan one special activity with each family member; establish a weekly family game night or walk
- **Side Business**: Dedicate 1 hour every Saturday morning to business planning; start with market research or competitor analysis; set up a simple workspace
- **Financial Planning**: Schedule 2 hours this Sunday to review all accounts; use apps like Mint or YNAB to track spending; set up automatic savings transfers
- **Online Learning**: Schedule 20 minutes daily for coursework; watch one lesson during lunch breaks; set a completion deadline and track progress
- **Writing Project**: Commit to writing 15 minutes every morning; set a daily word count goal (even 100 words); join a writing group for accountability

Question 4: What habit could you build to support your top priority?

Former Student Responses:
- "I could start my day by reviewing my top 3 priorities before checking email."
- "I could do a weekly planning session every Sunday evening."
- "I could set a timer for focused work blocks to avoid distractions."
- "I could prepare everything the night before to have smoother mornings."
- "I could batch similar tasks together instead of switching constantly."
- "I could take a 5-minute break every hour to stay energized."
- "I could end each day by planning tomorrow's priorities."

Possible Solutions:
- **Morning Priority Review**: Stack this habit onto your morning coffee routine; write priorities on sticky notes and place them where you'll see them; review them before opening any apps
- **Weekly Planning**: Schedule this like any important appointment; use the same day and time each week; create a simple template with goals, priorities, and schedule review
- **Focused Work Blocks**: Start with 25-minute Pomodoro sessions; use a physical timer or app; communicate your focus time to colleagues; turn off all notifications

- **Evening Preparation**: Set out clothes, prepare lunch, and review tomorrow's calendar; create a simple checklist; do this immediately after dinner
- **Task Batching**: Group similar activities (all phone calls, all emails, all errands); schedule specific times for each batch; resist the urge to mix different types of tasks
- **Regular Breaks**: Set hourly reminders; use breaks for movement, hydration, or brief meditation; step away from your workspace completely
- **Daily Planning**: Spend 10 minutes each evening reviewing the day and planning tomorrow; identify the next day's top priority; prepare your workspace for tomorrow's first task

Question 5: How will you remind yourself to focus on what matters most each day?

Former Student Responses:
- "I could put sticky notes with my goals on my computer monitor."
- "I could set phone reminders to check if I'm working on priorities."
- "I could start each day by asking myself 'What's most important today?'"
- "I could use my calendar to block time for important activities."
- "I could create a vision board to keep my goals visible."
- "I could find an accountability partner to check in with weekly."
- "I could review my goals every morning during my coffee routine."

Possible Solutions:
- **Visual Reminders**: Place your top 3 goals on your bathroom mirror, computer screen, and car dashboard; use colorful sticky notes that catch your attention; change locations weekly to maintain effectiveness
- **Phone Reminders**: Set 2-3 daily alarms with questions like "Am I working on what matters most?"; use motivational wallpapers; set calendar notifications for priority activities
- **Morning Questions**: Create a simple morning ritual asking "What are my top 3 priorities today?" and "Which one will have the biggest impact?" Write answers in a journal or planner
- **Calendar Blocking**: Color-code your calendar with different priorities; block time for important activities first; set reminders 15 minutes before priority work begins
- **Vision Board**: Create a visual representation of your goals; place it somewhere you'll see daily; include both images and words; update it quarterly

- **Accountability Partner**: Schedule weekly 15-minute check-ins; share your priorities and progress; ask them to remind you of your goals when you get off track
- **Goal Review Routine**: Stack goal review onto an existing habit like morning coffee; keep goals written in a place you'll see daily; spend 2 minutes each morning reconnecting with your "why"

Universal Solutions Across All Chapter 3 Questions:

Conduct Regular Time Audits: Track your activities weekly to identify patterns and time-wasters that need addressing.

Apply the Covey Matrix: Use the urgent/important framework to prioritize activities and spend more time in Quadrant II.

Start Small and Build: Choose one time management improvement to focus on for 30 days before adding another.

Create Systems, Not Just Goals: Build routines and habits that make good time management automatic rather than relying on willpower.

Use Visual and Environmental Cues: Make your priorities visible and remove barriers to important activities while creating obstacles to time-wasters.

Build Accountability: Share your time management goals with others who can provide support and gentle reminders.

Regular Review and Adjustment: Schedule weekly reviews to assess what's working and what needs to change in your approach.

Focus on Progress, Not Perfection: Celebrate improvements in your time management rather than demanding flawless execution from day one.

Chapter 4 – Time, Change, and the Power of Prioritization

If you've read *Change That Matters* or *Goals That Matter*, you'll notice some familiar themes here. That's intentional: understanding change, clarifying your "why," and learning how to prioritize are the bedrock of effective time management. Here, we'll recap only the essentials, then quickly move into practical, time-focused strategies to help you turn intention into daily action.

Embracing Change—The Time Management Angle

Change is the only constant in life. Whether you're seeking to improve your health, relationships, or productivity, change is the gateway to growth. But without mastering your time, even the best intentions can get lost in the daily rush.

Why Change Fails Without Time Mastery

Many people set goals or make resolutions, but fail to follow through—not because they lack motivation, but because they haven't made time for change. Time management is the bridge between wanting to change and actually changing.

Clarifying Your "Why" for Time Management

"He who has a why to live can bear almost any how." – Friedrich Nietzsche

Before you can change how you use your time, you need a compelling reason—a "why." This is your anchor when distractions, setbacks, or busyness threaten your progress.

Quick Exercise: Use the "Five Whys" technique for any time management change you want to make. For example:

- I want to get up earlier.
- Why? To have a quiet time before work.
- Why? So I can plan my day.
- Why? So I feel less rushed and more in control.
- Why? Because I want to be present for my family in the evening.
- Why? Because family is my top priority.

The Power of Time Audits

You can't improve what you don't measure. A time audit is a simple, powerful tool to discover where your hours really go.

How to Do a Time Audit:

1. For one week, write down everything you do in 15–30 minute blocks.
2. At the end of the week, review your log.
    a. Where did your time go?

b. What surprised you?
   c. What activities gave you the most energy or value?

The Time Management Matrix

This is one of the most important tools of time management to help you prioritize what matters most.

Not all tasks are created equal, and treating them as if they are is a recipe for stress and inefficiency. Stephen Covey's Time Management Matrix is a simple but powerful tool that helps you sort your activities based on two criteria: urgency and importance. Visualize the matrix as a square divided into four quadrants:

Quadrant 1 Urgent & Important	Quadrant 2 Not Urgent but Important
Do First (Crises, deadlines) These are your true emergencies and pressing deadlines—think of a project due today, a medical emergency, or a last-minute crisis at work. These tasks demand immediate attention and can't be ignored. **Example:** Submitting a tax return on the deadline, handling a family emergency, or fixing a critical system failure.	**Schedule and Focus Here** (Planning, health, growth) This is where real growth and long-term success happen. These tasks are important for your goals and wellbeing, but because they aren't urgent, they're easy to neglect. This quadrant includes planning, relationship building, exercise, skill development, and self-care. **Example:** Scheduling regular exercise, planning your week, developing a new skill, or spending quality time with loved ones.
Quadrant 3 Urgent but Not Important	**Quadrant 4** Not Urgent & Not Important
Delegate or Minimize (Interruptions, some emails) These tasks feel pressing, but don't actually move you closer to your goals. They're often interruptions—like certain phone calls, meetings, or emails that demand your attention but aren't truly important. **Example:** Answering non-essential emails, attending meetings that don't require your input, or responding to someone else's minor crisis.	**Eliminate** (Time wasters, distractions) These are pure time wasters—activities that neither help you achieve your goals nor require immediate attention. They add little or no value and should be minimized or eliminated. **Example:** Mindless social media scrolling, binge-watching TV, or getting lost in internet rabbit holes.

How to Use the Matrix in Practice:
   1. At the start of each week, list your tasks and sort them into the four quadrants.
   2. Focus first on Quadrant I, but aim to spend most of your time in Quadrant II—these are the activities that prevent future crises and build a meaningful life.
   3. Delegate or batch Quadrant III tasks, and ruthlessly cut out Quadrant IV.

4. Review your matrix regularly. If you find yourself constantly in Quadrant I, ask what you could have done earlier (in Quadrant II) to prevent the crisis.

Example: Suppose you're a student with an upcoming exam (Quadrant I), regular study sessions (Quadrant II), group chat notifications (Quadrant III), and endless YouTube videos (Quadrant IV). By scheduling your study sessions in advance (Quadrant II), you reduce last-minute cramming (Quadrant I), mute group chats during study time (minimizing Quadrant III), and set a timer to avoid getting lost on YouTube (eliminating Quadrant IV).

By using Covey's Time Management Matrix, you'll make smarter choices about where to invest your energy, reduce stress, and create more space for what truly matters.

Action Step: After your time audit, sort your activities into these four quadrants. Where are you spending most of your time?

Aim to spend more time in Quadrant II—this is where real progress and fulfillment happen.

Reclaim an Hour This Week
- Identify one activity in Quadrant IV (not urgent, not important) and eliminate or reduce it.
- Use that reclaimed time for a Quadrant II activity (planning, learning, connecting).
- Example: Replace 30 minutes of social media with 30 minutes of exercise or reading.

The Power of Now: Making Present Actions Count

You can't change the past, and you can't act in the future. The only time you have any real power is right now. This is the essence of the Power of Now: recognizing that every meaningful change, every step toward your goals, and every improvement in your life happens in the present moment. Too often, people get stuck either dwelling on past mistakes or anxiously planning for a future that never quite arrives, missing the opportunity to act today. The truth is, your future is shaped by what you choose to do in the present. If you want a different outcome tomorrow, you must make different choices today.

A practical way to harness the Power of Now is to use your time audit and your list of priorities to guide your actions, moment by moment. Ask yourself throughout the day, "What am I doing right now, and why?" This question keeps you mindful and intentional, helping you avoid slipping into autopilot or wasting precious hours on distractions. When you focus on the present and consistently make small, conscious choices that align with your goals, you create momentum and progress. Whether it's starting a new habit, tackling a high-priority task, or simply choosing to focus on what matters instead of what's urgent, the actions you take now are the building blocks of your future success.

***Remember:** the only moment you can control is this one—so make it count.*

Building Habits That Support Prioritization

Habits are the engine of time management. Once you know your priorities, build routines that make them automatic.

- **Habit Stacking:** Attach a new priority habit to an existing routine. Example: "After I pour my morning coffee, I'll review my top three priorities for the day."
- **Visual Cues:** Use sticky notes, phone reminders, or a planner to keep your priorities visible.
- **Weekly Reviews:** Set aside 30 minutes each week to review your time audit, priorities, and progress.

Chapter Summary

- Change, priorities, and habits are the foundation of effective time management.
- Without time mastery, even the best intentions get lost in the busyness of life.
- Use a time audit to see where your hours really go, then use the Covey Matrix to prioritize.
- The "Power of Now" means making conscious choices in the present.
- Build supportive habits and routines to make your priorities automatic.

Reflection Questions

Question 1: What is your biggest time management challenge right now?

Former Student Responses:

- "I constantly feel like I'm putting out fires instead of working on important projects."
- "I get distracted by social media and emails throughout the day."
- "I have too many commitments and can't seem to say no to anything."
- "I procrastinate on big tasks until they become urgent and stressful."
- "I don't have a consistent routine - every day feels chaotic."
- "I spend too much time in meetings that don't seem productive."
- "I feel overwhelmed by my to-do list and don't know where to start."

Possible Solutions:

- **Crisis Management**: Use the Covey Matrix to identify Quadrant II activities (important but not urgent) and schedule time for them weekly to prevent future crises
- **Digital Distractions**: Set specific times for checking email and social media; use app blockers during focused work periods; turn off non-essential notifications

- **Over-Commitment**: Practice the "pause and check" method before saying yes; create criteria for what aligns with your priorities; schedule buffer time between commitments
- **Procrastination**: Use the 2-minute rule for small tasks; break large projects into 15-minute segments; apply the Pomodoro Technique for sustained focus
- **Lack of Routine**: Start with one consistent morning routine; use time-blocking to create structure; establish regular weekly planning sessions
- **Meeting Overload**: Decline optional meetings; suggest shorter durations; ask for agendas in advance; propose alternatives like quick calls or emails
- **Overwhelm**: Limit daily to-do lists to 3-5 items; use the 80/20 rule to identify high-impact activities; delegate or eliminate low-priority tasks.

Question 2: What did your time audit reveal about your current routines?

Former Student Responses:
- "I spend way more time on social media than I realized - almost 3 hours a day"
- "I'm constantly switching between tasks and never get into deep focus."
- "Most of my time goes to urgent but unimportant activities."
- "I waste a lot of time looking for things because I'm disorganized."
- "I don't have any time blocked for my most important goals."
- "I'm always available to others but never protect time for myself."
- "I underestimate how long tasks take and always run behind schedule."

Possible Solutions:
- **Excessive Social Media**: Use app timers to limit daily usage to 30 minutes; schedule specific times for checking (like 15 minutes after lunch); remove apps from phone and only check on computer
- **Task Switching**: Use time-blocking to dedicate specific hours to similar activities; batch email responses into 2-3 daily sessions; create "do not disturb" periods for deep work
- **Urgent vs. Important**: Apply the Covey Matrix daily; schedule Quadrant II activities first; learn to distinguish between what feels urgent and what's actually important.
- **Disorganization**: Implement the "everything has a home" principle; spend 10 minutes each evening organizing for tomorrow; use digital tools to reduce paper clutter
- **No Goal Time**: Block time for your top priority first thing each morning; treat goal work like unmovable appointments; protect this time from other requests

- **Always Available**: Set boundaries by communicating your availability; use "office hours" for non-urgent requests; practice saying, "I'm in a focus block right now, can we talk at 3 PM?"
- **Time Estimation**: Track how long tasks actually take for a week; add 25% buffer time to estimates; break large tasks into smaller, more predictable chunks

Question 3: Which Quadrant II (important but not urgent) activity will you schedule this week?

Former Student Responses:
- "I want to start exercising regularly, but I never seem to find the time."
- "I need to plan my career development and update my skills."
- "I should spend more quality time with my family without distractions."
- "I want to work on my side business idea, but keep putting it off."
- "I need to organize my finances and create a budget."
- "I should start that online course I bought months ago."
- "I want to begin writing the book I've been thinking about."

Possible Solutions:
- **Exercise**: Schedule 30 minutes three times this week at specific times; start with walking or simple bodyweight exercises; treat it like a doctor's appointment
- **Career Development**: Block 2 hours this weekend to research industry trends; schedule 30 minutes daily to work on one new skill; reach out to one professional contact weekly
- **Family Time**: Schedule device-free family dinners; plan one special activity with each family member; establish a weekly family game night or walk
- **Side Business**: Dedicate 1 hour every Saturday morning to business planning; start with market research or competitor analysis; set up a simple workspace
- **Financial Planning**: Schedule 2 hours this Sunday to review all accounts; use apps like Mint or YNAB to track spending; set up automatic savings transfers
- **Online Learning**: Schedule 20 minutes daily for coursework; watch one lesson during lunch breaks; set a completion deadline and track progress
- **Writing Project**: Commit to writing 15 minutes every morning; set a daily word count goal (even 100 words); join a writing group for accountability

Question 4: What habit could you build to support your top priority?

Former Student Responses:
- "I could start my day by reviewing my top 3 priorities before checking email."

- "I could do a weekly planning session every Sunday evening."
- "I could set a timer for focused work blocks to avoid distractions."
- "I could prepare everything the night before to have smoother mornings."
- "I could batch similar tasks together instead of switching constantly."
- "I could take a 5-minute break every hour to stay energized."
- "I could end each day by planning tomorrow's priorities."

Possible Solutions:
- **Morning Priority Review**: Stack this habit onto your morning coffee routine; write priorities on sticky notes and place them where you'll see them; review them before opening any apps
- **Weekly Planning**: Schedule this like any important appointment; use the same day and time each week; create a simple template with goals, priorities, and schedule review
- **Focused Work Blocks**: Start with 25-minute Pomodoro sessions; use a physical timer or app; communicate your focus time to colleagues; turn off all notifications
- **Evening Preparation**: Set out clothes, prepare lunch, and review tomorrow's calendar; create a simple checklist; do this immediately after dinner
- **Task Batching**: Group similar activities (all phone calls, all emails, all errands); schedule specific times for each batch; resist the urge to mix different types of tasks
- **Regular Breaks**: Set hourly reminders; use breaks for movement, hydration, or brief meditation; step away from your workspace completely
- **Daily Planning**: Spend 10 minutes each evening reviewing the day and planning tomorrow; identify the next day's top priority; prepare your workspace for tomorrow's first task

Question 5: How will you remind yourself to focus on what matters most each day?

Former Student Responses:
- "I could put sticky notes with my goals on my computer monitor."
- "I could set phone reminders to check if I'm working on priorities."
- "I could start each day by asking myself 'What's most important today?'"
- "I could use my calendar to block time for important activities."
- "I could create a vision board to keep my goals visible."
- "I could find an accountability partner to check in with weekly."

- "I could review my goals every morning during my coffee routine."

Possible Solutions:
- **Visual Reminders**: Place your top 3 goals on your bathroom mirror, computer screen, and car dashboard; use colorful sticky notes that catch your attention; change locations weekly to maintain effectiveness
- **Phone Reminders**: Set 2-3 daily alarms with questions like "Am I working on what matters most?"; use motivational wallpapers; set calendar notifications for priority activities
- **Morning Questions**: Create a simple morning ritual asking "What are my top 3 priorities today?" and "Which one will have the biggest impact?" Write answers in a journal or planner
- **Calendar Blocking**: Color-code your calendar with different priorities; block time for important activities first; set reminders 15 minutes before priority work begins
- **Vision Board**: Create a visual representation of your goals; place it somewhere you'll see daily; include both images and words; update it quarterly
- **Accountability Partner**: Schedule weekly 15-minute check-ins; share your priorities and progress; ask them to remind you of your goals when you get off track
- **Goal Review Routine**: Stack goal review onto an existing habit like morning coffee; keep goals written in a place you'll see daily; spend 2 minutes each morning reconnecting with your "why"

Universal Solutions Across All Chapter 4 Questions:

Conduct Regular Time Audits: Track your activities weekly to identify patterns and time-wasters that need addressing.

Apply the Covey Matrix: Use the urgent/important framework to prioritize activities and spend more time in Quadrant II.

Start Small and Build: Choose one time management improvement to focus on for 30 days before adding another.

Create Systems, Not Just Goals: Build routines and habits that make good time management automatic rather than relying on willpower.

Use Visual and Environmental Cues: Make your priorities visible and remove barriers to important activities while creating obstacles to time-wasters.

Build Accountability: Share your time management goals with others who can provide support and gentle reminders.

Regular Review and Adjustment: Schedule weekly reviews to assess what's working and what needs to change in your approach.

Focus on Progress, Not Perfection: Celebrate improvements in your time management rather than demanding flawless execution from day one.

Take Action

- Complete a one-week time audit using a printable or digital template.
- Sort your activities into the Covey Matrix and identify at least one thing to eliminate or delegate.
- Schedule a Quadrant II activity for this week.
- Start a habit tracker for your new priority routine.
- Share your commitment to prioritizing what matters with a friend or accountability partner.

"The key is not to prioritize what's on your schedule, but to schedule your priorities." –
Stephen R. Covey.

Looking Ahead: In the next chapter, we'll explore how to set goals that fit your life—and how to turn those goals into scheduled actions that actually get done.

Chapter 5 – Setting Goals That Fit Your Life

From Intention to Implementation

In the previous chapters, you learned how to clarify your "why," audit your time, and prioritize what truly matters. Now, it's time to bridge the gap between intention and action by setting goals that fit your unique life—and, crucially, by turning those goals into scheduled, achievable steps.

If you've read *Goals That Matter*, you'll recognize some familiar principles here. This chapter recaps only the essentials, then pivots to the practical side: how to translate your vision into daily and weekly reality using time management tools and strategies.

The SMART Way to Set Goals

SMART goals are:
- **Specific** (clear and well-defined)
- **Measurable** (trackable progress)
- **Achievable** (realistic for you)
- **Relevant** (aligned with your values and priorities)
- **Time-bound** (with a deadline)

From Goals to Action

A goal without a plan is just a wish. The key to achievement is moving your goals from a list into your actual schedule.

Step 1: Break Down Your Goal

Divide your goal into smaller steps or milestones.

Example: If your goal is to write a book, your steps might be: outline chapters, write 500 words daily, and complete one chapter per week.

Step 2: Assign Time Blocks

For each step, decide when you'll work on it. Block out time in your calendar—just as you would for a meeting or appointment.

Keep your goals and scheduled tasks visible—on your wall, in your planner, or using a digital tool.

Step 3: Review and Adjust Weekly

At the end of each week, review your progress. What worked? What needs to change? Adjust your schedule for the coming week.

Tools for Turning Goals Into Action

- **Digital Calendars:** Google Calendar, Outlook, Apple Calendar
- **Task Managers:** Todoist, Trello, Notion

- **Paper Planners:** Weekly or daily planners with space for priorities and time blocks
- **Habit Trackers:** Apps or printable charts to track daily actions

Case Study 1: The Busy Parent

Sarah wants to spend more quality time with her children. She sets a goal to have a family game night every Friday. She blocks out Friday evenings in her calendar, sets reminders, and protects that time from other commitments.

Case Study 2: The Freelancer

James wants to grow his business. He sets a goal to reach out to three new potential clients each week. He schedules 30 minutes every Monday, Wednesday, and Friday for outreach and tracks his progress in a spreadsheet.

Case Study 3: The Student

Maria wants to improve her grades. She sets a goal to study math for 45 minutes every weekday. She uses a habit tracker app to record her study streaks and adjusts her schedule based on upcoming exams.

Overcoming Common Challenges

- **Overwhelm:** Break big goals into the smallest possible steps. Focus on the next action, not the whole project.
- **Distractions:** Schedule focused work blocks and set "do not disturb" times.
- **Lack of Progress:** Review your plan weekly. If you're not moving forward, adjust your approach or ask for help.

Goal-to-Calendar Workflow

1. Write your goal
2. Break it into steps
3. Assign each step to a specific time block
4. Track progress
5. Review and adjust weekly

Chapter Summary

- SMART goals help you clarify and structure your intentions.
- The real secret is moving goals from a list into your calendar—making them visible and actionable.
- Use digital or paper tools to plan, track, and review your progress.
- Break goals into small steps, assign time blocks, and adjust as needed.
- Real-life examples show that this method works for any lifestyle.

Reflection Questions

Question 1: What specific, measurable outcomes do you want to achieve in the next 6-12 months?

Former Student Responses:
- "I want to get promoted to a senior position and increase my salary by at least 15%"
- "I want to save $10,000 for a down payment on a house by next December."
- "I want to lose 25 pounds and run a 5K race by my birthday in 8 months."
- "I want to complete my master's degree program and graduate with honors."
- "I want to launch my freelance consulting business and secure 5 regular clients."
- "I want to improve my relationship with my teenage daughter by having weekly one-on-one time."
- "I want to read 24 books this year and start a book club in my community."

Possible Solutions:
- **Career Advancement**: Create a professional development plan, identify required skills, seek mentorship, document achievements, and schedule regular check-ins with supervisors
- **Financial Goals**: Set up automatic transfers to savings, track expenses monthly, identify additional income sources, and create a realistic timeline with milestones
- **Health and Fitness**: Use a structured training program like Couch-to-5K, track daily food intake, schedule regular weigh-ins, and find an accountability partner
- **Education**: Create a study schedule, join study groups, utilize the professor's office hours, and break large assignments into smaller tasks
- **Business Launch**: Develop a business plan, build a professional network, create a portfolio, and start with part-time clients while maintaining current income
- **Relationship Building**: Schedule weekly activities in advance, put away devices during this time, and focus on active listening and shared interests
- **Personal Growth**: Set a reading schedule, join online book communities, and start small with local friends before expanding to community-wide

Question 2: How will you break down these larger goals into smaller, actionable steps?

Former Student Responses:
- "I know I need to break things down, but I'm not sure how small the steps should be."

- "I tend to create plans that look good on paper but are too overwhelming in practice."
- "I get stuck trying to figure out the perfect sequence of steps."
- "I break things down but then get distracted by other priorities."
- "I'm good at planning but struggle with following through on the small daily actions."
- "I make my action steps too vague, like 'work on business plan'"
- "I underestimate how long things will take and get discouraged."

Possible Solutions:
- **Step Size Guidance**: Make steps small enough to complete in 15-30 minutes; if a step takes longer, break it down further
- **Practical Planning**: Test your plan by doing the first few steps before committing to the entire sequence; adjust based on reality
- **Sequence Flexibility**: Start with obvious first steps and let the path become clearer as you progress; perfect planning isn't required
- **Priority Management**: Use time-blocking to protect time for goal-related activities; say no to non-essential commitments
- **Daily Action**: Focus on one small action per day rather than trying to do everything; consistency beats intensity
- **Specific Actions**: Replace vague steps like "work on business plan" with specific tasks like "write executive summary section."
- **Realistic Timing**: Add buffer time to estimates; track how long tasks actually take to improve future planning

Question 3: What resources, skills, or support do you need to succeed?

Former Student Responses:
- "I need to learn new technical skills, but don't know where to start."
- "I need more time in my schedule, but can't figure out where to find it."
- "I need financial resources to invest in my goals, but I have a tight budget."
- "I need emotional support from people who understand what I'm trying to achieve."
- "I need better organizational systems to keep track of everything."
- "I need to overcome my fear of networking and asking for help."
- "I need accountability because I tend to let myself off the hook too easily."

Possible Solutions:
- **Skill Development**: Start with free resources like YouTube and library books; take one online course at a time; find free workshops or webinars
- **Time Management**: Conduct a time audit to identify where time is currently spent; eliminate or delegate low-priority activities; wake up 30 minutes earlier
- **Financial Resources**: Look for low-cost alternatives; start with goals requiring minimal investment; consider earning extra income specifically for goals
- **Emotional Support**: Join online communities related to your goals; find one accountability partner; share goals with supportive friends or family
- **Organization Systems**: Start with simple tools like calendars and notebooks; use free apps before investing in premium versions; focus on one system at a time
- **Networking Confidence**: Start with online networking; attend small, local events; prepare conversation starters; focus on helping others rather than asking for help
- **Accountability**: Schedule regular check-ins with a trusted friend; join a mastermind group; hire a coach if budget allows; use apps with social features

Question 4: How will you maintain motivation when progress feels slow or obstacles arise?

Former Student Responses:
- "I usually start strong but lose steam after a few weeks when I don't see immediate results."
- "I get discouraged when I face setbacks and tend to give up completely."
- "I compare myself to others and feel like I'm not making progress fast enough."
- "I lose motivation when life gets busy and my goals feel less urgent."
- "I struggle with perfectionism and get demotivated when things don't go exactly as planned."
- "I don't know how to celebrate small wins - I always focus on what's left to do."
- "I need external validation to stay motivated, but don't always get it."

Possible Solutions:
- **Sustaining Momentum**: Track daily actions rather than just outcomes; create visual progress charts; set smaller milestones with quicker rewards
- **Setback Recovery**: Develop a specific "comeback plan" before you need it; practice self-compassion; reframe setbacks as learning opportunities
- **Comparison Management**: Focus on your own progress over time; limit social media exposure; remember that everyone's journey is different

- **Priority Maintenance**: Connect daily actions to your deeper "why"; schedule goal time like important appointments; review your vision regularly
- **Perfectionism Management**: Set "good enough" standards; celebrate progress over perfection; focus on consistency rather than flawless execution
- **Celebration Practice**: Plan specific rewards for milestones; share achievements with supportive people; keep a "wins journal" to review regularly
- **Internal Motivation**: Develop self-validation skills; focus on effort and growth rather than external recognition; connect with your personal values

Question 5: What potential obstacles do you anticipate, and how will you prepare for them?

Former Student Responses:
- "I always get derailed when work gets busy or family emergencies come up."
- "I tend to procrastinate on the most important tasks and focus on easier, less impactful activities."
- "I worry that people close to me won't understand or support my goals."
- "I'm concerned about not having enough money to pursue some of my goals."
- "I struggle with self-doubt and impostor syndrome, especially when trying new things."
- "I get overwhelmed when I have multiple goals and don't know which to prioritize."
- "I have a history of starting projects but not finishing them."

Possible Solutions:
- **Life Disruptions**: Build flexibility into your plans; have backup options for busy periods; focus on minimum viable progress during challenging times
- **Procrastination**: Use the "2-minute rule" for getting started; tackle the most important task first each day; break overwhelming tasks into tiny steps
- **Lack of Support**: Communicate your goals clearly to family; find supportive communities outside your immediate circle; prepare responses to criticism
- **Financial Constraints**: Start with low-cost or free approaches; look for scholarships or payment plans; consider earning extra income for goal funding
- **Self-Doubt**: Keep evidence of past successes; practice positive self-talk; start with smaller challenges to build confidence
- **Multiple Goals**: Limit yourself to 1-3 major goals at a time; use the "Rule of 3" - one goal per major life area; review priorities monthly

- **Follow-Through Issues**: Start with extremely small commitments; track completion rates; celebrate finishing small projects before tackling larger ones

Universal Solutions Across All Chapter 5 Questions:

Create Detailed Action Plans: Break every goal into specific, time-bound steps that are small enough to feel manageable and clear enough to execute without confusion.

Build Support Systems: Actively cultivate relationships with people who understand and encourage your goals, whether through existing relationships or new communities.

Plan for Obstacles: Anticipate likely challenges and create specific strategies to overcome them before they derail your progress.

Focus on Process Over Outcome: Track and celebrate the actions you take consistently rather than just the end results you achieve.

Maintain Flexibility: Be willing to adjust your approach, timeline, or even goals as you learn what works best for your situation.

Develop Internal Motivation: Connect your goals to your deeper values and vision so you can maintain momentum even without external validation.

Practice Self-Compassion: Treat setbacks as learning opportunities rather than failures, and speak to yourself with the same kindness you'd show a good friend.

Start Small and Build: Begin with goals and actions that stretch you without overwhelming you, then gradually increase the challenge as you build confidence and momentum.

Take Action

- Choose one goal and break it into steps.
- Block time for those steps in your calendar for this week.
- Make your goal and schedule visible.
- At the end of the week, review your progress and adjust as needed.
- Share your goal and plan with someone who can cheer you on.

> *"A goal without a plan is just a wish."* – **Antoine de Saint-Exupéry**

Looking Ahead: Next, you'll discover how to build habits, routines, and systems that make time mastery automatic—so you can keep moving forward, even on your busiest days.

Chapter 6 – Habits, Routines, and Systems for Time Mastery

If you've ever wondered why some people seem to "just get things done," the answer is rarely superhuman willpower—it's habits and routines. Habits are the invisible architecture of daily life. Once established, they run on autopilot, freeing up your energy for the things that matter most.

Habits: The Real Engine of Time Management

A habit is a behavior that's been repeated enough times to become automatic. Research shows that up to 40% of our daily actions are habits, not conscious decisions. That means your success with time management depends less on motivation and more on the systems you set up.

Building Keystone Habits

Not all habits are equal. Some, called "keystone habits," have a ripple effect, improving other areas of your life.

Examples include:

- Planning your day every morning
- Exercising regularly
- Doing a weekly review

Quick Win: Choose one keystone habit to focus on this month. Make it small and easy to start.

Habit Stacking: The Easiest Way to Build New Routines

Habit stacking means attaching a new habit to an existing one.
Formula: "After I [current habit], I will [new habit]."

Examples:

- After I pour my morning coffee, I'll review my top three priorities.
- After I finish dinner, I'll set out my clothes for tomorrow.

Morning, Evening, and Weekly Routines

Routines are simply groups of habits performed in sequence.

- **Morning routines** set the tone for your day.
- **Evening routines** help you wind down and prepare for tomorrow.
- **Weekly reviews** keep you on track and allow for adjustments.

Sample Morning Routine:

1. Wake up at 6:30
2. Drink a glass of water

3. Review calendar and priorities
4. 10 minutes of stretching or meditation

The Role of Environment and Triggers

Your environment shapes your habits more than you realize. Make good habits easy and bad habits hard:

- Keep your planner visible on your desk.
- Use alarms or reminders for new routines.
- Remove distractions from your workspace.

Tracking and Maintaining Habits

Use a habit tracker (digital or paper) to mark off each day you complete your habit.

- Apps: Habitica (https://habitica.com), Streaks (https://streaksapp.com), Loop Habit Tracker (https://loophabits.org)
- Paper: Printable habit tracker or wall calendar

When Habits Slip: Getting Back on Track

Everyone slips up. The key is not perfection, but persistence.

- If you miss a day, restart the next day.
- Review what triggered the lapse and adjust your environment or routine.

Chapter Summary

- Habits and routines are the foundation of effective time management.
- Keystone habits create positive ripple effects.
- Habit stacking and environmental design make change easier.
- Tracking progress builds momentum and accountability.
- Consistency beats intensity; focus on small, sustainable changes.

Reflection Questions

Question 1: What is one habit that, if established, would make the biggest difference in your time management?

Former Student Responses:

- "I need to start planning my day the night before instead of winging it every morning."
- "I should establish a consistent morning routine to start my day with intention."
- "I want to develop the habit of doing my most important task first thing in the morning."
- "I need to stop checking my phone constantly and set specific times for it."
- "I should create a weekly review habit to assess my progress and plan ahead."
- "I want to establish boundaries around work hours so I can have personal time."

- "I need to develop the habit of saying no to commitments that don't align with my priorities."

Possible Solutions:
- **Evening Planning**: Spend 10 minutes each evening writing down tomorrow's top 3 priorities; prepare everything needed for the next day; review your calendar and adjust expectations
- **Morning Routine**: Start with just 15 minutes of consistent activities (coffee + priority review); gradually expand as the habit becomes automatic; stack new habits onto existing ones like brushing teeth
- **First Things First**: Identify your most important task before checking email; block the first hour of your day for this priority; turn off notifications during this time
- **Phone Boundaries**: Use app timers to limit usage; designate phone-free zones and times; check messages only at scheduled intervals (e.g., 9 AM, 1 PM, 5 PM)
- **Weekly Reviews**: Schedule 30 minutes every Sunday evening; use a simple template to review goals, assess progress, and plan the upcoming week
- **Work-Life Boundaries**: Set specific start and stop times for work; communicate these boundaries to colleagues; create transition rituals between work and personal time
- **Strategic No**: Create criteria for what you'll say yes to; practice polite decline phrases; remember that every yes to something unimportant is a no to something that matters

Question 2: What existing habit could you "stack" a new habit onto?

Former Student Responses:
- "I could add goal review to my morning coffee routine."
- "I could do stretches right after I brush my teeth."
- "I could plan tomorrow while I'm eating lunch."
- "I could listen to educational podcasts during my commute."
- "I could do a quick tidy-up right after dinner."
- "I could write in a gratitude journal before I go to bed."
- "I could review my calendar while I'm waiting for my computer to start up."

Possible Solutions:
- **Morning Coffee + Goal Review**: Keep your goals written on a card next to your coffee maker; review them while the coffee brews; spend 2 minutes connecting your day's tasks to your bigger picture

- **Teeth Brushing + Stretching**: Do simple stretches like neck rolls or shoulder shrugs while brushing; use the 2-minute timer as your stretch duration; gradually add more movements.
- **Lunch + Planning**: Use the first 5 minutes of lunch to review your afternoon priorities; plan tomorrow's top task; keep a small notebook or use your phone for quick planning
- **Commute + Learning**: Download educational podcasts or audiobooks; use driving/transit time for skill development; choose content related to your goals
- **Post-Dinner Tidying**: Set a 10-minute timer for family cleanup; make it a game or play music; focus on just clearing surfaces and putting things back in place
- **Bedtime + Gratitude**: Keep a journal by your bed; write down three things you're grateful for; reflect on one positive moment from the day
- **Computer Startup + Calendar Review**: Use the boot-up time to scan your calendar; adjust priorities based on meetings and deadlines; prepare mentally for the day ahead

Question 3: How can you adjust your environment to support better routines?

Former Student Responses:
- "I could set up a dedicated workspace that's always ready for focused work."
- "I should put my workout clothes out the night before to make morning exercise easier."
- "I could remove junk food from my kitchen and stock healthy snacks instead."
- "I should charge my phone outside my bedroom to avoid late-night scrolling."
- "I could set up visual reminders of my goals around my house."
- "I should organize my workspace so everything has a designated place."
- "I could use apps to block distracting websites during work hours."

Possible Solutions:
- **Dedicated Workspace**: Clear a specific area for important work; keep necessary supplies always available; remove distractions from this space; make it comfortable and inviting
- **Exercise Preparation**: Lay out workout clothes, shoes, and water bottle the night before; set up equipment in a visible location; create a playlist ready to go
- **Healthy Environment**: Stock fruits and vegetables in visible places; move unhealthy snacks to hard-to-reach locations; prep healthy snacks in advance; keep water bottles readily available

- **Phone Boundaries**: Charge phone in another room; use a traditional alarm clock; create a charging station away from your bed; establish phone-free zones
- **Visual Cues**: Post your goals where you'll see them daily (bathroom mirror, refrigerator, computer monitor); use sticky notes for reminders; create a vision board
- **Organization Systems**: Implement "everything has a home" principle; use containers and labels; spend 10 minutes each evening organizing for tomorrow; create simple filing systems
- **Digital Environment**: Install website blockers during focus time; organize digital files and folders; use apps that support your goals; turn off non-essential notifications

Question 4: What's your plan for tracking and celebrating progress?

Former Student Responses:
- "I want to use a simple habit tracker, but I'm not sure what format works best."
- "I tend to forget to track my progress consistently."
- "I don't know what milestones are worth celebrating."
- "I feel like celebrating small wins is premature when I haven't reached my big goal yet."
- "I've tried tracking apps before, but I always abandon them after a few weeks."
- "I'm not sure how often I should review my progress."
- "I don't know what kinds of rewards would actually motivate me."

Possible Solutions:
- **Simple Tracking**: Start with a basic calendar and checkmarks; use your phone's notes app; try a simple paper chart; focus on tracking just one habit initially
- **Tracking Consistency**: Link tracking to an existing habit (track after morning coffee); set daily phone reminders; place tracking tools in visible locations; use habit stacking
- **Milestone Identification**: Set weekly mini-goals; celebrate consistency streaks (7 days, 30 days); acknowledge effort, not just outcomes; recognize overcoming obstacles
- **Celebration Mindset**: Understand that celebrating progress creates momentum; small rewards reinforce positive behavior; progress deserves recognition regardless of the final destination

- **App Sustainability**: Choose the simplest app possible; focus on one metric at a time; use apps with minimal setup required; consider switching back to paper if apps feel overwhelming

- **Review Frequency**: Start with weekly 10-minute reviews; schedule monthly deeper assessments; use daily micro-check-ins (2 minutes); adjust frequency based on what works

- **Meaningful Rewards**: Choose rewards that align with your goals (fitness goal = new workout gear); use experience-based rewards (movie, nature walk); celebrate with time-based treats (extra sleep, hobby time)

Question 5: How will you recover and restart if you miss a day?

Former Student Responses:
- "I usually give up completely when I break my streak."
- "I feel so guilty about missing a day that it's hard to get back on track."
- "I tend to think 'I'll start again on Monday' and then lose momentum."
- "I get discouraged and think I'm not disciplined enough to maintain habits."
- "I try to make up for missed days by doing extra, which usually leads to burnout."
- "I don't have a plan for getting back on track when life gets busy."
- "I take missing one day as evidence that I'm not capable of change."

Possible Solutions:
- **Streak Recovery**: Remember that missing one day doesn't erase previous progress; focus on getting back on track immediately rather than waiting for a "fresh start"; use the "never miss twice" rule

- **Guilt Management**: Practice self-compassion; speak to yourself as you would a good friend; remember that setbacks are normal parts of the process; focus on learning rather than self-criticism

- **Immediate Restart**: Get back on track the very next day; don't wait for Monday or the first of the month; treat each day as a new opportunity; avoid the "all or nothing" mentality

- **Self-Efficacy Building**: Remind yourself of past successes; start with an even smaller version of the habit; focus on building confidence through small wins; challenge negative self-talk with evidence

- **Avoid Overcompensation**: Don't try to "make up" for missed days; return to your normal routine rather than doing extra; maintain consistency rather than intensity; prevent the boom-bust cycle.

- **Contingency Planning**: Identify likely obstacles in advance; create "minimum viable" versions of your habits for busy days; have backup plans for common scenarios; build flexibility into your routine
- **Identity vs. Behavior**: Separate your identity from your actions; one missed day doesn't define your character; focus on who you're becoming rather than perfect performance; view habits as practice, not tests

Universal Solutions Across All Chapter 6 Questions:

Start Ridiculously Small: Choose habits so small they seem almost trivial - this builds momentum without triggering resistance.

Use Environmental Design: Make good habits easy and bad habits hard by adjusting your physical and digital environment.

Focus on Systems Over Goals: Build processes that naturally lead to your desired outcomes rather than relying on willpower alone.

Practice Self-Compassion: Treat yourself with kindness during the habit-building process, especially when facing setbacks.

Stack Habits Strategically: Attach new habits to existing strong routines to increase the likelihood of consistency.

Track Progress Simply: Use the easiest possible tracking method that you'll actually maintain over time.

Celebrate Small Wins: Acknowledge and reward progress to reinforce positive behavior patterns and maintain motivation.

Plan for Obstacles: Anticipate challenges and have specific strategies ready for getting back on track when you inevitably face setbacks.

Take Action

- Choose one keystone habit to start this week.
- Write out a simple morning or evening routine.
- Set up a habit tracker (digital or paper).
- Tell a friend or accountability partner about your new habit.
- Celebrate your first streak—no matter how small!

"We are what we repeatedly do. Excellence, then, is not an act, but a habit." **– Aristotle.**

Looking Ahead: In the next chapter, you'll discover how to overcome procrastination and Overwhelm.

Chapter 7 – Conquering Procrastination and Overwhelm

Procrastination and overwhelm are the twin enemies that stand between intention and action. Everyone faces them, regardless of age, experience, or ambition. Mastering your time means learning to recognize, manage, and overcome both.

Part 1: Procrastination – Why We Delay (and How to Stop)

What Is Procrastination?

Procrastination is the act of delaying or postponing tasks, even when you know they are important. It's not laziness, it's often a way to avoid discomfort, uncertainty, or fear of failure.

Why Do We Procrastinate?

- Task feels too big or unclear (overwhelming)
- Fear of failure or imperfection
- Lack of motivation or unclear goals
- Distractions and lack of boundaries

The Science of Procrastination

Procrastination is a coping mechanism. When a task feels unpleasant or daunting, your brain seeks short-term relief by doing something easier or more enjoyable. But the relief is temporary, and the task (and anxiety) only grows.

Practical Tools to Beat Procrastination

Overcoming procrastination isn't about willpower alone—it's about using proven techniques that make starting and sustaining focus easier. Here are four of the most effective tools, each with clear explanations and real-life examples:

1. *The Pomodoro Technique*

The Pomodoro Technique is a time management method developed by Francesco Cirillo. It breaks work into focused intervals—traditionally 25 minutes—called "Pomodoros," followed by a short 5-minute break. After four Pomodoros, you take a longer break (15–30 minutes).

- Short bursts of focus feel manageable, making it easier to start.
- Regular breaks prevent burnout and help maintain energy.
- The ticking timer creates a sense of urgency and helps block distractions.

How to use it:
1. Choose a task you want to work on.
2. Set a timer for 25 minutes (use a kitchen timer, phone, or Pomodoro app).

3. Work on the task until the timer rings—no interruptions!
4. Take a 5-minute break. Move, stretch, or grab a drink.
5. Repeat. After four Pomodoros, take a longer break.

Example: Maria struggles to start her monthly report. She sets a Pomodoro timer for 25 minutes and tells herself she only has to work until the bell rings. The time flies, and she often finds herself wanting to continue after the break.

Recommended tools:
- Focus Booster (https://www.focusboosterapp.com)
- Pomodone (https://pomodoneapp.com)
- TomatoTimer (https://tomato-timer.com)

2. Timeboxing

Timeboxing means allocating a fixed, pre-determined amount of time to an activity and then stopping when the time is up, regardless of whether the task is "finished."

- Creates boundaries for tasks that could otherwise drag on.
- Reduces perfectionism and "analysis paralysis."
- Helps you make progress on big or intimidating projects.

How to use it:
1. Decide how much time you'll spend on a task (e.g., 45 minutes to write a proposal).
2. Set a timer or mark it on your calendar.
3. Work on the task until the time is up, then stop—even if you're not "done."
4. Review what you accomplished and schedule more time if needed.

Example: James needs to prepare a presentation but keeps putting it off. He schedules a 60-minute timebox on Tuesday morning. When the hour is up, he's surprised by how much he's accomplished—and he feels less overwhelmed about finishing it later.

Recommended tools:
- Google Calendar or Outlook (for scheduling time blocks)
- Toggl Track (for tracking time spent) (https://toggl.com/track)
- Clockify (for timeboxing and reporting) (https://clockify.me)

3. The 2-Minute Rule

Popularized by David Allen in *Getting Things Done*, the 2-Minute Rule states: "If a task will take two minutes or less, do it immediately." For larger tasks, it means starting with just two minutes of effort to overcome inertia.

- Knocks out small tasks before they pile up and become overwhelming.
- Makes starting a big or dreaded task feel less intimidating.
- Builds momentum: once you begin, you're likely to keep going.

How to use it:
1. As you review your to-do list, identify tasks that can be done in two minutes or less (reply to an email, file a document, make a quick call).
2. Do them right away.

3. For bigger tasks, commit to just two minutes of focused work—often, you'll keep going.

Example: Sarah's desk is cluttered, and she's been avoiding cleaning it. She tells herself, "I'll just tidy up for two minutes." Once she starts, she finds it easy to keep going and finishes the whole task in ten minutes.

No special tools needed, just awareness and a timer if you want to limit yourself.

4. *Digital Blockers*

Digital blockers are apps or browser extensions that block access to distracting websites, apps, or notifications during work periods.

- Removes temptation—if you can't access social media or news sites, you're less likely to procrastinate.
- Helps you create focused, distraction-free work sessions.
- Builds awareness of your digital habits.

How to use it:
1. Choose a digital blocker app or extension.
2. Set up a list of distracting sites or apps to block (e.g., Facebook, YouTube, Instagram).
3. Schedule focused work sessions during which these sites are inaccessible.
4. Use the freed-up time for your priority tasks.

Example: A student, Alex, finds himself constantly checking social media while studying. He installs Freedom and schedules it to block all social sites from 7–9 p.m. each night. He finds it much easier to focus and gets his homework done faster.

Recommended tools:
- Freedom (blocks websites and apps across devices) (https://freedom.to)
- Forest (gamifies focus by growing a virtual tree) (https://www.forestapp.cc)
- RescueTime (tracks and blocks distractions) (https://www.rescuetime.com)
- StayFocusd (browser extension for Chrome)

Putting It All Together

You don't need to use every tool at once. Experiment with each technique and see which works best for your personality and workflow. Many people find that combining two or more (for example, Pomodoro + digital blockers) creates a powerful system for staying on track.

Quick Reference Table

Tool	Best For	How to Start	Example Use Case
Pomodoro Technique	Getting started, maintaining focus	Set a timer for 25 minutes, then break	Writing, studying, and admin tasks
Timeboxing	Limiting perfectionism, big projects	Schedule a fixed time block	Preparing a presentation

| 2-Minute Rule | Tackling small tasks, overcoming inertia | Do any task under 2 minutes immediately | Email, tidying, quick calls |
| Digital Blockers | Reducing digital distractions | Install the app, block sites during work | Studying, writing, and deep work sessions |

Take Action
- Choose one tool from this list and use it today on a task you've been avoiding.
- Track your results and note any changes in your focus, productivity, or stress.
- Share your experience with a friend or accountability partner for extra motivation.

"You don't have to see the whole staircase, just take the first step." — **Martin Luther King Jr.**

Breaking Down Big Projects

Overwhelm often comes from seeing the whole mountain at once.

- Break projects into the smallest possible steps.
- Focus on the next action, not the whole project.
- Celebrate each small win to build momentum.

Quick Win: Pick one task you've been avoiding. Set a timer for 10 minutes and work on it—just to get started. Often, action leads to motivation.

Part 2: Overwhelm – When There's Just Too Much

Overwhelm is the feeling that there's too much to do and not enough time, energy, or clarity to do it. It's a major cause of procrastination and burnout.

Why Do We Get Overwhelmed?
- **Too many priorities** (or no clear priorities)
- **Lack of boundaries**—saying yes to everything
- **Perfectionism**—believing everything must be done perfectly
- **No system for organizing tasks**

Practical Strategies to Beat Overwhelm

1. Prioritize Ruthlessly

Use the Covey Matrix (Urgent/Important) to identify what truly matters. Focus on Quadrant II (important but not urgent) and delegate/eliminate the rest.

2. Limit Your To-Do List

Each day, pick your top 3 priorities. If you finish those, move on to the next.

3. *Set Boundaries and Learn to Say No*

Protect your time by declining tasks that don't align with your priorities.

4. *Delegate or Outsource*

You don't have to do everything yourself. Ask for help or use tools to automate routine tasks.

5. *Schedule Breaks and Recovery*

Build short breaks into your day to recharge your energy and prevent burnout.

When You're Already Overwhelmed: The Reset
- Stop and breathe. Step away from your work for a few minutes.
- Write down everything on your mind or to-do list.
- Circle the one thing that, if done, would make the biggest difference.
- Do that one thing first. Then reassess.

Quick Win: Do a "brain dump" of everything on your mind, then pick just one thing to focus on. Give yourself permission to do only that for the next hour.

Chapter Summary

- Procrastination and overwhelm are normal—but manageable—challenges on the path to time mastery.
- Procrastination is best tackled with small steps, clear boundaries, and practical tools like Pomodoro, timeboxing, and the 2-minute rule.
- Overwhelm is reduced by ruthless prioritization, limiting your to-do list, setting boundaries, and scheduling recovery.
- When in doubt, start small and focus on one thing at a time.

Reflection Questions

Question 1: What tasks do you procrastinate on most, and why?

Former Student Responses:
- "I avoid writing reports because I'm a perfectionist and worry they won't be good enough."
- "I put off difficult conversations with my team members because I hate conflict."
- "I delay starting big projects because they feel overwhelming, and I don't know where to begin."
- "I procrastinate on administrative tasks like filing and organizing because they're boring."
- "I avoid making important phone calls because I'm afraid of rejection or bad news."
- "I put off exercise because I'm tired after work and would rather watch TV."

- "I delay financial planning because numbers stress me out, and I feel incompetent."

Possible Solutions:
- **Perfectionism**: Set "good enough" standards and time limits; use the 2-minute rule to start imperfectly; focus on progress over perfection
- **Conflict Avoidance**: Practice having small, low-stakes difficult conversations; prepare talking points in advance; reframe conversations as problem-solving opportunities
- **Overwhelming Projects**: Break large projects into 15-minute tasks; use the Pomodoro Technique; focus only on the very next step
- **Boring Tasks**: Batch similar tasks together; reward yourself after completion; listen to music or podcasts while doing routine work
- **Fear-Based Avoidance**: Start with less intimidating versions; practice scripts beforehand; remind yourself that avoiding makes anxiety worse
- **Energy Management**: Schedule exercise during higher-energy times; start with just 10 minutes; choose activities you actually enjoy
- **Skill Gaps**: Start with basic tutorials; ask for help from knowledgeable friends; break complex tasks into smaller learning steps

Question 2: Which tool or technique (Pomodoro, timeboxing, 2-minute rule) will you try this week?

Former Student Responses:
- "I want to try the Pomodoro Technique because I get distracted easily and need structure."
- "Timeboxing appeals to me because I tend to spend too much time perfecting things."
- "The 2-minute rule sounds good for tackling all the small tasks that pile up."
- "I'm not sure which one would work best for my personality and work style."
- "I've tried some of these before but didn't stick with them consistently."
- "I want to try digital blockers because social media is my biggest distraction."
- "I think I need a combination approach rather than just one technique."

Possible Solutions:
- **Pomodoro Interest**: Download a timer app; start with 25-minute sessions; take real breaks between sessions; track how many Pomodoros you complete daily

- **Timeboxing Appeal**: Schedule specific time blocks in your calendar; set clear start and stop times; resist the urge to continue past the time limit
- **2-Minute Rule Adoption**: Keep a list of quick tasks; do them immediately when they arise; use this rule to start larger projects with just 2 minutes of effort
- **Technique Uncertainty**: Try each method for one week; track your productivity and stress levels; choose the one that feels most natural
- **Consistency Issues**: Start smaller than before; attach the technique to existing habits; track your usage to build accountability
- **Digital Distraction**: Install Freedom or similar apps; schedule specific times for social media; remove apps from your phone during work hours
- **Combination Approach**: Use Pomodoro for deep work, the 2-minute rule for quick tasks, and timeboxing for meetings; don't overwhelm yourself with too many systems at once

Question 3: What's one source of overwhelm you can reduce or eliminate?

Former Student Responses:
- "I say yes to too many commitments and then feel stressed about everything I have to do."
- "My email inbox is constantly overflowing, and I feel like I can never catch up."
- "I try to multitask everything and end up doing nothing well."
- "I don't have clear priorities, so everything feels equally urgent and important."
- "My workspace is cluttered and disorganized, which makes me feel scattered."
- "I take on tasks that other people could do because I think I can do them better."
- "I worry about things that are completely outside my control."

Possible Solutions:
- **Over-Commitment**: Practice saying "Let me check my calendar and get back to you"; create criteria for what you'll say yes to; schedule buffer time between commitments
- **Email Overwhelm**: Check email only 2-3 times daily; unsubscribe from unnecessary lists; use filters and folders; set up auto-responses about response times
- **Multitasking Habit**: Focus on one task at a time; batch similar activities together; turn off notifications during focused work; use time-blocking
- **Priority Confusion**: Use the Covey Matrix to categorize tasks; limit daily to-do lists to 3-5 items; ask "What would happen if I didn't do this today?"

- **Workspace Clutter**: Spend 10 minutes daily organizing; implement "everything has a home" principle; clear your desk at the end of each day
- **Delegation Resistance**: Identify tasks others can do 80% as well; provide clear instructions and deadlines; resist the urge to redo delegated work
- **Control Worries**: Make a list of what you can and can't control; focus energy only on controllable items; practice acceptance of uncertain outcomes

Question 4: Where do you need to set better boundaries or say no?

Former Student Responses:
- "I need to stop checking work emails after hours and on weekends."
- "I should say no to social events when I'm already overcommitted."
- "I need boundaries with family members who constantly ask for favors."
- "I should stop accepting every meeting request that comes my way."
- "I need to limit how much time I spend helping colleagues with their work."
- "I should say no to volunteer opportunities when my plate is already full."
- "I need to set boundaries around my time for personal goals and self-care."

Possible Solutions:
- **Work-Life Boundaries**: Set specific work hours and communicate them; turn off work notifications after hours; create physical separation between work and personal spaces
- **Social Obligations**: Evaluate invitations against your priorities; suggest alternative ways to connect; remember that saying no to one thing means saying yes to something more important
- **Family Boundaries**: Have honest conversations about your availability; suggest alternative solutions; set specific times when you're available to help
- **Meeting Overload**: Ask for agendas before accepting; suggest shorter durations; decline optional meetings; propose alternatives like quick calls or emails
- **Colleague Assistance**: Set "office hours" for helping others; teach people to solve problems independently; refer them to other resources when appropriate
- **Volunteer Limits**: Choose one cause to focus on rather than spreading yourself thin; set term limits for commitments; remember that you can't help others if you're burned out
- **Personal Time Protection**: Schedule self-care and goal time like important appointments; communicate your needs to family and friends; start with small boundaries and build up

Question 5: How will you celebrate your next small win?

Former Student Responses:
- "I never really celebrate small wins - I just move on to the next task."
- "I don't know what a meaningful celebration would feel like."
- "I feel guilty celebrating when there's still so much left to do."
- "I prefer experiences over material rewards."
- "I want celebrations that don't contradict my goals (like food rewards for fitness goals)"
- "I'd like to celebrate with other people, but I'm embarrassed about my goals."
- "I'm on a tight budget, so I can't afford expensive rewards."

Possible Solutions:
- **No Celebration Habit**: Schedule celebration time in your calendar; set reminders to acknowledge progress; create a "wins journal" to track accomplishments
- **Celebration Uncertainty**: Try different types of rewards to see what motivates you; ask friends what they do; focus on activities that energize you
- **Guilt About Celebrating**: Reframe celebration as fuel for continued progress; remember that acknowledging wins increases motivation; celebrate effort, not just outcomes
- **Experience Preferences**: Plan special outings, try new activities, or visit places you've wanted to explore; attend events related to your interests
- **Goal-Aligned Rewards**: Celebrate fitness progress with new workout gear; reward learning goals with advanced courses; treat financial goals with small investments in your future
- **Social Celebration Needs**: Share wins with supportive friends and family; join communities where you can celebrate others' successes too; start small with one trusted person
- **Budget-Conscious Options**: Use free activities like nature walks or library visits; create homemade treats; celebrate with time-based rewards like sleeping in or taking a relaxing bath

Universal Solutions Across All Chapter 7 Questions:

Start Small: Choose one anti-procrastination technique and one boundary to focus on this week, rather than trying to change everything at once.

Address Root Causes: Identify whether procrastination stems from perfectionism, fear, overwhelm, or lack of clarity, then use targeted strategies.

Use Environmental Design: Remove barriers to important tasks and create obstacles to procrastination triggers.

Build Support Systems: Share your anti-procrastination goals with others who can provide accountability and encouragement.

Practice Self-Compassion: Treat setbacks as learning opportunities rather than evidence of personal failure.

Focus on Progress: Celebrate any movement forward, no matter how small, to build momentum and motivation.

Create Systems: Use tools and techniques that make good choices easier and bad choices harder.

Regular Review: Schedule weekly check-ins to assess what's working and adjust your approach as needed.

Take Action

- Choose one procrastination-busting tool and use it today.
- Break a big project into the smallest possible steps and schedule the first one.
- Do a "brain dump" and pick your top 3 priorities for tomorrow.
- Set a "do not disturb" block for focused work.
- Share your win with someone who will cheer you on.

"You may delay, but time will not." – **Benjamin Franklin**

Looking Ahead: In the next chapter, you'll discover how to manage stress and energy for sustainable productivity, so you can keep moving forward, even when life gets busy.

Chapter 8 – Stress, Energy, and Sustainable Productivity

Time management isn't just about getting more done; it's about doing what matters, with less stress and more energy. Even the best plans and tools can fall apart if you're overwhelmed, exhausted, or burned out. Sustainable productivity means learning to manage both your stress and your energy, so you can keep moving forward without sacrificing your well-being.

Understanding Stress

Stress is your body's response to demands or threats. Some stress is normal, even helpful, but chronic stress drains your energy, clouds your thinking, and sabotages your goals.

Types and Sources of Stress
- **Acute stress:** Short-term, from immediate pressures (deadlines, traffic jams)
- **Chronic stress:** Ongoing, from unresolved issues (workload, relationships)
- **Internal stress:** Self-imposed, from perfectionism or negative self-talk
- **External stress:** From outside events or people

Example: Sarah finds herself anxious every Sunday night. When she looks closer, she realizes she's been saying "yes" to too many projects at work and isn't blocking out time for rest or family.

How Poor Time Management Amplifies Stress
- Overcommitting and underestimating how long tasks take
- Failing to prioritize, leading to last-minute rushes
- Not scheduling breaks or downtime
- Neglecting self-care in the pursuit of productivity

Four Steps to Control and Manage Stress

1. **Awareness:** Notice your stress signals (tight shoulders, racing thoughts, irritability)
2. **Identify the Source:** Is it external (work, people) or internal (expectations, beliefs)?
3. **Take Action:** Use stress-reducing strategies (see below)
4. **Reflect and Adjust:** What worked? What can you do differently next time?

Stress Management Strategies for Busy People

1. Mindfulness and Micro-Breaks

Take a few minutes each day to breathe, meditate, or simply be present. Try the "4-7-8" breathing technique: inhale for 4 seconds, hold for 7, exhale for 8.

2. Physical Activity

Move your body daily—walk, stretch, dance, or exercise. Physical movement reduces stress hormones and boosts mood.

3. Sleep and Nutrition

Prioritize rest and eat nourishing foods. Fatigue and poor diet make stress harder to manage.

4. Social Support

Connect with friends, family, or colleagues. Sharing your experiences can lighten your emotional load.

Energy Management: The Key to Sustainable Productivity

Managing your energy—not just your time—helps you do your best work and avoid burnout.

Align Tasks with Your Natural Rhythms
- Identify your peak energy times (morning, afternoon, evening).
- Schedule your most important or demanding tasks during those times.
- Save low-energy tasks (email, admin) for your natural dips.

Example: James is a morning person, so he schedules creative work before noon and reserves meetings for the afternoon.

The Importance of Rest and Recovery
- Build short breaks into your day to recharge.
- Take a walk, listen to music, or simply step away from your desk.
- Plan regular days off and longer breaks to recover fully.

The Myth of "Always On" and the Power of Focused Sprints
- Productivity doesn't mean working nonstop.
- Use focused sprints (e.g., 90 minutes of deep work, then a break) for your most important projects.

Chapter Summary
- Stress and energy management are essential for sustainable productivity and well-being.
- Chronic stress and poor energy habits undermine even the best time management systems.
- Use awareness, prioritization, and simple strategies (mindfulness, movement, rest, social support) to reduce stress and boost energy.
- Align your most important work with your natural rhythms and protect your recovery time.
- Sustainable productivity means doing what matters most, without burning out.

Reflection Questions

Question 1: What are your top sources of stress right now?

Former Student Responses:
- "I'm constantly worried about meeting deadlines at work and feel like I'm always behind."
- "My family responsibilities are overwhelming - kids' activities, household tasks, and caring for aging parents."
- "I have no work-life balance - I check emails at night and work weekends."
- "Financial pressure is keeping me up at night - bills, debt, and no emergency savings."
- "I feel guilty about not spending enough time with my family because of work demands."
- "I'm burned out from saying yes to everything and having no time for myself."
- "The constant notifications and interruptions make me feel scattered and anxious."

Possible Solutions:
- **Work Deadlines**: Use time-blocking to schedule focused work periods; break large projects into smaller tasks; communicate realistic timelines with supervisors
- **Family Overwhelm**: Delegate age-appropriate tasks to children; create shared family calendars; ask for help from extended family or hire services when possible
- **Work-Life Boundaries**: Set specific work hours and stick to them; turn off work notifications after hours; create physical separation between work and personal spaces
- **Financial Stress**: Create a simple budget; automate savings, even if small amounts; seek financial counseling or education resources
- **Family Guilt**: Schedule dedicated family time and protect it; focus on quality over quantity; communicate your work demands to family members
- **Overcommitment**: Practice saying no to new requests; review current commitments and eliminate non-essential ones; schedule buffer time between activities
- **Digital Overwhelm**: Turn off non-essential notifications; batch check emails at set times; create phone-free zones and times

Question 2: When during the day do you have the most energy? The least?

Former Student Responses:
- "I'm definitely a morning person - I feel sharp and focused until about 2 PM, then I crash."
- "I'm a night owl - I don't really wake up until 10 AM, but I'm productive until midnight"
- "My energy is highest mid-morning around 10 AM, and I hit a wall after lunch."
- "I have bursts of energy throughout the day but struggle with consistency."
- "I feel drained all the time - I can't identify when I have peak energy."
- "My energy depends entirely on how much sleep I got and what I ate."
- "I have good energy in the morning, but afternoon meetings drain me completely."

Possible Solutions:
- **Morning People**: Schedule most important tasks before 2 PM; use afternoons for routine tasks like email and admin work; plan demanding meetings for morning hours
- **Night Owls**: Protect late evening hours for important work; use mornings for lighter tasks; negotiate flexible work schedules when possible
- **Mid-Morning Peak**: Block 10 AM-12 PM for your most challenging work; avoid scheduling meetings during this time; use early morning for planning and preparation
- **Inconsistent Energy**: Track energy patterns for two weeks to identify trends; ensure consistent sleep and meal times; identify what activities energize vs. drain you
- **Chronic Fatigue**: Evaluate sleep quality and quantity; assess nutrition and hydration; consider medical evaluation; start with a gentle exercise routine
- **Sleep/Food Dependent**: Prioritize consistent sleep schedule; eat regular, balanced meals; avoid energy crashes from caffeine and sugar
- **Meeting Drain**: Limit back-to-back meetings; schedule breaks between meetings; suggest shorter meeting durations; prepare thoroughly to reduce mental load

Question 3: Which stress-reduction strategy will you try this week?

Former Student Responses:
- "I want to try meditation, but I don't think I have time for long sessions."
- "I'd like to exercise more, but I'm too tired after work."
- "I should probably limit my news and social media consumption."
- "I need to get better sleep, but my mind races when I try to go to bed."

- "I want to spend more time in nature, but I live in the city."
- "I should talk to someone about my stress, but I don't want to burden others."
- "I need to learn to say no, but I feel guilty disappointing people."

Possible Solutions:
- **Meditation Interest**: Start with just 5 minutes daily; use guided meditation apps; try mindful breathing during commute or breaks
- **Exercise Barriers**: Start with 10-minute walks; try morning workouts when energy is higher; find activities you enjoy rather than forcing gym workouts
- **Media Overwhelm**: Set specific times for news/social media; use app timers to limit usage; choose one trusted news source instead of multiple feeds
- **Sleep Issues**: Create a bedtime routine; write down worries before bed; avoid screens 1 hour before sleep; try progressive muscle relaxation
- **Nature Access**: Visit local parks; bring plants into your living space; take lunch breaks outside; plan weekend nature trips
- **Social Support**: Start with one trusted friend or family member; consider professional counseling; join support groups; remember that sharing helps others, too
- **Boundary Setting**: Practice saying "Let me check my calendar and get back to you"; start with small, low-stakes situations; remember that boundaries protect your ability to help others

Question 4: How can you better align your tasks with your natural energy rhythms?

Former Student Responses:
- "I do my hardest work when I'm tired and save easy tasks for when I'm energized."
- "I schedule meetings randomly throughout the day without considering my energy."
- "I don't really know what my natural rhythms are - every day feels the same."
- "I try to power through low-energy times instead of working with them."
- "My schedule is controlled by others, so I don't think I can change much."
- "I waste my high-energy time on email and administrative tasks."
- "I fight my natural rhythms because I think I should be productive all day."

Possible Solutions:
- **Backwards Scheduling**: Flip your current schedule - do creative/challenging work during high energy, routine tasks during low energy.

- **Random Meeting Scheduling**: Block your peak energy hours for focused work; suggest meeting times during your moderate energy periods; batch similar meetings together
- **Unclear Rhythms**: Track energy levels hourly for two weeks; note patterns related to meals, sleep, and activities; identify your personal prime time
- **Fighting Low Energy**: Plan easier tasks for low-energy periods; use these times for planning, organizing, or learning; take breaks instead of forcing productivity.
- **External Control**: Negotiate where possible; protect at least one hour daily during peak energy; communicate your needs to supervisors or family
- **Energy Waste**: Batch administrative tasks during lower energy times; check email only during designated periods; protect your prime time fiercely
- **All-Day Productivity Myth**: Accept that energy naturally fluctuates; plan recovery time; focus on working smarter during peak hours rather than longer overall

Question 5: What's one boundary you can set to protect your rest and recovery?

Former Student Responses:
- "I need to stop checking work emails after 8 PM, but I worry about missing something urgent."
- "I should take actual lunch breaks instead of eating at my desk while working."
- "I need to say no to weekend social events sometimes so I can recharge."
- "I should stop letting family members interrupt my personal time constantly."
- "I need to protect my morning routine from being hijacked by urgent requests."
- "I should stop feeling guilty about taking breaks during the workday."
- "I need to create a boundary around my sleep time, no more late-night scrolling."

Possible Solutions:
- **Evening Email**: Set an auto-response explaining your hours; turn off work notifications after 8 PM; designate one person for true emergencies only
- **Lunch Break Protection**: Block lunch time in your calendar, leave your workspace, turn off notifications, and communicate that you're unavailable during this time.
- **Social Event Balance**: Give yourself permission to decline; suggest alternative ways to connect; explain that you need downtime to be your best self
- **Family Interruptions**: Communicate your need for uninterrupted time; create visual signals when you're not available; schedule specific times for family interaction

- **Morning Routine**: Wake up earlier to create buffer time; communicate your morning needs to household members; prepare everything the night before
- **Break Guilt**: Remember that breaks improve productivity; schedule breaks like appointments; start with short 5-10 minute breaks to build the habit
- **Sleep Boundaries**: Charge phone outside bedroom; set a digital curfew 1 hour before bed; create a relaxing bedtime routine; use blue light filters

Universal Solutions Across All Chapter 8 Questions:

Conduct a Stress Audit: Identify your specific stress triggers, energy patterns, and current coping mechanisms to create targeted solutions.

Start Small with Stress Management: Choose one simple stress-reduction technique and practice it consistently before adding others.

Honor Your Natural Rhythms: Work with your energy patterns rather than against them to maximize both productivity and well-being.

Create Non-Negotiable Boundaries: Protect your rest and recovery time as fiercely as you would protect important work commitments.

Build Support Systems: Share your stress management goals with others who can provide accountability and encouragement.

Practice Self-Compassion: Treat stress management as self-care, not selfishness, and be patient with yourself as you build new habits.

Regular Review and Adjustment: Schedule weekly check-ins to assess what's working and adjust your stress management strategies as needed.

Focus on Sustainable Practices: Choose stress management techniques you can maintain long-term rather than quick fixes that aren't sustainable.

Take Action

- Identify your peak energy window and schedule a priority task during that time tomorrow.
- Choose one stress management technique and use it daily for a week.
- Block out time for a real break this week—even 15 minutes counts.
- Share your energy and stress insights with a friend or accountability partner.

"Almost everything will work again if you unplug it for a few minutes… including you." –
Anne Lamott

Looking Ahead: Next, you'll discover the best tools and technology for modern time management, so you can put all your new habits and strategies into practice with confidence.

Chapter 9 – Tools and Technology

Time management isn't just about discipline or willpower—it's about setting up systems that make the right actions easy and the wrong ones hard. In today's digital world, the right tools and technology can help you organize, automate, and streamline your routines, freeing up your energy for what matters most.

Choosing the Right Tools for You

There's no one-size-fits-all solution. The best tools are the ones you'll actually use, that fit your personality and lifestyle, and that support your unique goals. This chapter will introduce a range of options—from simple paper planners to powerful digital apps—so you can build your own productivity "stack."

Digital Tools for Time Management

1. Calendars

- **Google Calendar / Outlook / Apple Calendar:** Schedule appointments, block time for deep work, set recurring reminders, and share calendars with family or team members.
- Best for: People who want everything in one place and accessible from any device.

Example: Sarah uses Google Calendar to block out "focus time" for her top priorities every morning and color-codes her events for work, family, and personal projects.

2. Task Managers

- **Todoist / Microsoft To Do / Things / TickTick:** Create and organize tasks by project, set deadlines, and use recurring reminders.
- Best for: Anyone who juggles multiple projects or wants to break big goals into small, actionable steps.

Example: James uses Todoist to track daily, weekly, and monthly tasks. He uses labels like "@work," "@home," and "@errands" to stay organized.

3. Project Boards

- **Trello / Asana / Notion:** Visualize projects with boards, lists, and cards. Move tasks from "To Do" to "Doing" to "Done."
- Best for: Visual thinkers, teams, or anyone managing complex projects.

Example: Maria uses Trello to manage her freelance design projects, with boards for each client and cards for each stage of the design process.

4. Time Tracking & Focus Apps

- **RescueTime / Clockify / Toggl:** Track how you spend your time on your computer and mobile devices. Get reports on your habits and set focus goals.
- **Forest / Focusmate / Freedom:** Block distracting websites, gamify focus sessions, or work alongside a virtual accountability partner.

Example: Alex uses RescueTime to discover he spends too much time on email. He sets a goal to limit email to two 30-minute blocks per day and uses Freedom to block social media during deep work.

5. **Note-Taking and Knowledge Management**
   - **Evernote / OneNote / Notion / Google Keep:**
     Capture ideas, meeting notes, and reference material in one searchable place.
   - Best for: Anyone who wants to keep information organized and accessible.

6. **Hybrid Systems: Paper + Digital**

Many people find that a combination of digital and paper tools works best. For example:

- Use a digital calendar for scheduling and reminders.
- Use a paper planner or bullet journal for daily priorities, habit tracking, and reflection.

Example: Lisa schedules appointments in Google Calendar but uses a paper planner each morning to set her top three priorities and reflect on her progress.

Setting Up Your Personal Productivity Stack

Step 1: Identify Your Needs
- Do you need help remembering appointments? (Calendar)
- Do you want to organize projects and tasks? (Task manager or project board)
- Do you need to limit distractions? (Focus apps)
- Do you want to track habits or time spent? (Habit tracker or time tracker)

Step 2: Start Simple

Pick one tool for each need. Don't try to implement everything at once.

Step 3: Customize and Iterate

Experiment with features, integrations, and workflows. Adjust as your needs change.

Tool Comparison Chart:

Tool	Best For	Example Use Case
Google Calendar	Scheduling & reminders	Block focus time
Todoist	Task management	Daily/weekly tasks
Trello	Visual project planning	Freelance/client work
RescueTime	Time tracking	Limit email/social media
Forest	Focus & distraction block	Gamify focus sessions
Paper Planner	Reflection & priorities	Morning routine/daily plan

Reflection Questions

Question 1: Which tool(s) have you tried before, and what worked or didn't?

Former Student Responses:
- "I've tried multiple task management apps but always abandon them after a few weeks."
- "I used Google Calendar for appointments, but never blocked time for important projects."
- "I tried habit tracking apps but found them too complicated and overwhelming."
- "I've used paper planners, but they get messy and I lose track of them."
- "I downloaded productivity apps but never took time to set them up properly."
- "I tried time tracking software, but it felt like micromanaging myself."
- "I used to-do list apps, but they just became endless lists that stressed me out."

Possible Solutions:
- **App Abandonment**: Start with the simplest possible tool; focus on one feature at a time; choose tools with minimal setup required
- **Calendar Underuse**: Begin blocking just one hour daily for your most important task; gradually expand time-blocking as the habit develops
- **Habit Tracking Overwhelm**: Track only one habit initially; use simple checkmark systems; focus on consistency over perfection.
- **Paper Planner Issues**: Designate a specific home for your planner; use simple formats; consider hybrid digital-paper approaches
- **Setup Procrastination**: Schedule dedicated time for tool setup; start with basic features only; watch tutorial videos for guidance
- **Time Tracking Resistance**: Use automatic tracking tools; focus on patterns rather than minute-by-minute details; set specific tracking periods
- **To-Do List Stress**: Limit daily lists to 3-5 items; use time-blocking instead of endless lists; regularly review and purge old tasks

Question 2: What's your biggest challenge—remembering appointments, staying focused, tracking habits, or organizing projects?

Former Student Responses:
- **Remembering Appointments**: "I constantly double-book myself or forget important meetings."
- **Staying Focused**: "I get distracted by notifications and lose hours to social media."

- **Tracking Habits**: "I start tracking new habits, but forget to maintain the system."
- **Organizing Projects**: "I have multiple projects but no clear system to manage them all."
- **All of the Above**: "I struggle with everything and don't know where to start."

Possible Solutions:
- **Appointment Management**: Use one primary calendar with notifications; set up recurring reminders; sync across all devices; add buffer time between meetings
- **Focus Issues**: Turn off non-essential notifications; use website blockers during work time; try the Pomodoro Technique; create distraction-free workspaces
- **Habit Tracking**: Start with one simple habit; use visual cues and reminders; link new habits to existing routines; celebrate small wins
- **Project Organization**: Choose one project management tool; break projects into small tasks; use simple folder structures; schedule regular project reviews
- **Multiple Challenges**: Focus on one area for 30 days; choose the challenge that would have the biggest impact if solved; start with the simplest solution

Question 3: Do you prefer digital, paper, or a hybrid system?

Former Student Responses:
- "I love the feel of writing on paper, but worry about losing information."
- "Digital tools are convenient, but I find them distracting."
- "I want to use both, but struggle to keep them synchronized."
- "I'm not sure what would work best for my lifestyle."
- "I prefer paper for planning, but need digital for reminders."
- "Digital tools have too many features that overwhelm me."
- "I like paper for creativity, but digital for organization."

Possible Solutions:
- **Paper Preference with Loss Concerns**: Take photos of important pages; use bound notebooks instead of loose sheets; create simple backup systems
- **Digital Distraction**: Use focus modes; choose simple apps with minimal features; set specific times for checking digital tools
- **Hybrid Synchronization**: Use digital calendar for appointments, paper for daily planning; take photos of paper notes to store digitally; keep systems simple
- **Uncertainty**: Experiment with each approach for one week; consider your lifestyle (travel, work environment, tech comfort); start with what feels most natural

- **Mixed Needs**: Use paper for morning planning, digital for reminders and scheduling; leverage the strengths of each system
- **Digital Overwhelm**: Start with basic features only; choose tools with clean, simple interfaces; ignore advanced features until basics are mastered
- **Different Purposes**: Use paper for brainstorming and reflection, digital for scheduling and task management; play to each medium's strengths

Question 4: What's one tool you'll experiment with this week?

Former Student Responses:
- "I want to try time-blocking in Google Calendar for my most important tasks."
- "I'm going to experiment with the Forest app to reduce phone distractions."
- "I'll try using a simple paper planner for daily priority setting."
- "I want to test Todoist for organizing my work projects."
- "I'm interested in trying RescueTime to see where my time actually goes."
- "I'll experiment with the Pomodoro Technique using a basic timer."
- "I want to try a hybrid approach with digital calendar and paper notes."

Possible Solutions:
- **Time-Blocking Experiment**: Start with blocking just one hour daily; choose your peak energy time; protect this time from interruptions; track how it affects your productivity
- **Focus App Trial**: Install Forest and use it for one focused work session daily; start with 25-minute sessions; track your distraction patterns
- **Paper Planner Test**: Choose a simple format; use it for morning priority setting only; keep it visible on your desk; review effectiveness after one week
- **Task Management Trial**: Set up Todoist with just one project; add only this week's tasks; focus on the basic features; evaluate ease of use
- **Time Tracking Experiment**: Install RescueTime and let it run passively; review the weekly report; identify your biggest time-wasters
- **Pomodoro Trial**: Use a simple timer for 25-minute work blocks; take 5-minute breaks; try it for one important task daily
- **Hybrid System Test**: Use digital calendar for appointments, paper for daily planning; sync them each morning; assess which works better for different needs

Question 5: How will you measure success with your chosen tool?

Former Student Responses:
- "I'm not sure how to know if a tool is actually helping me."

- "I want to feel less stressed and more organized."
- "I hope to waste less time on distractions."
- "I want to complete my important tasks more consistently."
- "I'd like to feel more in control of my schedule."
- "I want to stop forgetting important things."
- "I hope to have a better work-life balance."

Possible Solutions:

- **Unclear Success Metrics**: Define specific, measurable outcomes like "complete 3 priority tasks daily" or "reduce social media time by 50%"
- **Stress and Organization**: Rate your stress level 1-10 daily; track how often you feel "in control" of your day; measure time spent looking for things
- **Distraction Reduction**: Use time tracking to measure actual distraction time; count how often you check your phone; track focus session completion
- **Task Completion**: Track percentage of priority tasks completed; measure how often you finish what you planned; note quality of work produced
- **Schedule Control**: Measure how often your day goes according to plan; track buffer time usage; assess meeting and deadline management
- **Memory and Organization**: Count missed appointments or forgotten tasks; track how often you have to search for information; measure preparation time for meetings
- **Work-Life Balance**: Track hours worked vs. personal time; measure family/personal activity completion; assess evening and weekend work frequency

Universal Solutions Across All Chapter 9 Questions:

Start Simple: Choose tools with minimal features and setup requirements rather than complex systems that might overwhelm you.

Focus on One Tool at a Time: Don't try to implement multiple new tools simultaneously; master one before adding another.

Match Tools to Your Lifestyle: Consider your work environment, travel needs, tech comfort level, and personal preferences when selecting tools.

Measure and Adjust: Track specific metrics to determine if tools are actually helping you achieve your goals.

Build Habits Around Tools: The best tool is useless without consistent usage habits; focus on building routines that incorporate your chosen tools.

Keep Backups Simple: Whether digital or paper, have basic backup systems to prevent loss of important information.

Regular Review and Cleanup: Schedule time to review, organize, and optimize your tool usage to prevent digital or physical clutter.

Don't Over-Engineer: Resist the temptation to create overly complex systems; the best productivity system is the one you'll actually use consistently.

Take Action

- Choose one new tool or template and use it for a week.
- Block time on your calendar to set up your system.
- Review your results and tweak your setup as needed.
- Share your favorite tool or tip with a friend or colleague.

"The best tool is the one you'll actually use. Start simple, build habits, and let your system evolve as you do."

Looking Ahead: In the next chapter, you'll see how real people put these strategies into practice through case studies, before-and-after stories, and lessons learned from a variety of life situations.

Chapter 10 – Real-World Case Studies

You've learned the principles, tools, and strategies of effective time management. But how do these ideas play out in real life? In this chapter, you'll see how people from different walks of life—students, parents, freelancers, retirees, and managers—apply these concepts to overcome their unique challenges. Through their stories, you'll discover practical ways to adapt time management to your own circumstances and see that there's no single "right" way—only what works for you.

Mini-Profiles: Time Management in Action

1. Sarah, the Busy Parent

Challenges: Balancing work, family, and personal time; constant interruptions; guilt about not doing enough for her kids.

What Worked:

- Uses Google Calendar to block out "family time" and "focus time."
- Implements the 2-Minute Rule for quick household tasks.
- Says "no" to extra commitments that don't align with her top priorities.
- Schedules a weekly planning session every Sunday night.

Result: Sarah feels less overwhelmed, is more present with her children, and gets more done at work, without sacrificing her sanity.

2. James, the Freelancer

Challenges: Juggling multiple clients, inconsistent workload, and frequent procrastination.

What Worked:

- Uses Trello boards to visualize projects and deadlines.
- Applies the Pomodoro Technique for deep work sessions.
- Timebox administrative tasks to avoid perfectionism.
- Sets boundaries with clients about response times.

Result: James delivers projects on time, feels more in control, and has more free time for creative pursuits.

3. Maria, the University Student

Challenges: Balancing classes, part-time work, and social life; distracted by social media.

What Worked:

- Uses a paper planner for daily priorities and a digital calendar for class schedules.
- Installs Freedom app to block social media during study sessions.
- Breaks big assignments into small steps and schedules them over several days.

- Joins a study group for accountability.

Result: Maria's grades improve, she feels less stressed, and she still has time for friends.

4. Lisa, the Retiree

Challenges: Transitioning from a structured work life to an unstructured retirement; wants to stay active and engaged.

What Worked:

- Creates a weekly routine with time for volunteering, hobbies, and exercise.
- Uses a habit tracker to build new routines.
- Schedules regular social activities and learning opportunities.
- Limit TV and "mindless" time by planning meaningful activities.

Result: Lisa feels fulfilled, maintains her health, and enjoys a vibrant social life.

5. David, the Team Manager

Challenges: Managing meetings, delegating tasks, and avoiding burnout.

What Worked:

- Schedules "no meeting" blocks for deep work.
- Delegates tasks using Asana and sets clear expectations.
- Uses the Covey Matrix to prioritize urgent vs. important work.
- Block time for lunch and short walks to recharge.

Result: David's team is more productive, meetings are shorter, and he models healthy boundaries for his staff.

Before and After

Before Time Management:

- Constantly putting out fires
- Missing deadlines and appointments
- Feeling guilty about neglected priorities
- No time for self-care or reflection

After Applying Principles:

- Starts each day with a clear plan
- Handles urgent issues without neglecting important goals
- Schedules breaks and personal time
- Ends each week with a sense of accomplishment

Lessons Learned and Pitfalls to Avoid

- **Start small:** Don't try to overhaul your life overnight. Begin with one or two changes.
- **Adjust as you go:** Your system should evolve with your needs and circumstances.

- **Beware of perfectionism:** Progress beats perfection. Celebrate small wins.
- **Don't go it alone:** Accountability—whether through a friend, group, or app—makes a big difference.
- **Review regularly:** Weekly reviews help you spot what's working and what needs to change.

"What I Wish I'd Known Sooner"

- "Blocking time for myself isn't selfish—it's necessary."
- "The right tool is the one I'll actually use, not the fanciest app."
- "It's okay to say no, even to good things, if they don't fit my priorities."
- "Tracking my time for a week was eye-opening—I found hours I didn't know I had."
- "Habits take time to build, but once they're in place, everything gets easier."

Reflection Questions

Question 1: Which profile do you relate to most? Why?
Former Student Responses:

- "I relate most to Sarah, the busy parent - I'm constantly juggling work and family responsibilities and feel guilty about not being present enough."
- "James the freelancer resonates with me because I struggle with multiple projects and procrastination when working from home."
- "I see myself in Maria, the student - social media is my biggest distraction, and I leave assignments until the last minute."
- "David, the manager speaks to me - I'm in back-to-back meetings all day and never have time for strategic thinking."
- "I'm like Lisa the retiree - I have all this free time but feel unproductive and lack structure in my days."
- "I relate to multiple profiles - I feel like I have elements of the overwhelmed parent and the distracted student."

Possible Solutions:

- **Busy Parent Identification:** Implement Sarah's strategies - use calendar blocking for family time, apply the 2-minute rule for household tasks, practice saying no to non-essential commitments
- **Freelancer Connection:** Adopt James's approach - use project management tools like Trello, implement the Pomodoro Technique, set clear boundaries with clients about response times
- **Student Struggles:** Follow Maria's example - use digital blockers during study time, break large assignments into smaller tasks, and join study groups for accountability

- **Manager Overwhelm**: Apply David's methods - schedule "no meeting" blocks, delegate using project management tools, use the Covey Matrix for prioritization.
- **Retiree Structure**: Use Lisa's strategies - create weekly routines, use habit trackers, schedule meaningful activities, and social connections
- **Multiple Profile Recognition**: Choose one profile's strategies to focus on for 30 days, then gradually incorporate elements from others

Question 2: What's one idea or tool from these stories that you could try in your own life?

Former Student Responses:
- "I want to try time-blocking like Sarah does - scheduling family time and focus time in my calendar."
- "James's use of the Pomodoro Technique for deep work sounds like it could help my concentration issues."
- "I'm interested in Maria's approach of using both digital and paper tools - digital calendar with paper daily planning."
- "David's 'no meeting' blocks appeal to me - I need protected time for important work."
- "I like Lisa's idea of using a habit tracker to build new routines."
- "The idea of color-coding my calendar like Sarah does could help me see where my time really goes."
- "Setting boundaries with response times like James does could reduce my stress about always being available."

Possible Solutions:
- **Time-Blocking Interest**: Start with blocking just one hour daily for your most important task; gradually expand as the habit develops; protect this time from interruptions
- **Pomodoro Technique Trial**: Download a timer app, start with 25-minute focused sessions, take real 5-minute breaks, track how many sessions you complete daily
- **Hybrid System Experiment**: Use digital calendar for appointments and reminders, paper planner for daily priorities and reflection; sync them each morning
- **No-Meeting Blocks**: Schedule 2-3 hour blocks weekly for deep work; communicate these boundaries to colleagues; use this time for your most important projects
- **Habit Tracking**: Choose one simple habit to track (like daily planning or exercise); use a basic calendar or app; celebrate consistency streaks

- **Calendar Color-Coding**: Assign colors to different life areas (work, family, personal); review weekly to see if time allocation matches your priorities
- **Response Time Boundaries**: Set specific times for checking email and messages; communicate your availability to others; use auto-responses to set expectations

Question 3: What's your biggest time management challenge right now, and what's one small step you could take this week to address it?

Former Student Responses:
- "I'm constantly distracted by notifications and social media - I could try turning off non-essential notifications for one week."
- "I procrastinate on important tasks - I could use the 2-minute rule to start one dreaded task each day."
- "I say yes to everything and feel overwhelmed - I could practice saying 'let me check my calendar and get back to you' before committing to anything new."
- "I don't have a consistent routine - I could establish one simple morning routine and stick to it for a week."
- "I waste time looking for things because I'm disorganized - I could spend 10 minutes each evening organizing my workspace."
- "I don't prioritize effectively - I could start each day by identifying my top 3 priorities before checking email."
- "I work too many hours and have no work-life balance - I could set a firm stop time for work and stick to it for one week."

Possible Solutions:
- **Notification Distraction**: Turn off all non-essential app notifications; check messages only at scheduled times (9 AM, 1 PM, 5 PM); use "Do Not Disturb" modes during focused work
- **Procrastination Issues**: Apply the 2-minute rule - if something takes less than 2 minutes, do it immediately; for larger tasks, commit to just 2 minutes to get started
- **Over-Commitment**: Practice the pause - never say yes immediately; use phrases like "Let me check my priorities and get back to you"; create criteria for what deserves your time
- **Routine Absence**: Start with one simple 15-minute morning routine (coffee + priority review); do it at the same time daily; gradually expand as it becomes automatic

- **Disorganization**: Implement the "everything has a home" principle; spend 10 minutes each evening preparing for tomorrow; clear your workspace before leaving
- **Poor Prioritization**: Use the "Rule of 3" - identify your top 3 priorities each morning before opening email; focus on these before anything else
- **Work-Life Imbalance**: Set a specific work end time and stick to it; create a transition ritual between work and personal time; communicate boundaries to colleagues

Question 4: With whom can you share your goals or progress for accountability?

Former Student Responses:
- "I have a close friend who's also trying to improve her time management - we could check in weekly."
- "My spouse is supportive but doesn't really understand my work challenges - I might need to find a professional accountability partner."
- "I'm part of an online community for freelancers - I could share my goals there."
- "I don't really have anyone in my life who would understand these goals - I feel like I need to find new connections."
- "My team at work might be interested in improving productivity together."
- "I have a mentor who's great at time management - I could ask for their guidance."
- "I'm hesitant to share goals because I've failed before and felt embarrassed."

Possible Solutions:
- **Friend Partnership**: Schedule weekly 15-minute check-ins; share specific goals and progress; celebrate each other's wins; be honest about setbacks
- **Spouse Communication**: Explain your time management goals and how they benefit the family; ask for support during your focused work times; share your wins and challenges
- **Online Community**: Join groups on platforms like Reddit, Facebook, or Discord focused on productivity; share weekly progress updates; offer support to others
- **New Connections**: Join local meetups, professional associations, or online mastermind groups; attend productivity workshops or seminars; consider hiring a coach
- **Workplace Collaboration**: Suggest team productivity challenges; share time management tips during meetings; create accountability partnerships with colleagues

- **Mentor Relationship**: Schedule monthly check-ins; ask for specific advice on time management challenges; share your progress and ask for feedback
- **Fear of Failure**: Start with one trusted person; focus on sharing effort rather than just outcomes; remember that accountability increases success rates dramatically

Question 5: How will you celebrate your next small win?

Former Student Responses:
- "I never really celebrate small wins - I just move on to the next thing on my list."
- "I don't know what would feel like a meaningful celebration for time management progress."
- "I tend to reward myself with things that contradict my goals, like binge-watching TV when I should be productive."
- "I feel guilty celebrating when there's still so much left to do."
- "I prefer experiences over material rewards, but I'm not sure what would work for time management."
- "I'd like to celebrate with others, but I'm embarrassed about my goals."
- "I'm on a tight budget, so I can't afford expensive rewards."

Possible Solutions:
- **No Celebration Habit**: Schedule celebration time like any other appointment; set reminders to acknowledge progress; create a "wins journal" to review regularly
- **Celebration Uncertainty**: Experiment with different types of rewards - extra sleep, favorite coffee, nature walk, or hobby time; ask friends what motivates them
- **Contradictory Rewards**: Choose celebrations that support your goals - reward productivity with a new planner or app; celebrate focus time with a relaxing activity
- **Guilt About Celebrating**: Reframe celebration as fuel for continued progress; remember that acknowledging wins increases motivation; celebrate effort, not just outcomes
- **Experience Preferences**: Plan special outings like visiting a museum, trying a new restaurant, or taking a scenic drive; attend events related to your interests
- **Social Celebration Needs**: Share wins with supportive friends and family; join communities where you can celebrate others' successes too; start small with one trusted person
- **Budget Constraints**: Use free activities like library visits, park walks, or home spa time; celebrate with time-based rewards like sleeping in or pursuing a hobby

Universal Solutions Across All Chapter 10 Questions:

Learn from Others: Study the strategies that work for people in similar situations and adapt them to your unique circumstances.

Start Small and Experiment: Choose one new strategy or tool to try for a week rather than attempting to implement everything at once.

Build Support Systems: Actively seek out people who can provide accountability, encouragement, and shared learning experiences.

Celebrate Progress: Acknowledge and reward effort and improvement, not just perfect execution or final achievements.

Stay Flexible: Be willing to adjust your approach based on what you learn about yourself and what works best for your situation.

Focus on Systems: Build processes and habits that make good time management automatic, rather than relying on willpower alone.

Practice Self-Compassion: Treat setbacks as learning opportunities rather than evidence of personal failure.

Regular Review: Schedule time to assess what's working and what needs adjustment in your time management approach.

Take Action

- Choose one strategy or tool from this chapter and apply it for a week.
- Track your results and reflect on what changes.
- Share your experience with someone who can support or encourage you.

"Don't compare your behind-the-scenes to someone else's highlight reel. Build a system that works for you, and let your progress be your guide."

Looking Ahead: In the next chapter, you'll learn how to put all these elements together into your own Personal Time Mastery Plan—so you can keep growing, adapting, and thriving long after you finish this book.

Chapter 11 – Putting It All Together

You've explored the principles, tools, and real-world stories that make time management possible and meaningful. Now it's time to bring everything together into a practical, personal plan—a roadmap you can use to keep growing, adapting, and thriving long after you finish this book.

Step 1: Self-Audit – Where Are You Now?

Start with honest reflection. Review your time audit (from earlier chapters) and ask:

- Where is my time really going?
- What are my biggest time robbers and distractions?
- Which habits or routines support my goals, and which undermine them?
- How am I managing stress, energy, and overwhelm?

Action: Complete a one-week time audit if you haven't already. Use a printable or digital template to record your activities and feelings throughout the week.

Step 2: Clarify Your Vision and Goals – Where Do You Want to Be?

Revisit your vision for a life that matters (see *Goals That Matter* for a deep dive).

- What does your ideal day or week look like?
- What are your top 3–5 goals for the next 3–12 months?
- How do these goals align with your values and priorities?

Action: Write down your vision and goals. Make them visible—on your wall, in your planner, or as a digital wallpaper.

Step 3: Analyze Your Time – What Needs to Change?

Compare your current time use to your vision and goals.

- What's missing? (e.g., no time for exercise, family, or creative work)
- What's crowding out what matters? (e.g., too many meetings, social media, or low-value tasks)

Action: Circle or highlight activities in your time audit that don't align with your priorities. Decide which to reduce, delegate, or eliminate.

Step 4: Build Your Habit Plan – What Needs to Start (or Stop)?

Identify 1–3 keystone habits that will have the biggest impact on your time and goals.

- What new routines will support your vision?
- Which old habits need to be replaced or reworked?

Action: Use habit stacking and tracking tools (see Chapter 5) to build your new routines. Start small and celebrate consistency.

Step 5: Select Your Tools and Systems – What Will Help You Most?

Choose the digital and/or paper tools that fit your style (see Chapter 8).

- Calendar for appointments and time blocking
- Task manager for projects and daily priorities
- Habit tracker for consistency
- Focus apps for distraction-free work

Action: Set up your productivity "stack." Block time for weekly reviews and system tweaks.

Step 6: Create Your First 7-Day Experiment

Don't try to overhaul everything at once. Instead, design a one-week experiment:

- Pick one new habit or routine to try.
- Block time for your top priority each day.
- Use your chosen tools to track progress.

Action: At the end of the week, review what worked, what didn't, and what you'll adjust.

Step 7: Review, Adjust, and Celebrate

Time mastery is a process of continuous improvement.

- Schedule weekly and monthly reviews.
- Adjust your routines, tools, and priorities as needed.
- Celebrate progress—no matter how small.

Action: Share your wins with an accountability partner or group. Reflect on your growth and set your next experiment.

The 10 Bold Guarantees Revisited

If you consistently apply what you've learned in this book, you can expect:

1. More time for what matters most
2. Greater clarity about your priorities
3. Less stress and overwhelm
4. More consistent progress toward your goals
5. Stronger relationships
6. Improved health and well-being
7. Increased productivity and satisfaction
8. Better work-life balance
9. Greater confidence and self-esteem
10. A sense of fulfillment and purpose in your daily life

Reflection Questions

Question 1: What's the biggest insight you've gained about your time and priorities?

Former Student Responses:
- "I realized I spend way more time on urgent but unimportant tasks than on my actual goals."
- "I discovered that I have more time than I thought - I was just wasting it on distractions."
- "I learned that my priorities weren't actually reflected in how I spend my time."
- "I found out that I'm constantly in crisis mode because I don't plan ahead."
- "I realized that saying yes to everything means saying no to what matters most."
- "I discovered that my energy levels affect my productivity more than the amount of time I have."
- "I learned that without a clear vision, I'm just busy but not productive."

Possible Solutions:
- **Urgent vs. Important Confusion**: Use the Covey Matrix daily to categorize tasks; schedule Quadrant II activities first; learn to distinguish between what feels urgent and what's actually important
- **Hidden Time Discovery**: Continue tracking time weekly to maintain awareness; use reclaimed time for Quadrant II activities; eliminate or batch low-value tasks
- **Priority-Action Misalignment**: Schedule your top priorities first in your calendar; review weekly whether your time allocation matches your stated values
- **Crisis Mode Living**: Implement weekly planning sessions; build buffer time into schedules; focus on prevention through Quadrant II activities
- **Over-Commitment**: Create criteria for saying yes; practice the pause before committing; remember that boundaries protect your ability to serve your priorities
- **Energy Awareness**: Track energy patterns and align important tasks with peak energy times; protect rest and recovery time; use low-energy periods for routine tasks
- **Vision Clarity**: Revisit your vision regularly; connect daily tasks to larger goals; use visualization to maintain motivation and direction

Question 2: Which habit, tool, or strategy are you most excited to implement?

Former Student Responses:
- "I want to try time-blocking my calendar to protect time for my most important goals."
- "I'm excited about implementing a weekly review habit to stay on track."
- "I want to start using the Pomodoro Technique to improve my focus."
- "I'm going to try the 2-minute rule to stop small tasks from piling up."
- "I want to establish morning and evening routines to bookend my days."
- "I'm excited to use the 80/20 rule to identify my highest-impact activities."
- "I want to implement digital boundaries to reduce distractions."

Possible Solutions:
- **Time-Blocking**: Start with blocking just one hour daily for your top priority; gradually expand as the habit develops; protect this time from interruptions and treat it like an important meeting
- **Weekly Reviews**: Schedule 30 minutes every Sunday evening; create a simple template covering what worked, what didn't, and priorities for the coming week
- **Pomodoro Technique**: Download a timer app; start with 25-minute focused sessions; take real breaks; track how many Pomodoros you complete daily
- **2-Minute Rule**: Apply immediately when reviewing tasks; if something takes less than 2 minutes, do it now; for larger tasks, commit to just 2 minutes to get started
- **Daily Routines**: Start with a simple 15-minute morning routine; stack new habits onto existing ones; gradually expand as routines become automatic
- **80/20 Analysis**: Review your activities weekly to identify high-impact tasks; eliminate or delegate low-value activities; focus more time on the vital few
- **Digital Boundaries**: Set specific times for checking email and social media; use app timers or blockers; create phone-free zones and times

Question 3: What will your first 7-day experiment focus on?

Former Student Responses:
- "I want to experiment with waking up 30 minutes earlier to have quiet planning time."
- "I'll try blocking 2 hours every morning for deep work before checking email."
- "I want to test using a paper planner alongside my digital calendar."
- "I'll experiment with saying no to one non-essential commitment each day."

- "I want to try the Pomodoro Technique for all my focused work sessions."
- "I'll test scheduling all my priorities first, then fitting other things around them."
- "I want to experiment with a complete digital detox during family time."

Possible Solutions:
- **Early Morning Experiment**: Prepare everything the night before; start with just 15 minutes earlier; use the time for priority review and planning; track how it affects your day
- **Morning Deep Work**: Block the time in your calendar; turn off all notifications; communicate your unavailability to colleagues; start with 1 hour if 2 feels overwhelming
- **Hybrid Planning System**: Use a digital calendar for appointments and reminders, paper for daily priorities and reflection; sync them each morning; evaluate which works better for different needs
- **Strategic No Practice**: Identify one current commitment that doesn't align with your priorities; practice polite decline phrases; track how saying no affects your stress and goal progress
- **Pomodoro Trial**: Use a simple timer for 25-minute work blocks; take 5-minute breaks; try it for one important task daily; track focus and productivity changes
- **Priority-First Scheduling**: Schedule your top 3 priorities before anything else; protect this time from other requests; evaluate how this affects your goal progress
- **Digital Detox**: Put devices in another room during family time; use a traditional alarm clock; create engaging alternative activities; track relationship quality changes

Question 4: Who will you share your plan with for accountability?

Former Student Responses:
- "I have a close friend who's also working on productivity - we could check in weekly."
- "My spouse is supportive and could help remind me of my new boundaries."
- "I want to find an online community of people with similar goals."
- "I don't really have anyone who would understand these goals - I need to find new connections."
- "My team at work might be interested in improving our collective productivity."
- "I have a mentor who's great at time management - I could ask for their guidance."
- "I'm hesitant to share because I've failed at goals before and felt embarrassed."

Possible Solutions:
- **Friend Partnership**: Schedule weekly 15-minute check-ins; share specific goals and progress; celebrate each other's wins; be honest about setbacks and challenges
- **Spouse Support**: Explain how your time management goals benefit the family; ask for support during focused work times; share your wins and challenges regularly
- **Online Community**: Join groups on platforms like Reddit, Facebook, or Discord focused on productivity; share weekly progress updates; offer support to others
- **New Connections**: Join local meetups, professional associations, or online mastermind groups; attend productivity workshops or seminars; consider hiring a coach
- **Workplace Collaboration**: Suggest team productivity challenges; share time management tips during meetings; create accountability partnerships with colleagues
- **Mentor Relationship**: Schedule monthly check-ins; ask for specific advice on time management challenges; share your progress and ask for feedback
- **Fear of Failure**: Start with one trusted person; focus on sharing effort rather than just outcomes; remember that accountability increases success rates dramatically

Question 5: How will you celebrate your progress and keep your momentum going?

Former Student Responses:
- "I never really celebrate small wins - I just move on to the next thing."
- "I don't know what would feel like a meaningful celebration for productivity improvements."
- "I tend to reward myself with things that contradict my goals, like binge-watching TV."
- "I feel guilty celebrating when there's still so much left to improve."
- "I prefer experiences over material rewards, but I'm not sure what would work."
- "I'd like to celebrate with others, but I'm embarrassed about my time management struggles."
- "I'm on a tight budget, so I can't afford expensive rewards."

Possible Solutions:
- **No Celebration Habit**: Schedule celebration time like any other appointment; set reminders to acknowledge progress; create a "wins journal" to review regularly

- **Celebration Uncertainty**: Experiment with different types of rewards - extra sleep, favorite coffee, nature walk, or hobby time; ask friends what motivates them
- **Contradictory Rewards**: Choose celebrations that support your goals - reward productivity with a new planner or app; celebrate focus time with a relaxing activity that energizes you
- **Guilt About Celebrating**: Reframe celebration as fuel for continued progress; remember that acknowledging wins increases motivation; celebrate effort and systems, not just outcomes
- **Experience Preferences**: Plan special outings like visiting a museum, trying a new coffee shop, or taking a scenic drive; attend events related to your interests
- **Social Celebration Needs**: Share wins with supportive friends and family; join communities where you can celebrate others' successes too; start small with one trusted person
- **Budget Constraints**: Use free activities like library visits, park walks, or home spa time; celebrate with time-based rewards like sleeping in or pursuing a hobby

Universal Solutions Across All Chapter 11 Questions:

Start Immediately: Choose the smallest possible first step and take it today - action creates momentum that sustains motivation and builds confidence.

Build Support Systems: Actively cultivate relationships with people who understand and encourage your time management goals, whether through existing relationships or new communities.

Track What Matters: Monitor the actions you take (inputs) as much as the results you achieve (outputs) for better motivation and course correction.

Celebrate Progress: Acknowledge and reward effort and improvement, not just perfect execution or final achievements, to maintain motivation throughout your journey.

Learn from Experience: Use each time management experiment to understand your patterns, strengths, and areas for improvement.

Stay Connected to Your Why: Regularly revisit the deeper reasons behind your time management goals to maintain motivation and ensure continued relevance.

Practice Self-Compassion: Treat setbacks as learning opportunities rather than evidence of personal failure, and speak to yourself with the same kindness you'd show a good friend.

Embrace the Journey: Remember that mastering time management is a process, not a destination - focus on who you're becoming, not just what you're accomplishing.

Stay Flexible: Be willing to adjust your approach based on what you learn about yourself and what works best for your unique circumstances and goals.

Take Action

- Complete your self-audit and write down your vision and goals.
- Choose one habit or routine to implement this week.
- Set up your tools and schedule your first review.
- Share your commitment with a friend, mentor, or group.
- Celebrate your first win—no matter how small!

*"The future depends on what we do in the present." – **Mahatma Gandhi***

Final Encouragement

This is not the end, but the beginning of your journey. Every day offers a new chance to make your time matter. Keep learning, keep adjusting, and keep moving forward—one mindful, intentional step at a time.

Thank you for allowing us to be part of your story. Your next chapter starts now.

Appendices & Resources

Appendix A: Activity and Time Audit Template

Purpose:
To help you discover where your time really goes and identify opportunities to reclaim hours for what matters.

How to Use:
- Print or copy the template for a full week.
- Record your activities in 15–30 minute blocks.
- At the end of each day, highlight activities that felt productive, draining, or unnecessary.
- At week's end, review for patterns and time robbers.

Sample Template:

Time	Activity	Productive?	Notes/Feelings
7:00–7:30	Breakfast & news	Yes	Relaxed start
7:30–8:00	Social media scrolling	No	Felt distracted
8:00–9:00	Project work	Yes	Good focus

Download:
Find printable and digital versions at Canva or Smartsheet.

Appendix B: Weekly and Monthly Planner Templates

Purpose:
To help you schedule your priorities, block time, and review your progress.

Weekly Planner Sample:

Day	Top 3 Priorities	Time Blocks	Notes/Reflection
Monday	1. Client meeting	9–10am: Meeting	
	2. Write a proposal	11–12: Proposal	
	3. Exercise	5–5:30pm: Walk	

Monthly Planner Sample:
- Space for goal review, habit tracking, and key milestones.

Download:
Use Canva or Notion for customizable templates.

Appendix C: Quick Reference – 7 Concepts, 8 Commandments, Top Tools

7 Critical Concepts:
1. You can't manage time, only your actions.
2. Time is the great equalizer.
3. Time is like money—budget it.
4. Schedule, don't just "to-do."
5. The 80/20 rule (Pareto Principle).
6. You have more time than you think.
7. Always know what you're doing with your time.

8 Commandments for Time Managers:
1. Kick the robbers out.
2. Priority determines what matters.
3. Learn to say "No."
4. Juggling is an illusion (no multitasking).
5. Take the "I" out (delegate/teamwork).
6. Do the right thing right the first time.
7. Use the 4WH strategy (What, Why, Who, When, How).
8. Plan everything.

Top Tools:
- Digital: Google Calendar, Todoist, Trello, Notion, RescueTime, Forest, Focusmate
- Paper: Weekly/monthly planners, habit tracker grids
- Hybrid: Digital calendar + paper planner for daily review

Appendix D: Recommended Books, Podcasts, and Websites

Books:
- *Atomic Habits* by James Clear
- *Deep Work* by Cal Newport
- *Essentialism* by Greg McKeown
- *Eat That Frog!* by Brian Tracy

Podcasts:
- *The Productivity Show* (Asian Efficiency)
- *The Tim Ferriss Show*
- *Beyond the To-Do List*

Websites:
- James Clear's Blog
- Zen Habits
- Todoist Blog

Appendix E: Further Reading for Specific Roles

Students:
- *Make It Stick* by Peter C. Brown
- Notion Student Templates

Parents:
- *The Organized Mind* by Daniel J. Levitin
- Parenting Time Management Tips

Professionals/Managers:
- *Getting Things Done* by David Allen
- Harvard Business Review Productivity

Freelancers/Entrepreneurs:
- *The ONE Thing* by Gary Keller
- Trello Freelance Templates

Appendix F: Worksheets, Checklists, and Habit Trackers

- **Printable Habit Tracker:**

Rows for habits, columns for days, checkboxes for completion.

- **Goal Setting Worksheet:**

Vision → Goals → Steps → Schedule → Review.

- **Weekly Review Checklist:**
    - What worked?
    - What didn't?
    - What will I do differently next week?
- **SWOT Analysis Template:**

Four quadrants for Strengths, Weaknesses, Opportunities, Threats.

Appendix G: Quick-Start Action Checklist

1. Complete your one-week time audit.
2. Identify your top 3 time robbers and make a plan to address them.
3. Set your top 3 priorities for the next week.
4. Choose one new habit to build and track it daily.
5. Schedule a weekly review session.
6. Experiment with one new tool or technique.
7. Share your goals and progress with an accountability partner.

Final Encouragement & Series Roadmap

- **Keep this section handy** as you implement your plan and adjust your systems.
- **Revisit the appendices** whenever you need a refresher, a new template, or inspiration.
- **Continue your journey** with the next book in the About Things That Matter series: *Relations That Matter*.

*"The secret of getting ahead is getting started. The secret of getting started is breaking your complex, overwhelming tasks into small, manageable tasks, and then starting on the first one." – **Mark Twain.***

Bibliography

Primary Source

Allen, James. *As A Man Thinketh*. 1903. Reprint, New York: Dover Publications, 1999.

Neuroscience and Brain Research

Davidson, Richard J., et al. "Alterations in Brain and Immune Function Produced by Mindfulness Meditation." *Psychosomatic Medicine* 65, no. 4 (2003): 564-570.

Dietrich, Arne. "Neurocognitive Mechanisms Underlying the Experience of Flow." *Consciousness and Cognition* 13, no. 4 (2004): 746-761.

Doidge, Norman. *The Brain That Changes Itself: Stories of Personal Triumph from the Frontiers of Brain Science*. New York: Penguin Books, 2007.

Lazar, Sara W., et al. "Meditation Experience Is Associated with Increased Cortical Thickness." *NeuroReport* 16, no. 17 (2005): 1893-1897.

Ochsner, Kevin N., et al. "Rethinking Feelings: An fMRI Study of the Cognitive Regulation of Emotion." *Journal of Cognitive Neuroscience* 14, no. 8 (2002): 1215-1229.

Siegel, Daniel J. *The Developing Mind: How Relationships and the Brain Interact to Shape Who We Are*. 2nd ed. New York: Guilford Press, 2012.

Simons, Daniel J., and Christopher F. Chabris. "Gorillas in Our Midst: Sustained Inattentional Blindness for Dynamic Events." *Perception* 28, no. 9 (1999): 1059-1074.

Emotional Intelligence and Regulation

Barrett, Lisa Feldman. *How Emotions Are Made: The Secret Life of the Brain*. Boston: Houghton Mifflin Harcourt, 2017.

Beck, Aaron T. *Cognitive Therapy and the Emotional Disorders*. New York: International Universities Press, 1976.

Damasio, Antonio. *Descartes' Error: Emotion, Reason, and the Human Brain*. New York: Putnam, 1994.

Ekman, Paul. *Emotions Revealed: Recognizing Faces and Feelings to Improve Communication and Emotional Life*. New York: Times Books, 2003.

Goleman, Daniel. *Emotional Intelligence: Why It Matters More Than IQ*. New York: Bantam Books, 1995.

Gross, James J. "Emotion Regulation: Affective, Cognitive, and Social Consequences." *Psychophysiology* 39, no. 3 (2002): 281-291.

Neff, Kristin D. "Self-Compassion: An Alternative Conceptualization of a Healthy Attitude Toward Oneself." *Self and Identity* 2, no. 2 (2003): 85-101.

Pert, Candace B. *Molecules of Emotion: The Science Behind Mind-Body Medicine*. New York: Scribner, 1997.

Positive Psychology and Resilience

Fredrickson, Barbara L. "The Role of Positive Emotions in Positive Psychology: The Broaden-and-Build Theory of Positive Emotions." *American Psychologist* 56, no. 3 (2001): 218-226.

Kabat-Zinn, Jon. "An Outpatient Program in Behavioral Medicine for Chronic Pain Patients Based on the Practice of Mindfulness Meditation." *General Hospital Psychiatry* 4, no. 1 (1982): 33-47.

Maddi, Salvatore R. "The Story of Hardiness: Twenty Years of Theorizing, Research, and Practice." *Consulting Psychology Journal* 54, no. 3 (2002): 173-185.

Tedeschi, Richard G., and Lawrence G. Calhoun. "Posttraumatic Growth: Conceptual Foundations and Empirical Evidence." *Psychological Inquiry* 15, no. 1 (2004): 1-18.

Waldinger, Robert J., and Marc S. Schulz. "What's Love Got to Do with It? Social Functioning, Perceived Health, and Daily Happiness in Married Octogenarians." *Psychology and Aging* 25, no. 2 (2010): 422-431.

Cognitive Psychology and Decision-Making

Csikszentmihalyi, Mihaly. *Flow: The Psychology of Optimal Experience*. New York: Harper & Row, 1990.

Kahneman, Daniel. *Thinking, Fast and Slow*. New York: Farrar, Straus and Giroux, 2011.

Narrative Psychology and Meaning-Making

Frankl, Viktor E. *Man's Search for Meaning*. Boston: Beacon Press, 1946.

McAdams, Dan P. "The Psychology of Life Stories." *Review of General Psychology* 5, no. 2 (2001): 100-122.

Park, Crystal L. "Making Sense of the Meaning Literature: An Integrative Review of Meaning Making and Its Effects on Adjustment to Stressful Life Events." *Psychological Bulletin* 136, no. 2 (2010): 257-301.

White, Michael, and David Epston. *Narrative Means to Therapeutic Ends.* New York: Norton, 1990.

Habit Formation and Behavioral Change

Duhigg, Charles. *The Power of Habit: Why We Do What We Do in Life and Business.* New York: Random House, 2012.

Fogg, BJ. "A Behavior Model for Persuasive Design." *Proceedings of the 4th International Conference on Persuasive Technology.* ACM, 2009.

Lally, Phillippa, et al. "How Are Habits Formed: Modelling Habit Formation in the Real World." *European Journal of Social Psychology* 40, no. 6 (2010): 998-1009.

Classical References

Henley, William Ernest. "Invictus." 1875.

Lao Tzu. *Tao Te Ching.* Translated by Stephen Mitchell. New York: Harper & Row, 1988.

Contemporary Applications

Clear, James. *Atomic Habits: An Easy & Proven Way to Build Good Habits & Break Bad Ones.* New York: Avery, 2018.

Covey, Stephen R. *The 7 Habits of Highly Effective People.* New York: Free Press, 1989.

Dweck, Carol S. *Mindset: The New Psychology of Success.* New York: Random House, 2006.

PART 4 - RELATIONSHIPS THAT MATTER

To everyone who understands that success is never a solo journey, and to those who choose to invest in others even when the returns aren't immediately visible. Your commitment to connection creates ripples of positive change that extend far beyond what you'll ever know.

"We are wired for connection. It's in our biology." — **Brené Brown.**

Relationships That Matter
Building Social Wealth for a Life of Connection and Impact

About Things That Matter
A Self-Improvement Series for Success

Book 4

JC Ryan

About Relationships That Matter

Relationships That Matter is your guide to building social wealth, deepening your connections, and creating a life of lasting impact. In a world that often values achievement and productivity above all else, this book reminds you that your relationships—family, friends, colleagues, mentors, and community—are the foundation for happiness, resilience, and success.

This book is for anyone who wants to strengthen existing bonds, form new connections, or repair relationships that matter. Whether you're an introvert or extrovert, a leader or a learner, you'll find practical strategies, reflection prompts, and real-world examples to help you build a rich, supportive network.

You'll learn how to:
- Map your relationship landscape and identify the roles that support your growth
- Build trust, empathy, and authenticity in every interaction
- Communicate with clarity, confidence, and compassion
- Set healthy boundaries and manage your social energy
- Find or build your tribe and foster a sense of belonging
- Navigate digital relationships with intention and balance
- Give, receive, and grow together—through all of life's changes

Relationships That Matter builds on the foundations of *Change That Matters*, *Goals That Matter*, and *Time That Matters*, but focuses on the people who will walk with you on your journey. Each chapter ends with reflection questions and action steps, so you can immediately apply what you learn.

It's About Social Wealth

In a world that often celebrates independence and self-sufficiency, it's easy to forget that no one achieves greatness alone. Behind every meaningful accomplishment, every moment of resilience, and every story of transformation, you'll find the quiet strength of relationships with family, friends, mentors, colleagues, and communities who walk beside us, lift us up, and remind us of who we are.

The About Things That Matter series began with a simple premise: that a life of meaning, momentum, and fulfillment is built on a foundation of clarity, purpose, and action. *Change That Matters* showed you how to embrace growth. *Goals That Matter* helped you turn vision into reality. *Time That Matters* taught you how to make space for what's truly important. Now, *Relationships That Matter* invites you to focus on the people who make the journey worthwhile.

Why relationships? Because success is a team sport. Because joy is multiplied when shared. Because, in the end, the quality of your connections shapes the quality of your life. Social wealth—the trust, support, and belonging you build with others—is the most enduring asset you can possess. It's what sustains you in hard times, inspires you to grow, and gives your achievements lasting meaning.

This book is your invitation to invest intentionally in the people who matter most. Whether you're seeking deeper friendships, stronger partnerships, or a greater sense of community, you'll find practical wisdom, real-world stories, and actionable steps to help you build, nurture, and sustain the relationships that will support you through every season of life.

Let's begin the journey together.

The Power of Social Wealth

What if your greatest resource wasn't your skills, your knowledge, or your achievements but the relationships you cultivate along the way?

Think back on the most meaningful moments in your life. Chances are, they weren't defined by what you accomplished alone, but by who was with you—celebrating your victories, comforting you in setbacks, or simply sharing the ordinary days that become extraordinary in the company of others.

In today's fast-paced, hyper-connected world, we are surrounded by people and yet often feel more isolated than ever. We chase productivity, accumulate followers, and fill our calendars, but sometimes neglect the deeper connections that bring true fulfillment. Research is clear: strong, healthy relationships are the single greatest predictor of happiness, resilience, and even longevity. Social wealth is not measured in likes or contacts, but in trust, empathy, and shared growth.

Relationships That Matter is the fourth pillar in the About Things That Matter series. It builds on the foundations of personal change, purpose-driven goals, and intentional time management, and turns your attention outward—to the people who shape your life. Here, you'll learn how to:

> Map your relationship landscape and identify the roles that support your growth
> Build trust, empathy, and authenticity in every interaction
> Communicate with clarity, confidence, and compassion
> Set healthy boundaries and manage your social energy
> Find or build your tribe and foster a sense of belonging
> Navigate digital relationships with intention and balance
> Give, receive, and grow together—through all of life's changes

Each chapter ends with reflection questions and action steps, so you can immediately apply what you learn. You'll find exercises, scripts, and real-life stories to help you deepen existing bonds, form new connections, and repair relationships that matter.

Your journey to a life of connection and impact starts here. The people you choose to walk with will shape your future as much as any goal you set or habit you build. This book is your guide to building social wealth, one act of kindness, one courageous step at a time.

Are you ready to invest in the relationships that matter most? Turn the page, and let's begin—together.

Chapter 1 – Why Relationships Are the Ultimate Wealth

The Role of Relationships in Personal Fulfillment, Health, and Achievement

When you look back on the most meaningful moments of your life, chances are they are defined not by what you accomplished alone, but by who was with you. Relationships are the foundation of fulfillment—offering support in tough times, amplifying joy in good times, and giving life its deepest sense of purpose. Research consistently shows that strong, healthy relationships are the single greatest predictor of happiness and well-being. People with rich social connections live longer, recover more quickly from setbacks, and experience greater resilience in the face of adversity.

Achievement, too, is rarely a solo pursuit. Behind every personal or professional milestone stands a network of supporters—family, friends, mentors, colleagues, and communities—who offer encouragement, accountability, and practical help. Whether you're striving for personal growth, career advancement, or simply a sense of belonging, relationships are the invisible force that moves you forward.

Social Wealth vs. Material Wealth

In a world that often measures success by what you own or achieve, it's easy to overlook the value of social wealth. Material wealth—money, possessions, status—can provide comfort and opportunity, but it is social wealth that truly enriches your life. Social wealth is the trust, goodwill, and support you build with others over time. It's the network of people you can count on, the sense of community you belong to, and the feeling of being seen, valued, and understood.

Unlike material wealth, social wealth cannot be hoarded or lost in a market crash. It grows the more you give, share, and invest in others. When you nurture your relationships, you create a reservoir of support that sustains you through life's inevitable ups and downs. In the end, it is not the size of your bank account, but the strength of your connections that determines the richness of your life.

The Science of Connection: Belonging, Loneliness, and Well-Being

Human beings are wired for connection. From our earliest days, our brains and bodies are shaped by our relationships with others. Neuroscience shows that social connection releases oxytocin, the "bonding hormone," which reduces stress and increases feelings of trust and safety. Conversely, chronic loneliness and isolation are linked to increased risk of depression, anxiety, and even physical illness.

A landmark study by Harvard University found that the quality of a person's relationships at age 50 was a better predictor of health at age 80 than cholesterol levels or income. Belonging is not just a "nice to have"—it is a fundamental human need. When you invest in relationships, you are investing in your own well-being and longevity.

How Relationships Amplify (or Undermine) Your Progress in Change, Goals, and Time Management

Relationships are not just a source of comfort—they are a catalyst for growth. In *Change That Matters*, you learned that lasting transformation is rarely achieved in isolation. Supportive relationships provide encouragement, honest feedback, and accountability, making it easier to step outside your comfort zone and sustain new habits.

In *Goals That Matter*, we explored how sharing your goals with others increases your chances of success. Friends, mentors, and colleagues can offer perspective, resources, and connections that accelerate your progress. And as *Time That Matters* teaches, how you spend your time is often a reflection of who you spend it with. The people in your life can either help you protect your priorities or pull you away from what matters most.

But relationships can also undermine your progress if they are negative, draining, or misaligned with your values. That's why it's essential to cultivate connections that inspire and support you—and to set boundaries with those that don't.

Reflection: Who Are the Five People Shaping Your Life Right Now?

Take a moment to reflect on your closest relationships. Jim Rohn famously said, "You are the average of the five people you spend the most time with." Who are your five? How do they influence your mindset, habits, and aspirations? Do they encourage your growth, challenge you to be better, or hold you back from your potential?

Write down the names of your five closest connections. Next to each name, note one way this person supports or challenges you. This simple exercise can reveal patterns—both positive and negative—in your relationship landscape.

Action: Quick Relationship Audit

To begin building your social wealth, start with a quick relationship audit:

- **List Your Key Relationships:** Family, friends, colleagues, mentors, community members.
- **Assess the Quality:** For each, rate the relationship on a scale from 1 (draining) to 10 (energizing).
- **Identify Gaps:** Are there important roles missing (e.g., a mentor, a confidant, a collaborator)?
- **Spot Opportunities:** Who would you like to spend more time with? Who might you need to set boundaries with?

Use this audit as a starting point for the journey ahead. As you move through this book, you'll learn how to deepen existing connections, form new ones, and create a network that supports your best life.

Chapter Summary

- Relationships are the foundation of fulfillment, health, and achievement.
- Social wealth—your network of trust and support—is more valuable than material wealth.
- Connection is a biological and psychological need; loneliness is a serious health risk.
- The people around you can amplify or undermine your progress in change, goals, and time management.
- Start your journey by reflecting on who shapes your life and auditing the quality of your relationships.

Reflection Questions

Question 1: Who are the five people you spend the most time with, and how do they influence you?

Former Student Responses:
- "I spend most of my time with family, but sometimes feel they don't understand my goals."
- "My closest friends support me, but I wish I had more mentors."
- "I have colleagues who challenge me, but also some who drain my energy."
- "I feel disconnected from my community and want to build new relationships."
- "I don't know who my true supporters are."

- "My five people are mostly from work, and I realize I need more diversity in my network."
- "I spend time with people who complain a lot, and I notice it affects my mood negatively."

Possible Solutions:
- Reflect on your current relationships and identify their impact on your growth.
- Seek to strengthen relationships that support your goals
- Consider finding new mentors or joining communities aligned with your values
- Set boundaries with those who drain your energy
- Actively seek out people who inspire and challenge you positively
- Join professional associations or hobby groups to expand your network
- Practice gratitude for supportive relationships while addressing toxic ones

Question 2: Which relationships energize and support you? Which ones drain or distract you?

Former Student Responses:
- "My partner and close friends energize me, but some family members are emotionally draining."
- "Work relationships can be both supportive and stressful, depending on the person."
- "I feel distracted by social media connections that don't add real value."
- "My mentor energizes me, but I don't have enough people like that in my life."
- "I realize I give more energy than I receive in most of my relationships."
- "Some friends only contact me when they need something."
- "I feel exhausted after spending time with certain people, but guilty about limiting contact."

Possible Solutions:
- Prioritize spending time with energizing people
- Limit exposure to draining relationships through boundaries
- Curate your social media and digital connections intentionally
- Seek out more mentors and positive influences
- Practice reciprocity - both giving and receiving support
- Have honest conversations about one-sided relationships
- Use the "energy audit" to evaluate relationships regularly

Question 3: What role does social wealth play in your definition of success?

Former Student Responses:
- "I believe success includes having strong, supportive relationships."
- "Without good relationships, achievements feel hollow."
- "Social wealth is as important as financial wealth to me."
- "I used to focus only on career success, but now I see relationships matter more."
- "I want to be remembered for how I treated people, not just what I accomplished."
- "I'm starting to realize that networking isn't just about career advancement."
- "I've achieved a lot professionally, but feel lonely - that's not real success."

Possible Solutions:
- Recognize the importance of social connections in overall well-being
- Invest time and energy in building meaningful relationships
- Redefine success to include relationship quality alongside other achievements
- Create goals that include both personal accomplishments and relationship building
- Practice gratitude for the social wealth you already have
- Share your achievements with others to make them more meaningful
- Consider how your success can benefit and include others

Question 4: Where do you see opportunities to deepen or expand your connections?

Former Student Responses:
- "I want to reconnect with old friends I've lost touch with."
- "I wish to join local groups or clubs related to my interests."
- "I want to be more intentional in my interactions."
- "I'd like to find a mentor in my field."
- "I need to build stronger relationships with my colleagues."
- "I want to contribute more to my community."
- "I should reach out to people instead of waiting for them to contact me."

Possible Solutions:
- Reach out to people you haven't connected with recently
- Join interest-based or values-based communities
- Practice active listening and authentic communication
- Attend networking events or professional meetups
- Volunteer for causes you care about
- Schedule regular check-ins with important people
- Take initiative in planning social activities or gatherings

Universal Solutions Across All Chapter 1 Questions:

Conduct a Relationship Audit: Regularly assess the quality and impact of your relationships on your well-being and growth.
Practice Intentional Connection: Be deliberate about who you spend time with and how you invest your social energy.
Build Diverse Networks: Seek relationships across different areas of life - professional, personal, community, and mentorship.
Set Healthy Boundaries: Protect your energy by limiting time with draining relationships while nurturing supportive ones.
Invest in Social Wealth: Recognize that relationships are an asset that requires time, attention, and care to grow.
Seek Reciprocity: Aim for balanced relationships where both giving and receiving occur naturally.
Expand Your Definition of Success: Include relationship quality and social impact in how you measure a successful life.
Take Initiative: Don't wait for others to reach out - be proactive in building and maintaining connections.

Take Action

- Complete your quick relationship audit today.
- Reach out to one person who energizes you and express your appreciation.
- Identify one relationship you'd like to improve or invest in over the coming weeks.

Chapter 2 – Mapping Your Relationship Landscape

The Relationship Ecosystem: Family, Friends, Colleagues, Mentors, Community, Online and Offline

Your relationships form a living ecosystem—an interconnected web that shapes your sense of belonging, support, and growth. This ecosystem isn't limited to just family or close friends; it includes colleagues at work, mentors who guide you, community members who share your interests or values, and even people you connect with online. Each relationship plays a distinct role in your life, contributing to your well-being, resilience, and opportunities for growth.

Think of your relationship ecosystem as having multiple layers:

- **Inner circle:** Family and closest friends—those you trust deeply and turn to in times of need.
- **Professional circle:** Colleagues, mentors, collaborators—people who challenge and support your ambitions.
- **Community circle:** Neighbors, interest groups, faith or volunteer communities—those who create a sense of belonging.
- **Digital connections:** Online friends, networks, and communities that provide learning, support, or inspiration.

A healthy relationship ecosystem is diverse, dynamic, and intentional. It evolves as your life changes, and it requires regular attention to remain strong and supportive.

The 5 Essential Roles in Your Network

Not all relationships are the same. To thrive, you need a variety of roles filled in your network. Here are the five essential types:

1. **Champions:** The cheerleaders—these are the people who believe in your potential, celebrate your wins, and encourage you through setbacks.
2. **Challengers:** The truth-tellers—those who push you to grow, offer honest feedback, and aren't afraid to question your assumptions.
3. **Collaborators:** The partners—people who share your goals or passions and work alongside you to achieve something greater.

4. **Companions:** The sources of joy and rest are friends or family who bring comfort, laughter, and a sense of home.
5. **Catalysts:** The connectors—individuals who introduce you to new ideas, people, or opportunities, helping you expand your horizons.

Reflect on your current network: Do you have each of these roles represented? Are there gaps that need to be filled?

Relationship Mapping Exercise: Visualizing Your Current Network

To truly understand your relationship landscape, it helps to see it visually.

Try this exercise:
1. Draw yourself at the center of a blank page.
2. Around you, create circles for each layer: inner circle, professional, community, and digital.
3. Write the names of people in each circle, noting their primary role (champion, challenger, collaborator, companion, catalyst).
4. Use lines or colors to indicate the strength and frequency of each connection.

Downloadable/Printable Template: You can find a free relationship mapping worksheet online or create your own using tools like Canva or a simple spreadsheet.

Identifying Gaps, Energy Drains, and Missing Connections

Once your map is complete, review it with a critical eye:

- **Gaps:** Are there roles that aren't filled? For example, do you lack a mentor (challenger) or a creative collaborator?
- **Energy Drains:** Are there relationships that consistently leave you feeling depleted, anxious, or unsupported?
- **Missing Connections:** Is there someone you'd like to know better, or a type of relationship (e.g., community, spiritual, professional) that's missing altogether?

Awareness is the first step to positive change. By identifying these areas, you can begin to nurture what's working, adjust what isn't, and seek out new connections that support your growth.

Reflection: Who Lifts You Up? Who Drains You? Who's Missing?

Take a moment to reflect on your map:
- Who are your greatest sources of encouragement and energy?
- Who challenges you to grow, even when it's uncomfortable?

- Are there people in your life who consistently drain your energy, distract you from your goals, or hold you back?
- Who would you like to connect with, or what kind of relationship would you like to cultivate in the future?

Chapter Summary

- Your relationship ecosystem is made up of many layers—family, friends, colleagues, mentors, community, and online connections.
- Thriving networks include champions, challengers, collaborators, companions, and catalysts.
- Mapping your relationships helps you see strengths, gaps, and opportunities for growth.
- Identifying energy drains and missing connections is the first step to building a network that truly supports you.

Reflection Questions

Question 1: Which roles are well-represented in your current network? Which are missing?

Former Student Responses:
- "I have plenty of companions (friends for fun), but I'm missing challengers who push me to grow."
- "My network is mostly colleagues and family, but I don't have any real mentors or catalysts."
- "I have champions who support me, but I lack collaborators to work on projects with."
- "Most of my relationships are companions and champions, but I need people who will challenge me honestly."
- "I realize I have collaborators at work, but no real champions in my personal life."
- "I'm missing catalysts - people who introduce me to new opportunities and ideas"
- "I have all the roles, but they're not balanced - too many energy-draining relationships"

Possible Solutions:
- **Missing Challengers**: Seek out mentors, join mastermind groups, or ask trusted friends to give you honest feedback; look for people who have achieved what you aspire to
- **Lacking Mentors/Catalysts**: Attend industry events, join professional associations, or reach out to people you admire on LinkedIn; offer value in exchange for guidance
- **Need Collaborators**: Join hobby groups, volunteer organizations, or start a side project; look for people with complementary skills and shared interests.
- **Want More Champions**: Invest in existing relationships by being more vulnerable and authentic; join supportive communities where encouragement is the norm.
- **Seeking Catalysts**: Expand your network beyond your usual circles; attend diverse events, conferences, or online communities; be open to unexpected connections

Question 2: Who in your life consistently lifts you up, and who tends to drain your energy?

Former Student Responses:
- "My best friend always believes in me, but my coworker constantly complains and brings negativity."
- "My spouse is incredibly supportive, but my mother criticizes everything I do."
- "I have a mentor who inspires me, but some friends only contact me when they need something."
- "My workout buddy motivates me, but my neighbor always gossips and creates drama."
- "My book club friends energize me, but my old college friends just want to party and waste time."
- "My business partner challenges me positively, but my brother is always pessimistic about my goals."
- "I feel lifted up by my faith community, but drained by certain family members who don't understand my values."

Possible Solutions:
- **Energy Lifters**: Prioritize spending more time with these people; express gratitude for their support; reciprocate their positive energy; schedule regular connection time

- **Energy Drainers**: Set boundaries with time and emotional investment; limit exposure when possible; practice not taking their negativity personally; redirect conversations to positive topics
- **Mixed Relationships**: Acknowledge that some people serve different purposes; accept family members as they are while protecting your energy; find ways to appreciate their positive qualities
- **One-Sided Relationships**: Have honest conversations about reciprocity; gradually reduce investment in relationships that consistently take without giving; seek more balanced connections

Question 3: What's one relationship you'd like to strengthen or one new connection you'd like to make?

Former Student Responses:
- "I want to reconnect with my sister - we've grown apart since we both got busy with our careers."
- "I'd like to find a mentor in my industry who can guide my professional development."
- "I want to strengthen my relationship with my teenage daughter - we used to be close."
- "I'd like to make friends with people who share my interest in hiking and outdoor activities."
- "I want to build a better relationship with my new manager at work."
- "I'd like to connect with other entrepreneurs who understand the challenges I'm facing."
- "I want to deepen my friendship with my neighbor - we have great conversations, but only see each other occasionally."

Possible Solutions:
- **Family Reconnection**: Schedule regular one-on-one time; start with low-pressure activities; share what's happening in your life; ask about their experiences and listen actively
- **Finding Mentors**: Research people in your field; attend industry events; reach out with specific questions; offer to help with their projects; join professional mentorship programs.

- **Strengthening Parent-Child Relationships**: Plan activities based on their interests; put away devices during time together; ask open-ended questions; share appropriate stories from your own life
- **Interest-Based Connections**: Join clubs, meetups, or online groups; attend local events; take classes; use apps like Meetup or Bumble BFF to find like-minded people
- **Professional Relationships**: Schedule informal coffee meetings; ask thoughtful questions about their goals; offer assistance with projects; find common ground beyond work
- **Peer Communities**: Join entrepreneur groups, online forums, or local business networks; attend startup events; consider joining or creating a mastermind group
- **Neighbor Relationships**: Invite them for coffee or a meal; suggest shared activities like walking or gardening; offer help with projects; create opportunities for regular interaction

Question 4: How does your relationship landscape support—or hinder—your goals and well-being?

Former Student Responses:
- "My family supports my personal goals but doesn't understand my business ambitions."
- "Most of my friends encourage me, but a few make me feel guilty for prioritizing my health and growth."
- "My professional network helps with career goals, but I lack emotional support for personal challenges."
- "Some relationships energize me toward my goals, while others make me doubt myself."
- "I have great support for my creative pursuits, but no one who understands my financial goals."
- "My relationships are mostly supportive, but I don't have anyone who really challenges me to grow."
- "I'm surrounded by people who care about me, but they don't share my values around personal development."

Possible Solutions:
- **Mixed Support**: Communicate your goals clearly to family and friends; help them understand why these goals matter to you; find additional support in communities that share your ambitions
- **Guilt-Inducing Relationships**: Set boundaries around your personal growth time; explain how your development benefits your relationships; limit time with people who consistently discourage your progress
- **Compartmentalized Support**: Work to integrate your support network; introduce different groups of friends; seek people who can support multiple aspects of your life
- **Confidence Undermining**: Identify specific people or situations that trigger self-doubt; prepare responses to negative comments; strengthen relationships with people who believe in you.
- **Value Misalignment**: Find communities that share your values; join groups focused on personal development; consider that not everyone needs to understand all your goals
- **Lack of Challenge**: Actively seek out people who will push you; ask trusted friends to give you honest feedback; join groups where high standards are the norm

Universal Solutions Across All Chapter 2 Questions:

Conduct Regular Relationship Audits: Schedule quarterly reviews of your relationship landscape to identify changes, gaps, and opportunities for growth.
Diversify Your Network: Actively seek relationships across different areas of life—professional, personal, community, and interest-based connections.
Invest in Quality Over Quantity: Focus on deepening meaningful relationships rather than accumulating many superficial connections.
Practice Reciprocity: Both give and receive support; be the kind of friend, colleague, or community member you want to attract.
Set Healthy Boundaries: Protect your energy by limiting time with draining relationships while nurturing those that support your growth.
Communicate Your Needs: Help others understand how they can support you by being clear about your goals and values.
Seek Growth-Oriented Connections: Actively look for people who challenge you, inspire you, and share your commitment to personal development.

Be Patient with Relationship Building: Understand that meaningful connections take time to develop; consistency and authenticity are key to building trust.

Take Action

- Complete the relationship mapping exercise using the template provided.
- Reach out to one person who energizes you and express your appreciation.
- Identify one gap in your network and brainstorm ways to fill it through community events, professional groups, or online platforms.

Chapter 3 – Foundations of Lasting Connection

The Principles of Trust, Empathy, Authenticity, and Reciprocity

At the heart of every strong relationship are four foundational principles: trust, empathy, authenticity, and reciprocity. **Trust** is the bedrock of connection—without it, relationships remain superficial and fragile. It grows through reliability, honesty, and keeping your word, even in small matters. **Empathy** is the ability to step into another's shoes, to genuinely understand and feel what they're experiencing. When you listen with empathy, you create a safe space for others to share and be themselves. **Authenticity** means showing up as your true self, not hiding behind masks or pretending to be someone you're not. Authenticity invites others to do the same, deepening mutual respect and closeness. **Reciprocity** is the give-and-take that keeps relationships balanced and healthy. It's about both giving support and being willing to receive it, ensuring that the connection is a two-way street.

Transactional vs. Transformational Relationships

Not all relationships are created equal. **Transactional relationships** are based on exchanges—"I'll help you if you help me," or "What can I get from this person?" While these connections may be useful in certain contexts, they rarely lead to deep fulfillment. In contrast, **transformational relationships** are rooted in mutual growth, trust, and genuine care. These are the bonds where both people are changed for the better, supporting each other's dreams, learning from challenges, and celebrating successes together. Transformational relationships are what truly build social wealth, providing not just resources or opportunities but meaning, resilience, and a sense of belonging.

Self-Awareness in Relationships (Link to Book 1)

Lasting connection begins with self-awareness. As explored in *Change That Matters*, knowing your own values, needs, and patterns is essential for building healthy relationships. When you understand your triggers, communication style, and emotional landscape, you can show up more intentionally for others. Self-awareness also helps you recognize when you're falling into old habits—such as withdrawing, people-pleasing, or becoming defensive—and gives you the power to choose a new response. Relationships are mirrors: they reflect not just who others are, but who you are in connection with them. The more you know yourself, the more you can bring your best self to every interaction.

The Four Stages of Building Connection: Curiosity, Consistency, Vulnerability, Reciprocity

Strong relationships don't happen by accident; they're built over time, through a series of stages:

1. **Curiosity:** Every connection begins with curiosity; a genuine interest in another person's story, perspective, or experience. Asking thoughtful questions and listening deeply lays the groundwork for trust.
2. **Consistency:** Relationships deepen through regular, reliable contact. Consistency builds safety and shows you value the connection, whether it's a weekly call, a monthly lunch, or simply checking in with a message.
3. **Vulnerability:** As trust grows, so does the willingness to share more of yourself, your hopes, fears, struggles, and dreams. Vulnerability is the gateway to intimacy and real support, but it requires courage and discernment.
4. **Reciprocity:** The healthiest relationships are balanced. Both people give and receive, support and are supported. Reciprocity ensures that neither party feels used or neglected, and that the relationship remains nourishing for both.

Practical: Moving Beyond Small Talk and Building Depth

Many relationships stall at the surface level—polite greetings, weather updates, or work talk. To move beyond small talk and build depth, try these strategies:

- **Ask open-ended questions:** Instead of "How was your day?" try "What was the best part of your week?" or "What's something you're looking forward to?"
- **Share something real:** Offer a glimpse of your own life—an honest challenge, a recent joy, or a lesson learned. Authenticity invites authenticity.

- **Listen without fixing:** Sometimes, the most powerful gift is simply listening without judgment or advice. Reflect back what you hear and validate the other person's feelings.
- **Follow up:** Remember details from previous conversations and ask about them later. This shows you care and are truly invested in the relationship.
- **Create rituals:** Regular coffee dates, shared hobbies, or group traditions help relationships grow roots.

Chapter Summary

- Trust, empathy, authenticity, and reciprocity are the pillars of lasting connection.
- Transformational relationships, not just transactional ones, are the true source of social wealth.
- Self-awareness is the foundation for healthy, intentional relationships.
- Building connection is a process: curiosity, consistency, vulnerability, and reciprocity.
- Moving beyond small talk means asking better questions, sharing honestly, and listening deeply.

Reflection Questions

Question 1: Which of the four principles—trust, empathy, authenticity, or reciprocity—do you find most natural? Which is most challenging?

Former Student Responses:
- "Empathy comes naturally to me - I can easily understand how others feel, but I struggle with authenticity because I worry about being judged."
- "I'm good at reciprocity and giving back, but trust is hard for me because I've been hurt before."
- "Authenticity feels natural because I hate pretending, but empathy is challenging when people make choices I don't understand."
- "Trust comes easily to me - maybe too easily - but reciprocity is hard because I tend to give more than I receive"
- "I find all of them challenging because I'm naturally guarded and have trouble opening up to people."
- "Empathy and authenticity feel natural, but I struggle with reciprocity because I feel guilty asking for help."

- "Trust and reciprocity come naturally in my family, but empathy and authenticity are harder with colleagues and acquaintances."

Possible Solutions:
- **Authenticity Challenges**: Start small by sharing one genuine thought or feeling daily; practice with low-stakes relationships first; remember that vulnerability invites connection
- **Trust Difficulties**: Begin with small acts of trust; recognize that past hurts don't predict future relationships; consider therapy to work through trust issues
- **Empathy Struggles**: Practice active listening without trying to fix or judge; ask questions to understand different perspectives; remember that empathy doesn't require agreement
- **Reciprocity Issues**: Set boundaries around giving; practice asking for small favors; recognize that receiving help allows others to contribute meaningfully
- **Overall Guardedness**: Start with one principle at a time; find safe people to practice with; remember that connection requires some risk
- **Asking for Help**: Start with small requests; reframe help-seeking as giving others opportunities to contribute; practice gratitude when receiving support

Question 2: Are your key relationships more transactional or transformational? Why?

Former Student Responses:
- "Most of my work relationships are transactional - we help each other when needed, but don't really grow together."
- "My family relationships are transformational, but many of my friendships feel more surface-level and transactional."
- "I think I've been approaching relationships too transactionally - always thinking about what I can get rather than how we can grow together."
- "My closest friendships are transformational - we challenge and support each other's growth - but I wish I had more of these."
- "I'm realizing that some relationships I thought were transformational are actually pretty one-sided and transactional."
- "My romantic relationship is transformational, but I struggle to create that depth with friends and colleagues."
- "I tend to keep relationships transactional because transformational ones feel risky and vulnerable."

Possible Solutions:
- **Workplace Transformation**: Look for opportunities to mentor or be mentored; share personal growth goals with trusted colleagues; create deeper connections through shared projects
- **Family vs. Friends**: Apply the same vulnerability and investment you show family to friendships; seek friends who share your values and growth mindset
- **Transactional Mindset**: Shift focus from "what can I get" to "how can we both grow"; invest in relationships without expecting immediate returns
- **Seeking More Depth**: Join communities focused on personal development; initiate deeper conversations with existing friends; be willing to share your own growth journey.
- **One-Sided Recognition**: Have honest conversations about reciprocity; gradually reduce investment in consistently one-sided relationships
- **Expanding Transformation**: Use skills from your romantic relationship in other connections; practice vulnerability in small ways with friends.
- **Risk Aversion**: Start with small acts of vulnerability; choose trustworthy people for deeper sharing; remember that meaningful relationships require some risk

Question 3: How does your self-awareness shape the way you show up in relationships?

Former Student Responses:
- "I know I'm an introvert, so I make sure to recharge between social events and communicate my needs for alone time."
- "I'm aware that I tend to people-please, which means I often say yes when I should say no, and people don't always know my real opinions."
- "I know I get defensive when criticized, so I'm trying to pause and listen before reacting in difficult conversations."
- "I'm aware that I'm naturally competitive, which can sometimes make others feel like I'm not really listening to them."
- "I know I struggle with vulnerability, so I tend to keep relationships at a surface level even when I want them to be deeper."
- "I'm aware that I'm very direct, which some people appreciate but others find harsh or insensitive."
- "I know I have trust issues from past relationships, so I sometimes hold back even when people haven't given me reason to."

Possible Solutions:
- **Introversion Awareness**: Continue communicating your needs clearly; help others understand that your need for space isn't rejection; schedule social activities during your peak energy times
- **People-Pleasing**: Practice expressing your genuine opinions in low-stakes situations; remember that authentic disagreement can strengthen relationships; set small boundaries daily
- **Defensiveness**: Develop a pause practice before responding to feedback; ask clarifying questions instead of immediately defending; thank people for their honesty
- **Competitiveness**: Practice asking questions about others' experiences; focus on understanding rather than comparing; celebrate others' successes genuinely
- **Vulnerability Struggles**: Share one small, genuine thing about yourself each week; start with people who have already shown trustworthiness; remember that vulnerability builds intimacy
- **Direct Communication**: Learn to soften your delivery while maintaining honesty; ask if people want feedback before giving it; practice empathy alongside directness
- **Trust Issues**: Recognize when past experiences are influencing present relationships; practice giving people the benefit of the doubt; consider therapy to work through trust patterns

Question 4: What's one practical way you could move a relationship beyond small talk this week?

Former Student Responses:
- "I could ask my coworker about their weekend plans and actually listen to the details instead of just saying 'that's nice'"
- "I could share something real about my life with my neighbor instead of just talking about the weather."
- "I could ask my friend about what they're excited about lately instead of just complaining about work together."
- "I could tell my family member about a challenge I'm facing and ask for their perspective."
- "I could ask someone about their goals or dreams instead of just discussing daily logistics."

- "I could share a meaningful experience I had recently and see if they want to share something similar."
- "I could ask follow-up questions about something important they mentioned before instead of moving to a new topic."

Possible Solutions:
- **Deeper Listening**: Put away distractions during conversations; ask follow-up questions like "What was that like for you?" or "How did that make you feel?"
- **Authentic Sharing**: Share a current challenge, recent learning, or something you're grateful for; be genuine about your experiences
- **Future-Focused Questions**: Ask about hopes, dreams, goals, or what they're looking forward to; explore their values and what matters to them
- **Seeking Perspective**: Share a dilemma you're facing and genuinely ask for their thoughts; show that you value their wisdom and experience
- **Values Exploration**: Ask about what's important to them, what they're passionate about, or what gives their life meaning
- **Memory Sharing**: Share a meaningful memory and invite them to share one too; discuss formative experiences or lessons learned
- **Follow-Up Conversations**: Remember details from previous conversations and ask about them; show that you care about their ongoing experiences

Universal Solutions Across All Chapter 3 Questions:

Practice Self-Reflection: Regularly examine your own patterns, triggers, and tendencies in relationships to show up more intentionally.

Start Small: Begin with low-risk relationships when practicing new ways of connecting; build confidence before tackling more challenging relationships.

Focus on Growth: Approach relationships as opportunities for mutual development rather than just sources of comfort or utility.

Embrace Vulnerability: Recognize that authentic connection requires some emotional risk; start with small acts of openness and build gradually.

Balance the Four Principles: Work on developing all four foundations—trust, empathy, authenticity, and reciprocity—rather than relying on just your natural strengths.

Practice Active Curiosity: Ask genuine questions about others' experiences, thoughts, and feelings; show interest in their inner world.

Communicate Your Needs: Use self-awareness to clearly express your relationship needs and boundaries while respecting others'.

Seek Mutual Growth: Look for ways that relationships can help both people become better versions of themselves.

Take Action

- Identify one relationship where you'd like to build more depth. Practice asking open-ended questions and sharing something real.
- Reflect on your own patterns: Where are you most consistent? Where could you show more vulnerability or reciprocity?
- Choose one principle (trust, empathy, authenticity, or reciprocity) to focus on in your interactions this week.

Chapter 4 – Communication Mastery

The Four Communication Styles

Effective relationships are built on clear, respectful communication. Understanding your own style—and recognizing others'—is the first step to connecting deeply and navigating challenges. The four primary communication styles are:

- **Passive:** Avoids expressing needs or opinions, often to keep the peace. Passive communicators may say, "It doesn't matter to me," even when it does. Over time, this can lead to resentment or feeling unheard.
- **Aggressive:** Expresses needs or opinions in a forceful, sometimes disrespectful way. Aggressive communicators may interrupt, blame, or dominate conversations, often leaving others feeling attacked or dismissed.
- **Passive-Aggressive:** Appears passive on the surface but expresses anger or frustration indirectly—through sarcasm, silent treatment, or backhanded comments. This style breeds confusion and mistrust.
- **Assertive:** Clearly and respectfully expresses needs, feelings, and opinions while considering others'. Assertive communicators use "I" statements, listen actively, and seek win-win solutions. This is the healthiest, most effective style for building trust and resolving conflict.

Reflection: Which style do you default to under stress? Which would you like to strengthen?

Listening as a Superpower: Techniques and Scripts

Listening is more than waiting for your turn to speak—it's the foundation of true connection. When you listen deeply, you make others feel valued and understood.

Techniques for Active Listening:

- **Give full attention:** Put away distractions, make eye contact, and show you're present.
- **Reflect and clarify:** Paraphrase what you've heard ("So what I'm hearing is…"), and ask clarifying questions.
- **Validate feelings:** Acknowledge emotions, even if you don't agree ("That sounds really frustrating").
- **Pause before responding:** Give space for the other person's thoughts.

Sample Script: "I hear that you're feeling overwhelmed with work lately. Is there anything I can do to support you?"

Giving and Receiving Feedback

Feedback is essential for growth, but it can be hard to give—and even harder to receive. The key is to focus on behavior, not character, and to approach feedback as a gift, not a weapon.

Giving Feedback:
- Be specific: "When you interrupted me in the meeting, I felt frustrated."
- Focus on impact: "It made it hard for me to share my ideas."
- Offer a path forward: "In the future, could we agree to let each person finish before responding?"

Receiving Feedback:
- Listen without interrupting.
- Ask clarifying questions.
- Thank the person, even if it's hard to hear.
- Reflect before responding or defending.

Handling Conflict: Nonviolent Communication, "I Statements," and Repair Conversations

Conflict is inevitable in any meaningful relationship. The goal isn't to avoid it, but to handle it skillfully.

Nonviolent Communication (NVC):
1. **Observation:** State the facts, without judgment ("When you didn't call…").
2. **Feeling:** Express your emotion ("…I felt worried…").
3. **Need:** Share what you value or need ("…because I care about our plans…").
4. **Request:** Ask for a specific action ("…could you let me know if you'll be late next time?").

Using "I Statements": Instead of "You never listen," try "I feel unheard when I'm interrupted."

Repair Conversations: When things go wrong, initiate repair:
- Acknowledge the rupture ("I realize I hurt you when I…")
- Take responsibility
- Apologize sincerely
- Ask what's needed to move forward

Digital Etiquette: When to Text, Call, or Meet in Person

In our digital age, how you communicate is as important as what you say.
- **Text:** Best for quick updates, logistics, or low-stakes messages. Avoid using text for sensitive or emotionally charged topics.
- **Call:** Use for nuanced conversations, urgent matters, or when tone is important.
- **Meet in Person (or Video):** Choose face-to-face for conflict resolution, deep discussions, or when building trust.

Tip: If a message could be misunderstood, or if emotions are running high, pick up the phone or meet in person.

Practice: Conversation Starters, Reflection, and Repair Scripts

Conversation Starters:
- "What's been the highlight of your week?"
- "What's something you're looking forward to?"
- "Is there anything you wish we had talked about more?"

Reflection:

After a meaningful conversation, ask yourself:
- Did I listen more than I spoke?
- Did I express myself clearly and respectfully?
- Did I check for understanding?

Repair Script:
- "I realize our last conversation didn't go well. I'm sorry for my part in that. Can we talk about how to move forward together?"

Chapter Summary

- Communication mastery starts with understanding your style and striving for assertiveness.
- Active listening is the foundation of connection—practice giving your full attention and validating others' feelings.
- Give and receive feedback with clarity and compassion.
- Handle conflict with nonviolent communication, "I statements," and timely repair.
- Match your communication method to the message: sensitive topics deserve a call or an in-person meeting.
- Use scripts and reflection to build confidence and depth in every conversation.

Reflection Questions

Question 1: Which communication style do you use most often? Which would you like to strengthen?

Former Student Responses:
- "I'm definitely passive - I avoid expressing my needs because I don't want to create conflict or upset anyone."
- "I tend to be aggressive when I'm stressed, especially with my family, and I feel terrible about it afterward."
- "I'm passive-aggressive - I say everything is fine but then get resentful when people don't read my mind"
- "I try to be assertive but sometimes come across as aggressive, especially in professional settings."
- "I switch between passive and aggressive depending on the situation, which confuses people."
- "I'm not sure which style I use - I think it depends on who I'm talking to."
- "I want to be more assertive, but I'm afraid people will think I'm being demanding or selfish."

Possible Solutions:
- **Passive Communicators**: Practice expressing one small preference daily; use "I" statements to share feelings; remember that your needs matter too
- **Aggressive Tendencies**: Pause before responding when emotional; practice lowering your voice; focus on the issue, not the person
- **Passive-Aggressive Patterns**: Practice direct communication in low-stakes situations; express needs clearly rather than expecting others to guess
- **Assertiveness Development**: Learn the difference between assertive and aggressive; practice scripts for common situations; focus on win-win solutions
- **Inconsistent Styles**: Identify triggers that cause style changes; work on maintaining assertiveness across all relationships
- **Style Uncertainty**: Ask trusted friends for feedback; observe your communication patterns for a week; notice how others respond to you
- **Assertiveness Fears**: Start with small requests; remember that assertiveness shows respect for both yourself and others; practice with supportive people first

Question 2: When was the last time you truly listened without planning your response?

Former Student Responses:
- "I can't remember - I'm always thinking about what I'm going to say next."
- "I listen better with some people than others, but I struggle when the topic is something I have strong opinions about."
- "I think I'm a good listener, but my family says I interrupt them a lot."
- "I get distracted by my phone or other thoughts even when someone is talking to me."
- "I listen well when people are sharing problems, but not so much during casual conversations."
- "I realize I listen to respond rather than to understand."
- "I'm better at listening to strangers than to people close to me."

Possible Solutions:
- **Chronic Response Planning**: Practice the "pause" - count to three before responding; focus on understanding rather than being understood
- **Opinion-Triggered Distraction**: Notice when you stop listening and gently redirect attention back to the speaker; ask clarifying questions instead of arguing
- **Interrupting Habits**: Put your hand over your mouth as a physical reminder; wait for clear pauses before speaking; apologize when you catch yourself interrupting.
- **Digital Distractions**: Put devices away during conversations; make eye contact; use body language to show engagement
- **Selective Listening**: Practice active listening in all conversations, not just serious ones; value casual connection as much as problem-solving
- **Response-Focused Listening**: Shift your goal from "what should I say?" to "what are they really trying to tell me?"
- **Familiarity Bias**: Give loved ones the same attention you'd give a new acquaintance; don't assume you know what they're going to say

Question 3: How do you typically give and receive feedback? What could you improve?

Former Student Responses:
- "I avoid giving feedback because I don't want to hurt people's feelings."

- "I get defensive immediately when someone gives me feedback, even when they're trying to help."
- "I give feedback, but I'm probably too blunt and don't consider how it affects the other person."
- "I take all feedback as personal criticism, even when it's about my work."
- "I give feedback but then feel guilty about it and try to take it back."
- "I'm better at receiving feedback than giving it - I'm afraid of conflict."
- "I give feedback in the moment when I'm emotional, which doesn't go well."

Possible Solutions:
- **Feedback Avoidance**: Start with positive feedback to build comfort; use the "sandwich method" (positive-constructive-positive); remember that withholding helpful feedback isn't kind
- **Defensive Reactions**: Practice saying "thank you for the feedback" before responding; ask clarifying questions; take time to process before reacting
- **Blunt Delivery**: Focus on specific behaviors rather than personality; ask permission before giving feedback; consider timing and setting
- **Personal Criticism Interpretation**: Separate your identity from your actions; ask for specific examples; focus on what you can learn and improve
- **Guilt After Feedback**: Remember that honest feedback is a gift; check your motivation (helping vs. hurting); follow up to ensure understanding
- **Conflict Avoidance**: Practice giving feedback in low-stakes situations; focus on the relationship benefits of honest communication
- **Emotional Timing**: Implement a 24-hour rule for difficult feedback; practice calming techniques; focus on the behavior's impact rather than your emotions

Question 4: Is there a conversation you've been avoiding that could benefit from these tools?

Former Student Responses:
- "I need to talk to my manager about my workload, but I'm afraid they'll think I can't handle my job."
- "I should address my roommate's cleanliness habits, but I don't want to create tension in our living situation."
- "I need to have a conversation with my adult child about their financial decisions."
- "I've been avoiding talking to my partner about our different communication styles."

- "I should give feedback to a team member whose performance is affecting our projects."
- "I need to discuss boundaries with my mother-in-law about her involvement in our marriage."
- "I've been putting off a conversation with my friend about how they always cancel plans last minute."

Possible Solutions:
- **Workload Conversation**: Frame it as seeking solutions, not complaining; come with specific examples and potential solutions; emphasize your commitment to quality work
- **Roommate Issues**: Use "I" statements about how the situation affects you; suggest specific solutions; focus on creating a comfortable living environment for both
- **Parent-Adult Child Dynamics**: Approach with love and concern, not judgment; ask questions about their perspective; offer support rather than ultimatums
- **Partner Communication**: Schedule a calm time to discuss; focus on improving the relationship; use specific examples and avoid generalizations
- **Team Performance**: Document specific instances; focus on impact on team goals; offer support and resources for improvement
- **In-Law Boundaries**: Have your partner lead the conversation; be specific about what needs to change; emphasize your desire for a positive relationship
- **Friend Reliability**: Express how the cancellations affect you; ask if there's something you can do to help; be prepared to adjust your expectations

Universal Solutions Across All Chapter 4 Questions:

Practice Active Listening: Put away distractions, make eye contact, and focus on understanding rather than responding.
Develop Assertiveness Skills: Learn to express your needs clearly and respectfully while considering others' perspectives.
Master the Art of Feedback: Give specific, behavior-focused feedback with care, and receive feedback with curiosity rather than defensiveness.
Choose the Right Medium: Match your communication method to the message - sensitive topics deserve face-to-face or phone conversations.
Use "I" Statements: Express your feelings and needs without blaming or attacking the other person.

Practice Repair: When conversations go poorly, take responsibility for your part and work together to move forward.

Prepare for Difficult Conversations: Think through your main points, consider the other person's perspective, and choose appropriate timing and setting.

Build Communication Habits: Regular check-ins, appreciation expressions, and conflict resolution skills become easier with practice.

Take Action

- Practice active listening in your next conversation: put away distractions and reflect back what you hear.
- Use an "I statement" to express a need or feeling this week.
- Identify one digital conversation that would be better handled by phone or in person, and make it happen.
- Try one conversation starter or repair script with someone you care about.

Chapter 5 – Boundaries, Energy, and Healthy Relationships

Why Boundaries Matter for Social and Emotional Health

Healthy relationships don't just happen—they are built and maintained through clear boundaries. Boundaries are the invisible lines that define what is acceptable and what is not, both for yourself and others. They protect your emotional well-being, preserve your time and energy, and ensure that your needs are respected. Without boundaries, it's easy to become overwhelmed, resentful, or even burned out by the demands of others. Setting boundaries is not about shutting people out; it's about making space for genuine connection and mutual respect. When you communicate your limits with care, you create the foundation for trust and lasting, healthy relationships.

Scripts for Saying "No" and Setting Limits with Care

Saying "no" can feel uncomfortable, especially if you're used to prioritizing others' needs above your own. Yet, learning to say no is essential for protecting your energy and honoring your commitments. Here are a few scripts to help you set limits with kindness and clarity:

- "Thank you for thinking of me, but I can't commit to that right now."
- "I appreciate the invitation, but I need to focus on my current priorities."
- "I'd love to help, but my schedule is full this week. Can we revisit this another time?"
- "That doesn't work for me, but I hope you find the support you need."

Remember, you don't owe anyone a lengthy explanation. A polite, direct response is enough. Practice these scripts until they feel natural, and notice how your confidence grows as you protect your boundaries.

The Relationship Energy Budget: Allocating Time and Attention Intentionally

Just as you budget your money, you must also budget your energy and attention. Every relationship requires an investment of time, emotion, and presence. Some connections are energizing and restorative, while others can be draining or one-sided. Take stock of where your energy goes each week:

- Who leaves you feeling uplifted, inspired, or supported?
- Who consistently drains your energy or leaves you feeling depleted?
- Are you investing in relationships that align with your values and goals?

Try this exercise: List your key relationships and rate each from 1 (draining) to 10 (energizing). Aim to spend more time with those who fill your cup and less with those who empty it. If you notice a pattern of one-sided giving, consider whether the relationship needs to be rebalanced or, in some cases, released.

Recognizing and Addressing Toxic or One-Sided Relationships

Not all relationships are healthy. Some may become toxic, marked by manipulation, disrespect, or chronic negativity. Others may be simply one-sided, where you give far more than you receive. Signs of a toxic or draining relationship include:
- Feeling anxious or exhausted after interactions
- Being consistently criticized, dismissed, or controlled
- Having your boundaries ignored or violated
- Experiencing guilt or obligation rather than a genuine connection

Addressing these relationships requires courage. Start by communicating your needs and boundaries clearly. If the other person is unwilling or unable to respect them, it may be necessary to distance yourself or seek support from others. Remember: You are not responsible for fixing or carrying someone else's emotional burdens at the expense of your own well-being.

Case Study: Recovering from Burnout by Resetting Boundaries

Consider "Anna," a dedicated professional and friend who found herself constantly saying yes to every request, at work, at home, and in her community. Over time, she became exhausted, resentful, and disconnected from her own needs. After reaching a breaking point, Anna decided to audit her commitments and relationships. She identified the most draining connections and began practicing saying "no" using simple, respectful scripts. She also scheduled regular downtime and prioritized relationships that were mutually supportive. Within a few months, Anna felt more energized, present, and fulfilled. Her relationships improved—not because she did more, but because she invested her energy where it mattered most.

Action: Boundary-Setting Checklist

Use this checklist to strengthen your boundaries and protect your energy:
- Identify your top three energy-draining relationships or commitments.

- Practice saying "no" using a script that feels natural to you.
- Schedule regular time for self-care and restorative activities.
- Communicate your boundaries clearly and calmly, without apology.
- Reassess relationships that remain one-sided or toxic—even if it means stepping back.
- Celebrate each time you uphold a boundary, no matter how small.

Chapter Summary

- Boundaries are essential for social and emotional health; they protect your time, energy, and well-being.
- Saying "no" with care is a skill that can be learned and practiced.
- Treat your relationships like an energy budget—invest in those that nourish you, and limit those that drain you.
- Recognize and address toxic or one-sided relationships with clarity and courage.
- Resetting boundaries can lead to greater fulfillment, resilience, and deeper, healthier connections.

Reflection Questions

Question 1: Where in your life do you need stronger boundaries?

Former Student Responses:
- "I need boundaries with work - I check emails constantly and work weekends."
- "My family expects me to be available 24/7 for every crisis or favor."
- "I say yes to every social invitation, even when I'm exhausted."
- "I let friends vent to me for hours but never share my own struggles."
- "I give too much time to people who drain my energy."
- "I struggle to say no to volunteer commitments at church or school."
- "I don't protect my personal time for self-care and hobbies."

Possible Solutions:
- **Work Boundaries**: Set specific work hours and communicate them clearly; turn off work notifications after hours; create physical separation between work and personal spaces
- **Family Expectations**: Have honest conversations about your availability; suggest alternative solutions; set specific times when you're available to help

- **Social Over-Commitment**: Practice saying "I need to check my calendar and get back to you"; choose quality over quantity in social activities
- **One-Sided Support**: Set limits on venting sessions; practice asking for reciprocal support; redirect conversations to solutions rather than just problems
- **Energy Management**: Limit time with draining people; schedule recovery time after difficult interactions; prioritize relationships that energize you
- **Volunteer Overload**: Choose one cause to focus on rather than spreading yourself thin; set term limits for commitments; remember that saying no allows others to contribute
- **Personal Time Protection**: Schedule self-care like important appointments; communicate your needs to family and friends; start with small boundaries and build up

Question 2: Which relationships energize you, and which ones drain you?

Former Student Responses:
- "My best friend always makes me feel heard and supported, but my coworker constantly complains."
- "My mentor challenges me to grow, but my neighbor only gossips and creates drama."
- "My workout buddy motivates me, but some family members are always negative."
- "My book club friends inspire me, but my old college friends just want to party."
- "My business partner pushes me to be better, but my brother is pessimistic about everything."
- "My faith community lifts me up, but certain relatives criticize all my choices."
- "My spouse energizes me, but my mother-in-law makes me feel inadequate."

Possible Solutions:
- **Energy Givers**: Prioritize spending more time with these people; express gratitude for their support; reciprocate their positive energy; schedule regular connection time
- **Energy Drainers**: Set boundaries with time and emotional investment; limit exposure when possible; practice not taking their negativity personally; redirect conversations to positive topics
- **Mixed Family Relationships**: Accept that you can't change family members; focus on protecting your energy during interactions; find ways to appreciate their positive qualities while maintaining boundaries

- **Friend Group Evaluation**: Choose activities and gatherings that align with your current values and goals; it's okay to outgrow certain friendships
- **Professional Relationships**: Limit personal conversations with negative colleagues; find positive mentors and collaborators; create boundaries around work relationships
- **Community Connections**: Invest more time in communities that share your values and support your growth; reduce involvement in groups that consistently drain you

Question 3: What is one commitment or request you can say "no" to this week?

Former Student Responses:
- "I could decline the extra project my boss hinted at since I'm already overwhelmed."
- "I could say no to hosting the family dinner this weekend and suggest we order takeout instead."
- "I could skip the networking event, I don't really want to attend."
- "I could decline my friend's request to help them move since I just helped them last month."
- "I could say no to chaperoning the school field trip since I've done it three times this year."
- "I could decline the invitation to a party where I won't know anyone."
- "I could say no to taking on another volunteer role at church."

Possible Solutions:
- **Work Requests**: Use phrases like "I want to give quality work, and taking this on would compromise my current projects"; suggest alternative timelines or resources
- **Family Obligations**: Offer alternatives that still show care but require less of your energy; communicate your current capacity honestly
- **Social Events**: Remember that declining doesn't require a detailed explanation; "That doesn't work for me this time" is sufficient
- **Friend Favors**: Set boundaries around how often you help; suggest they ask other friends or hire professionals; offer emotional support instead of physical help.
- **School/Community Involvement**: Rotate responsibilities with other parents; suggest someone else who might benefit from the opportunity
- **Uncomfortable Social Situations**: Trust your instincts about events that won't serve you; suggest alternative ways to connect with the host

- **Additional Commitments**: Remember that saying yes to new things means saying no to current priorities; evaluate whether the new commitment aligns with your values and goals

Question 4: How do you feel after practicing a boundary-setting script?

Former Student Responses:
- "I felt guilty at first, but then relieved that I was honest about my limits."
- "It was scary to say no, but the person was actually understanding."
- "I felt empowered and more in control of my time and energy."
- "I was surprised that setting a boundary didn't damage the relationship."
- "I felt anxious before, but proud of myself afterward."
- "It was easier than I expected once I actually said the words."
- "I realized that most people respect boundaries when they're communicated clearly."

Possible Solutions:
- **Initial Guilt**: Remember that guilt is normal when changing patterns; the discomfort will decrease with practice; remind yourself that boundaries benefit both parties
- **Fear Response**: Start with low-stakes situations to build confidence; prepare scripts in advance; practice with supportive friends first
- **Empowerment**: Celebrate this feeling and use it as motivation to continue setting healthy boundaries; document how good it feels to honor your limits
- **Relationship Concerns**: Notice that healthy relationships actually improve with clear boundaries; people who respect your boundaries are worth keeping close
- **Anxiety Management**: Use breathing techniques before difficult conversations; remind yourself that you have the right to protect your energy
- **Confidence Building**: Each successful boundary-setting experience builds confidence for future situations; keep a record of positive outcomes
- **Respect Recognition**: Most people appreciate honesty and clarity; those who don't respect boundaries may not be the right people for your life

Question 5: What would your life look like if you consistently honored your own limits?

Former Student Responses:
- "I'd probably be less stressed and more present with the people I care about most."
- "I'd have more energy for my goals and the relationships that really matter."
- "I'd feel more authentic and less resentful in my interactions."
- "I'd be a better friend, partner, and parent because I wouldn't be constantly overwhelmed."
- "I'd have time for self-care and personal interests again."
- "I'd feel more confident and in control of my life."
- "I'd attract healthier relationships because I'd be modeling self-respect."

Possible Solutions:
- **Stress Reduction**: Continue practicing boundaries to create this reality; notice how each boundary reduces overall stress levels
- **Energy Management**: Use the energy you save from boundaries to invest in your most important relationships and goals
- **Authenticity**: Recognize that boundaries allow you to show up as your true self rather than a depleted version
- **Better Relationships**: Understand that taking care of yourself enables you to care better for others; model healthy boundaries for your family
- **Personal Time**: Schedule self-care and personal interests like important appointments; protect this time as fiercely as you would work commitments
- **Confidence Building**: Each boundary you maintain builds self-respect and confidence; this positive cycle reinforces healthy patterns
- **Relationship Quality**: Notice how boundaries attract people who respect you and filter out those who don't; this improves the overall quality of your social circle

Universal Solutions Across All Chapter 5 Questions:

Start Small: Begin with low-stakes boundary-setting situations to build confidence before tackling more challenging relationships.
Use Clear Communication: Be direct and honest about your limits without over-explaining or apologizing excessively.
Practice Self-Compassion: Remember that learning to set boundaries is a skill that takes time to develop; be patient with yourself.
Expect Resistance: Some people may push back against your boundaries initially; this is normal and doesn't mean you should abandon them.

Focus on Your Energy: Regularly assess which relationships and commitments energize versus drain you, and adjust accordingly.

Create Support Systems: Surround yourself with people who respect and encourage your boundary-setting efforts.

Celebrate Progress: Acknowledge each successful boundary-setting experience as a victory for your well-being and growth.

Remember Your Why: Connect boundary-setting to your larger goals and values to maintain motivation during difficult moments.

Take Action

- Complete the energy budget exercise and boundary-setting checklist.
- Choose one relationship or commitment to set a clear boundary with this week.
- Reflect on the results and adjust as needed.
- Remember: Healthy boundaries are a gift to yourself—and to those who truly value you.

Chapter 6 – Community, Belonging, and Social Capital

The Three Types of Community: Geographic, Interest-Based, and Values-Based

Community is more than just a group of people—it's a sense of belonging, shared purpose, and mutual support. There are three main types of communities that can enrich your life:

- **Geographic Community:** The people who live near you—neighbors, local businesses, and civic groups. These connections foster a sense of place and provide practical support in daily life.
- **Interest-Based Community:** Groups formed around shared hobbies, passions, or professions, like book clubs, sports teams, professional associations, or online forums. These communities spark creativity and growth by connecting you with like-minded individuals.
- **Values-Based Community:** Connections built on shared beliefs, causes, or missions, such as faith groups, advocacy organizations, or volunteer teams. Values-based communities offer deep meaning and a sense of contributing to something bigger than yourself.

A thriving life often draws from all three types, offering both rootedness and diversity.

How to Find or Build Your Tribe

Finding your "tribe" means seeking out people who energize, inspire, and support you. Here's how to get started:

- **Join Meetups and Groups:** Look for local or online meetups around your interests. Attend regularly to build familiarity and trust.
- **Participate in Masterminds:** Join or create a mastermind group—a small, committed circle that meets regularly to share goals, challenges, and support.
- **Volunteer:** Service is a powerful way to connect with others who share your values and to build relationships through shared action.
- **Engage in Faith or Spiritual Communities:** If relevant, faith groups offer belonging, shared rituals, and a support network.

- **Start Something New:** If you can't find the community you crave, consider starting a group—whether it's a book club, hiking circle, or online forum.

Tip: Building community takes time and vulnerability. Show up consistently, offer help, and be open to new connections.

The Role of Rituals, Traditions, and Shared Experiences

Rituals and traditions—whether weekly dinners, annual retreats, or simple check-in calls—are the glue that holds communities together. Shared experiences, even small ones, deepen bonds and create lasting memories. Consider:
- Hosting a monthly potluck or game night
- Celebrating birthdays and milestones together
- Creating annual traditions, like a volunteer day or group trip
- Establishing regular check-ins, even if just a text or call

These rituals build trust, foster belonging, and make your community resilient through life's ups and downs.

The Importance of Diversity and Bridging Social Capital

A strong community isn't just about similarity—it's about diversity. Seek out connections with people of different backgrounds, ages, professions, and perspectives. This "bridging social capital" expands your worldview, sparks innovation, and makes your network more resilient.

- **Bridging vs. Bonding:** Bonding capital is the trust within close-knit groups; bridging capital connects you to new ideas and opportunities.
- **Action:** Attend events or join groups outside your usual circles. Be curious and open-minded—you never know where your next great friendship or insight will come from.

Reflection: What Kind of Community Do You Crave?

Take a moment to reflect:
- Which type of community—geographic, interest-based, or values-based—do you feel most connected to right now?
- Where do you wish you had more belonging, support, or inspiration?
- What kind of people energize and challenge you? Who do you want to spend more time with?

Action: Community Blueprint Exercise

Design your ideal community using these steps:
1. **List the qualities you value in a community** (e.g., supportive, diverse, fun, purposeful).
2. **Identify the types of groups or communities you'd like to join or create.**
3. **Write down one action you'll take this month** to move closer to your ideal—whether it's attending a meetup, reaching out to a neighbor, or starting a new tradition.

Template:

Community Type	Group/Activity	Action to Take
Geographic	Neighborhood potluck	Invite 3 neighbors
Interest-Based	Local hiking club	Attend the next group hike
Values-Based	Volunteer at the shelter	Sign up for orientation

Chapter Summary

- Community comes in many forms: geographic, interest-based, and values-based.
- Finding or building your tribe takes intention, consistency, and openness.
- Rituals, traditions, and shared experiences deepen bonds and foster belonging.
- Diversity and bridging social capital make your network stronger and more innovative.
- Designing your ideal community starts with reflection and one small action.

Reflection Questions

Based on Chapter 6's reflection questions from "Relationships That Matter," here are student responses and corresponding solutions:

Question 1: Which type of community do you feel most drawn to right now?

Former Student Responses:
- "I'm most drawn to values-based community because I want to be around people who share my beliefs about making a positive impact."

- "Interest-based community appeals to me - I want to connect with people who share my passion for hiking and outdoor activities."
- "I feel most connected to geographic community right now because I want to know my neighbors and feel rooted in my local area."
- "I'm drawn to professional communities where I can grow my career and learn from others in my field."
- "I want a mix of all three types, but I'm not sure how to balance them or where to start."
- "I'm most interested in spiritual or faith-based community because I'm seeking deeper meaning in my life."
- "I want to find a creative community where I can express myself and be inspired by other artists."

Possible Solutions:
- **Values-Based Focus**: Research local volunteer organizations, advocacy groups, or faith communities that align with your core beliefs; attend their events or meetings to explore fit
- **Interest-Based Connection**: Join local clubs, meetups, or online groups focused on your hobbies; attend regular activities to build familiarity and friendships.
- **Geographic Community**: Attend neighborhood association meetings, organize block parties, or participate in local events; introduce yourself to neighbors during daily activities
- **Professional Development**: Join industry associations, attend networking events, or participate in professional development groups; seek mentorship opportunities within your field
- **Multiple Community Types**: Start with one type that feels most natural, then gradually expand; look for communities that might overlap multiple categories
- **Spiritual Seeking**: Visit different faith communities, meditation groups, or spiritual discussion circles; explore what resonates with your beliefs and values
- **Creative Expression**: Join art classes, writing groups, maker spaces, or online creative communities; participate in local arts events or open mic nights

Question 2: Where are you craving more connection, support, or inspiration?

Former Student Responses:
- "I need more professional support - I feel isolated in my career and don't have mentors or colleagues to learn from."

- "I'm craving emotional support from people who understand my struggles with anxiety and mental health."
- "I want more inspiration from people who are pursuing creative goals like I am."
- "I need practical support as a new parent - other parents who can share advice and understanding."
- "I'm looking for spiritual connection and people who share my faith journey."
- "I want more social connection - I've been isolated since moving to a new city."
- "I need accountability and motivation from people working on similar health and fitness goals."

Possible Solutions:
- **Professional Support**: Join industry associations, seek out mentorship programs, attend professional development workshops, or create informal coffee meetings with colleagues
- **Mental Health Community**: Look for support groups, therapy groups, or online communities focused on mental wellness; consider apps like 7 Cups or local NAMI chapters
- **Creative Inspiration**: Join artist collectives, writing groups, maker spaces, or online creative communities; attend gallery openings, poetry readings, or creative workshops
- **Parenting Support**: Join new parent groups, attend library story times, connect with other parents at playgrounds, or use apps like Peanut to find parent friends
- **Spiritual Connection**: Visit different faith communities, join Bible studies or spiritual discussion groups, attend retreats, or find online spiritual communities
- **Social Integration**: Use apps like Meetup or Bumble BFF, join hobby groups, take classes, volunteer, or attend community events regularly
- **Health Accountability**: Join fitness classes, running groups, weight loss support groups, or use apps with social features like MyFitnessPal or Strava

Question 3: What's one ritual or tradition you could start or join to deepen your sense of belonging?

Former Student Responses:
- "I could start hosting monthly potluck dinners for my neighbors to build community in my apartment building."
- "I want to join a weekly book club to connect with people who love reading as much as I do."

- "I could start a tradition of volunteering at the local food bank with my family every month."
- "I'd like to join a weekly hiking group to combine my love of nature with meeting new people."
- "I could start hosting game nights for my friends to create regular connection time."
- "I want to join a faith community's weekly service and small group meetings."
- "I could start a tradition of calling my elderly relatives every Sunday to strengthen family bonds."

Possible Solutions:
- **Neighborhood Potlucks**: Start small with 3-4 neighbors, rotate hosting duties, create a simple sign-up system for dishes, and make it a monthly recurring event
- **Book Club Participation**: Research existing clubs at libraries or bookstores, or start your own with friends; choose accessible books and create discussion questions
- **Family Volunteering**: Research local organizations that welcome families, schedule regular volunteer times, and make it a learning experience for children
- **Outdoor Groups**: Join existing hiking meetups, start with easier trails, bring extra water to share, and suggest post-hike coffee or meals
- **Game Night Hosting**: Choose simple, inclusive games, provide snacks, create a regular schedule (like the first Friday of each month), and rotate game selection
- **Faith Community Involvement**: Visit different congregations to find the right fit, participate in small groups or committees, and volunteer for community service projects
- **Family Connection Rituals**: Schedule calls at consistent times, prepare conversation topics in advance, and include multiple family members when possible

Question 4: How can you bring more diversity and new perspectives into your network?

Former Student Responses:
- "I realize most of my friends are from my same profession and background - I need to branch out."
- "I want to connect with people from different cultural backgrounds to learn about their experiences."

- "I'd like to build relationships with people of different ages - I mostly hang out with people my own age."
- "I want to connect with people who have different political or philosophical views to challenge my thinking."
- "I need to include people from different socioeconomic backgrounds in my social circle."
- "I'd like to connect with people who have different life experiences - different family structures, career paths, etc."
- "I want to build relationships across racial and ethnic lines in my predominantly homogeneous community."

Possible Solutions:
- **Professional Diversity**: Attend cross-industry networking events, join professional associations outside your field, or participate in community business groups
- **Cultural Connections**: Attend cultural festivals, join language exchange programs, participate in international student programs, or visit diverse places of worship
- **Age Diversity**: Volunteer with organizations that serve different age groups, join intergenerational programs, or participate in mentoring relationships
- **Ideological Diversity**: Join discussion groups focused on civil discourse, attend community forums, or participate in book clubs that explore different perspectives
- **Socioeconomic Bridging**: Volunteer with organizations serving different economic communities, participate in community service projects, or join mixed-income community groups
- **Life Experience Variety**: Join support groups for different life stages, participate in community education programs, or volunteer with diverse populations
- **Racial and Ethnic Diversity**: Attend community events in diverse neighborhoods, join multicultural organizations, or participate in racial justice or cultural competency programs

Question 5: What would help you feel more connected and supported in your daily life?

Former Student Responses:
- "I need people I can call when I'm having a bad day who will just listen without trying to fix everything."

- "I want regular social activities that I can count on - something consistent in my schedule."
- "I need practical support - people who can help with childcare, pet care, or household tasks when needed."
- "I want deeper conversations with people instead of always talking about surface-level things."
- "I need accountability partners who will check in on my goals and encourage me to keep going."
- "I want to feel useful and needed - ways to contribute to others' lives meaningfully."
- "I need a sense of belonging somewhere - a place where people know my name and care about me."

Possible Solutions:
- **Emotional Support Network**: Cultivate 2-3 close friendships through regular check-ins, practice vulnerability in small steps, and be the kind of listener you want to have
- **Consistent Social Structure**: Join weekly classes, clubs, or groups; create recurring social plans like monthly dinners; establish regular check-in calls with friends
- **Practical Support Systems**: Build reciprocal relationships with neighbors, join parent networks for childcare swaps, or create informal mutual aid groups
- **Meaningful Conversations**: Practice asking deeper questions, share something personal about yourself, and create environments conducive to real talk (walks, quiet cafes)
- **Accountability Partnerships**: Find goal-oriented friends, join mastermind groups, or use apps that connect you with accountability partners
- **Service Opportunities**: Volunteer regularly, mentor someone, offer your skills to help others, or join community improvement projects
- **Belonging Spaces**: Find a "third place" (not home or work) where you're a regular, join small groups where attendance matters, or create traditions that bring people together

Universal Solutions Across All Chapter 6 Questions:

Start Small and Consistent: Choose one type of community connection to focus on initially, then gradually expand your involvement and commitment.

Be Patient with Community Building: Meaningful connections and a sense of belonging take time to develop; show up consistently even when it feels awkward at first.

Contribute Before You Receive: Look for ways to add value to communities and relationships rather than focusing primarily on what you can get.

Embrace Discomfort: Stepping outside your usual social circles may feel uncomfortable initially, but this discomfort often leads to growth and new perspectives.

Create What You Seek: If you can't find the community you want, consider starting it yourself; others are likely looking for the same connections.

Practice Inclusive Behavior: Welcome newcomers, introduce people to each other, and help create the kind of inclusive environment you want to experience.

Balance Online and Offline: Use digital tools to find communities, but prioritize face-to-face interactions for deeper relationship building.

Maintain Multiple Communities: Don't put all your social needs on one group; cultivate diverse communities that serve different aspects of your life and growth.

Take Action

- Complete the community blueprint exercise.
- Reach out to one person or group you'd like to connect with this month.
- Start or join a new ritual, tradition, or shared experience.
- Reflect on how your sense of belonging shifts as you take these steps.

Chapter 7 – Relationships in the Digital Age

Navigating Social Media: Connection vs. Comparison

Social media has revolutionized the way we connect, making it possible to maintain relationships across distances and discover new communities with just a click. Yet, this constant connectivity comes with a hidden cost: the temptation to compare your life to the carefully curated highlight reels of others. While platforms like Facebook, Instagram, and LinkedIn can foster genuine connections, they can also fuel feelings of inadequacy, envy, or loneliness if you measure your worth against others' posts.

To use social media as a tool for connection rather than comparison, be mindful of your emotional responses. Ask yourself: "Does this interaction make me feel inspired and connected, or drained and less-than?" If you notice negative patterns, take a break, unfollow certain accounts, or limit your time online. Remember, a real connection is built on authenticity, not appearances.

Curating Your Digital Network: Unfollow, Mute, Prioritize

Your digital environment shapes your mindset just as much as your physical one. Take ownership of your online experience by curating your network:

- **Unfollow or mute** accounts that bring negativity, drama, or distraction into your feed.
- **Prioritize** connections that uplift, encourage, and align with your values.
- **Organize** your contacts into lists or groups so you can focus on meaningful interactions.
- **Review** your network regularly; relationships evolve, and so should your digital circles.

By intentionally shaping your digital environment, you make space for more positive, supportive, and energizing connections.

Maintaining Intimacy and Authenticity Online

It's possible to build deep, authentic relationships online—but it requires intention. Move beyond "likes" and surface-level comments by:

- Sending personal messages or voice notes to check in on friends.
- Scheduling regular video calls or virtual coffee dates.
- Sharing honestly about your own experiences, not just your achievements.
- Participating in online communities or groups where vulnerability and support are encouraged.

Remember, authenticity invites authenticity. When you show up as your real self, others are more likely to do the same.

Digital Boundaries: Tech for Connection, Not Distraction

Technology should serve your relationships, not sabotage them. Set digital boundaries to ensure your devices help you connect, rather than distract:

- **Designate "phone-free" times** (meals, family time, before bed) to be fully present.
- **Turn off notifications** for non-essential apps.
- **Communicate your boundaries** with others (e.g., "I don't check messages after 8 p.m.").
- **Use "Do Not Disturb" or focus modes** during deep work or quality time.

By setting clear boundaries, you reclaim your attention and show respect to the people you're with, both online and offline.

Digital Detox Challenge: Reclaiming Presence

If you feel overwhelmed by digital noise, try a digital detox:

- Choose a day (or even a few hours) to unplug from social media, email, and news.
- Use that time to connect with someone face-to-face, pursue a hobby, or simply rest.
- Notice how your mood, focus, and sense of connection shift.

A regular digital detox can help you reset your habits, reduce stress, and remind you of the value of real-world relationships.

Tool: App Comparison Chart for Intentional Connection

App/Platform	Best For	Connection Features	Potential Pitfalls
WhatsApp/Signal	Private messaging, groups	Voice/video calls, group chat	It can become overwhelming if there are too many groups
Zoom/Google Meet	Video calls, virtual meetups	Screen sharing, breakout rooms	"Zoom fatigue" from overuse
Facebook Groups	Community, shared interests	Events, group discussions	Distraction from the main feed

Slack/Discord	Professional or hobby communities	Channels, DMs, integrations	Notification overload
Marco Polo	Video messaging	Asynchronous, personal	Less immediate than live chat
Instagram	Visual storytelling	DMs, stories, comments	Comparison, curated feeds

Choose platforms that match your communication style and relational goals. Prioritize quality over quantity.

Chapter Summary

- Social media can connect or isolate—use it consciously to foster real relationships, not comparison.
- Curate your digital network by unfollowing, muting, and prioritizing connections that support your well-being.
- Authenticity and intimacy are possible online if you move beyond surface-level interactions.
- Set digital boundaries so technology serves your relationships, not the other way around.
- Regular digital detoxes help you reclaim your presence and deepen real-world connections.
- Choose digital tools intentionally—let them enhance, not replace, meaningful connection.

Reflection Questions

Based on Chapter 7's reflection questions from "Relationships That Matter," here are student responses and corresponding solutions:

Question 1: How does social media impact your sense of connection and self-worth?

Former Student Responses:
- "I find myself comparing my life to others' highlight reels and feeling inadequate afterwards."
- "Social media helps me stay connected with distant friends, but I often feel drained after scrolling."

- "I get caught up in seeking likes and validation, which makes me feel anxious when posts don't perform well."
- "I love connecting with like-minded communities online, but I spend too much time on my phone."
- "Social media makes me feel FOMO (fear of missing out) when I see others' experiences."
- "I use it to stay informed and connected, but sometimes the negativity and drama overwhelm me."
- "I feel more connected to acquaintances but less connected to close friends because we interact less in person."

Possible Solutions:
- **Comparison Issues**: Curate your feed to follow accounts that inspire rather than trigger comparison; unfollow accounts that consistently make you feel inadequate; practice gratitude for your own journey
- **Connection vs. Drain**: Set specific times for social media use; use it intentionally for connection rather than mindless scrolling; balance online interaction with face-to-face conversations
- **Validation Seeking**: Focus on creating content that reflects your authentic self rather than what gets likes; limit checking metrics; find validation through real-world relationships and personal achievements.
- **Screen Time Concerns**: Use app timers to limit daily usage; create phone-free zones and times; replace some social media time with in-person activities
- **FOMO Management**: Remember that social media shows curated highlights, not full reality; focus on your own goals and experiences; practice contentment with your current situation
- **Negativity Overload**: Unfollow or mute accounts that spread negativity; limit news consumption; seek out positive, uplifting content
- **Surface-Level Connections**: Use social media as a starting point for deeper conversations; prioritize quality interactions over quantity; schedule regular in-person meetups with close friends

Question 2: Who in your digital network energizes and supports you? Who drains you?

Former Student Responses:
- "My college friends' group chat always makes me laugh and feel supported."
- "I follow several motivational speakers and entrepreneurs who inspire me to grow."

- "My family WhatsApp group can be overwhelming with constant messages and drama."
- "I love the online writing community I'm part of - they give great feedback and encouragement."
- "Some old high school friends only post complaints and negativity."
- "My professional network on LinkedIn shares valuable insights and opportunities."
- "Certain influencers I follow make me feel bad about my lifestyle choices."

Possible Solutions:
- **Energizing Connections**: Prioritize time and engagement with these people; express gratitude for their positive impact; reciprocate their support and encouragement
- **Inspiring Content**: Engage more deeply with motivational content by commenting and sharing; apply insights to your own life; join communities around shared growth goals
- **Family Drama**: Set boundaries around family group participation; mute notifications during focused work time; redirect conversations to positive topics when possible
- **Supportive Communities**: Increase participation in communities that align with your goals; contribute value to these groups; build deeper relationships with key members
- **Negative Contacts**: Unfollow or mute consistently negative people; limit engagement with complaint-focused content; choose not to respond to drama
- **Professional Networks**: Actively engage with valuable professional content; share your own insights; build relationships through meaningful comments and messages
- **Draining Influencers**: Unfollow accounts that consistently make you feel inadequate; seek out influencers who promote realistic, positive messages; focus on content that aligns with your values.

Question 3: What boundaries could you set to make technology serve your relationships better?

Former Student Responses:
- "I could put my phone away during family dinners and conversations."
- "I should stop checking social media first thing in the morning and last thing at night."

- "I could set specific times for responding to messages instead of being available 24/7."
- "I should turn off work notifications after 7 PM to protect family time."
- "I could designate one day per week as a digital detox day."
- "I should stop scrolling mindlessly and use social media more intentionally."
- "I could create phone-free zones in my bedroom and dining room."

Possible Solutions:
- **Device-Free Meals**: Establish a family rule about phones during meals; create a designated phone parking area; focus on conversation and connection during eating times
- **Morning/Evening Boundaries**: Replace morning social media with meditation, exercise, or planning; create an evening routine that doesn't involve screens; charge phones outside the bedroom
- **Response Time Expectations**: Set specific times for checking and responding to messages; communicate your availability to others; use auto-responses to set expectations
- **Work-Life Separation**: Turn off work notifications after designated hours; create separate work and personal phone numbers or apps; communicate boundaries clearly to colleagues
- **Digital Detox**: Start with a few hours weekly and gradually increase; plan engaging offline activities; inform friends and family about your detox times
- **Intentional Usage**: Set specific purposes before opening social media apps; use timers to limit browsing sessions; ask yourself, "What am I hoping to accomplish?" before scrolling
- **Physical Boundaries**: Create phone-free zones in bedrooms, dining areas, or living rooms; use traditional alarm clocks instead of phones; designate specific areas for device charging

Question 4: When was the last time you had a meaningful, authentic conversation online?

Former Student Responses:
- "I had a deep conversation with an old friend via video call last month about life changes we're both going through."
- "I can't remember the last time - most of my online interactions are surface-level likes and comments."

- "I regularly have meaningful conversations in a private Facebook group about parenting challenges."
- "I had a great exchange with someone on LinkedIn about career transitions that really helped me."
- "I mostly just send memes and funny videos to friends - we don't really talk about serious stuff online."
- "I had a heart-to-heart with my sister over text when she was going through a difficult time."
- "I participate in thoughtful discussions in an online book club that feel very authentic."

Possible Solutions:
- **Video Call Connections**: Schedule regular video calls with important people; use video for sensitive conversations rather than text; create virtual coffee dates or dinner conversations
- **Surface-Level Interactions**: Move beyond likes and comments by sending personal messages; ask deeper questions in your responses; share something meaningful about your own experiences
- **Group Discussions**: Actively participate in online communities that encourage vulnerability and support; start meaningful conversations by asking thoughtful questions
- **Professional Networking**: Engage authentically on professional platforms by sharing personal insights and experiences; offer genuine help and support to others in your field
- **Casual Communication**: Balance light-hearted exchanges with occasional deeper conversations; ask friends about their goals, challenges, or meaningful experiences
- **Text Conversations**: Use voice messages for a more personal touch; call instead of texting for important conversations; share more than just logistics in family communications
- **Community Participation**: Join online groups that align with your interests and values; contribute thoughtfully to discussions; build relationships with regular participants

Question 5: What would a digital detox look like for you, and what might you gain from it?

Former Student Responses:
- "I'd love to spend a whole weekend without checking any social media or news."

- "I think I'd benefit from having phone-free evenings to focus on my family."
- "I want to try a week without Instagram to see how it affects my mood and self-esteem."
- "I'd like to take a break from all news and political content for a month."
- "I want to try working without any notifications for a full day."
- "I'd love to go on a vacation where I only use my phone for emergencies."
- "I think I need to stop checking my phone first thing in the morning for at least a week."

Possible Solutions:

- **Weekend Social Media Break**: Plan engaging offline activities; inform friends about your break; notice changes in mood, productivity, and relationships; use the time for hobbies, exercise, or face-to-face socializing

- **Phone-Free Evenings**: Create a charging station away from living areas; plan family activities that don't involve screens; read books, play games, or have conversations; notice improvements in sleep and family connection

- **Platform-Specific Detox**: Delete specific apps temporarily; ask friends to share important updates directly; focus on real-world activities and relationships; track changes in self-esteem and comparison tendencies

- **News and Politics Break**: Choose one trusted source for essential news; limit news consumption to specific times; focus on local community involvement; notice reduced anxiety and improved mental health

- **Notification-Free Work**: Turn off all non-essential notifications; use focus modes or airplane mode during deep work; batch check messages at designated times; experience improved concentration and productivity

- **Vacation Disconnect**: Inform contacts about limited availability; use out-of-office messages; engage fully in vacation activities; experience greater presence and relaxation

- **Morning Routine Change**: Replace phone checking with meditation, exercise, or journaling; keep phones out of the bedroom; start the day with intention rather than reaction; notice improved mood and focus throughout the day

Universal Solutions Across All Chapter 7 Questions:

Practice Intentional Usage: Before opening any app or device, ask yourself what you hope to accomplish and set a specific time limit.

Curate Your Digital Environment: Actively choose who and what you follow; unfollow accounts that consistently drain your energy or trigger negative emotions.

Prioritize Face-to-Face Connection: Use technology to facilitate in-person meetings rather than replace them; balance online interactions with real-world relationships.

Set Clear Boundaries: Establish specific times and places for technology use; communicate these boundaries to others; protect important relationship time from digital distractions.

Use Technology for Meaningful Connection: Move beyond surface-level interactions; use video calls for important conversations; participate in communities that align with your values.

Regular Digital Detoxes: Schedule regular breaks from technology to reset your relationship with devices and reconnect with offline life.

Monitor Your Emotional Response: Pay attention to how different digital interactions make you feel; adjust your usage based on what supports your well-being.

Focus on Quality Over Quantity: Prioritize meaningful connections over follower counts or likes; invest time in relationships that truly matter to you.

Take Action

- Curate your online network: unfollow or mute one account that doesn't serve you, and reach out to one person who does.
- Set a digital boundary this week (e.g., no devices at dinner, no checking email after 8 p.m.).
- Plan a mini digital detox—an evening, a day, or a weekend offline—and use the time to connect with someone face-to-face or by phone.
- Try a new app or platform that supports intentional, meaningful connections.

Chapter 8 – Giving, Receiving, and Growing Together

The Art of Support, Mentorship, and Asking for Help

No one achieves lasting success alone. The most resilient and fulfilled people are those who both give and receive support, building networks of trust and mutual aid. **Support** can be as simple as encouragement or as profound as standing by someone through a crisis. **Mentorship**—guiding or being guided—accelerates growth for both mentor and mentee, offering wisdom, perspective, and accountability. Just as important is the courage to **ask for help** when you need it. Many people struggle with this, fearing it shows weakness, but in truth, asking for support is a sign of strength and self-awareness. When you reach out, you give others the opportunity to contribute, deepening your bond and strengthening the relationship.

Practicing Gratitude and Recognition in Relationships

Gratitude is the glue that holds relationships together. Regularly expressing appreciation—whether for small favors or steadfast loyalty—nourishes trust and goodwill. Recognition doesn't have to be grand; a simple "thank you," a thoughtful note, or public acknowledgment of someone's contribution can make a lasting impact. When you practice gratitude, you not only lift others up but also shift your own mindset toward abundance and positivity. Over time, this habit transforms your relationships, making them more resilient and joyful.

Building "Circles of Support" and Mutual Aid

Strong relationships don't exist in a vacuum—they are part of a larger ecosystem of support. **Circles of support** are intentional groups of people who encourage, challenge, and help one another. These can be formal (mastermind groups, accountability partners, professional networks) or informal (close friends, family, neighbors). Mutual aid means everyone gives and receives, creating a culture where help flows freely and no one feels like a burden. To build your own circle, start by identifying people you trust and respect. Invite them to connect regularly, share goals, and offer support. Over time, these circles become powerful engines for growth, resilience, and shared achievement.

How to Be a Catalyst for Others' Growth

Great relationships are not just about what you get, but what you give. You can be a catalyst for others by:

- **Offering encouragement** when someone is struggling or doubting themselves.
- **Sharing resources**—books, contacts, opportunities—that might help a friend or colleague.
- **Celebrating others' wins** as enthusiastically as your own.
- **Challenging people** to stretch, try new things, or see their strengths more clearly.
- **Being present**—listening deeply, showing up, and following through on promises.

When you invest in others' growth, you multiply your own social wealth and create a ripple effect of positivity and achievement.

Reflection: Who Do You Support? Who Supports You?

Take a moment to reflect on your network:

- Who do you regularly encourage, mentor, or help?
- Who do you turn to for advice, comfort, or accountability?
- Are your relationships balanced, or do you tend to give more than you receive (or vice versa)?
- Where could you ask for more help, or offer more support?

Awareness of these patterns helps you nurture healthier, more reciprocal connections.

Action: 30-Day Gratitude and Outreach Challenge

To deepen your relationships and expand your circle of support, try this 30-day challenge:

1. **Each day, express gratitude to someone in your network.** This could be a quick text, a handwritten note, or a public shout-out.
2. **Once a week, reach out to someone you haven't connected with in a while.** Ask how they're doing, offer support, or simply listen.
3. **Identify one person you admire and offer encouragement or help, without expecting anything in return.**
4. **At the end of 30 days, reflect:**
   - How did these actions affect your relationships?
   - What did you learn about giving, receiving, and growing together?

Template:

Day	Person	Action (Gratitude/Support)	Notes/Reflection
1	Mom	Sent a thank-you text	She was touched
2	Colleague	Praised her project	Built rapport

Chapter Summary

- Support, mentorship, and asking for help are the cornerstones of strong, resilient relationships.
- Practicing gratitude and recognition transforms both your mindset and your connections.
- Circles of support and mutual aid create networks where everyone grows and thrives.
- Being a catalyst for others' growth multiplies your own social wealth.
- Regular outreach and gratitude keep your relationships vibrant and reciprocal.

Reflection Questions

Question 1: Who are your greatest supporters—and who do you support most?

Former Student Responses:
- "My spouse and best friend are my biggest supporters, but I realize I mostly support my children and don't reciprocate much to my friends."
- "I have great support from my mentor at work, but I'm not sure who I consistently support in return."
- "My family supports me emotionally, but I feel like I give more practical support than I receive."
- "I support my colleagues a lot with their projects, but when I need help, I tend to struggle alone."
- "My book club friends are incredibly supportive, and I try to be there for them too, but I could do more."
- "I realize I have more supporters than I thought, but I'm not great at asking for help when I need it."

- "I support my aging parents a lot, but I don't have many people supporting me through that challenge."

Possible Solutions:
- **Unbalanced Support**: Practice asking for help from those you support; express gratitude to supporters; create more reciprocal relationships by offering specific help to those who support you
- **Unclear Reciprocity**: Identify specific ways to support your mentor or other supporters; offer your skills or time; share resources or connections that might help them
- **Emotional vs. Practical Imbalance**: Communicate your need for practical support to family; offer emotional support to those who help you practically; find people who can provide both types of support
- **Self-Reliance Issues**: Practice asking for small favors first; remember that letting others help strengthens relationships; identify specific people to reach out to when struggling
- **Good Foundation**: Build on existing supportive relationships by being more intentional; schedule regular check-ins, look for opportunities to expand your support network
- **Hidden Support**: Acknowledge and thank people who support you; practice recognizing support in its various forms; express appreciation more frequently
- **Caregiver Stress**: Seek support groups for caregivers; ask family members to share responsibilities; find respite care options; connect with others in similar situations

Question 2: When was the last time you expressed genuine gratitude or recognition to someone?

Former Student Responses:
- "I can't remember the last time I actually told someone how much they mean to me."
- "I say 'thank you' all the time, but I don't think I express deep appreciation very often."
- "I wrote a thank-you note to my teacher last month, and it felt really good."
- "I tend to show gratitude through actions rather than words, but maybe people don't always notice."
- "I express gratitude to my family, but I rarely do it with friends or colleagues."

- "I'm better at recognizing people's efforts publicly at work than I am in my personal relationships."
- "I feel grateful, but I'm not good at expressing it - I worry it will seem awkward or forced."

Possible Solutions:
- **Unexpressed Gratitude**: Start with one person this week; write a heartfelt note or have a conversation expressing specific appreciation; practice makes it feel more natural
- **Surface-Level Thanks**: Move beyond "thank you" to specific appreciation like "I'm grateful for how you listened when I was struggling with my decision."
- **Positive Experience**: Continue the practice that felt good; set a goal to write one meaningful thank-you note monthly; notice how it affects your relationships
- **Action vs. Words**: Combine actions with verbal appreciation; help people understand that your actions are expressions of gratitude; use both methods for fuller communication
- **Selective Gratitude**: Expand appreciation to all areas of your life; practice expressing gratitude to colleagues and friends; notice how different relationships respond to appreciation
- **Professional vs. Personal**: Apply your professional recognition skills to personal relationships; practice giving specific, meaningful feedback to friends and family.
- **Expression Anxiety**: Start with written gratitude (texts, notes, emails); practice with people who are most supportive; remember that genuine appreciation is rarely unwelcome

Question 3: Are there relationships that feel one-sided? What could you do to rebalance them?

Former Student Responses:
- "I have a friend who always calls me with problems but never asks how I'm doing."
- "I feel like I'm always the one reaching out to my college friends to maintain contact."
- "My coworker asks for help constantly but never offers assistance when I need it."
- "I listen to my neighbor's complaints for hours, but when I try to share something, they change the subject."
- "I always host family gatherings and do all the planning, but no one else ever takes initiative."

- "I feel like I give more emotional support to my partner than I receive."
- "Several of my friendships feel like I'm the only one making an effort to stay connected."

Possible Solutions:
- **Problem-Focused Friend**: Set boundaries around venting sessions; practice redirecting conversations to include your experiences; ask directly for reciprocal support
- **Initiation Imbalance**: Stop being the only initiator for a period; see who reaches out; have honest conversations about maintaining the friendship
- **Workplace Imbalance**: Practice saying "I can't help right now, but I could use assistance with X"; set specific times when you're available to help; ask for help before offering it
- **Conversation Monopolizers**: Use phrases like "That reminds me of something I'm dealing with" to redirect, limit listening time, and practice assertive communication
- **Event Planning Burden**: Ask family members to take turns hosting; delegate specific tasks; communicate that you need others to share responsibility
- **Emotional Support Imbalance**: Communicate your need for emotional support; practice asking for what you need; consider couples counseling if the pattern persists
- **Multiple One-Sided Friendships**: Evaluate which relationships are worth rebalancing; practice asking for reciprocity; be willing to let some relationships fade if they remain consistently one-sided

Question 4: How could you be a catalyst for someone else's growth this month?

Former Student Responses:
- "I could introduce my two friends who have similar business goals."
- "I want to mentor a junior colleague who's struggling with confidence."
- "I could share some resources with my neighbor who's trying to get healthier."
- "I'd like to encourage my sister to pursue her art again - she's so talented."
- "I could offer to help my friend practice for job interviews."
- "I want to connect my book club friend with the writing group I know about."
- "I could share my experience with my cousin who's going through a similar life transition."

Possible Solutions:
- **Networking Catalyst**: Make the introduction via email or arrange a casual meeting; follow up to see how the connection went; continue facilitating valuable connections
- **Mentoring Opportunity**: Offer specific, regular support; share your experiences and lessons learned; help them set achievable goals; provide honest, constructive feedback
- **Resource Sharing**: Provide books, apps, or contacts that helped you; offer to be an accountability partner; share your own health journey, and what worked
- **Encouragement Provider**: Have a specific conversation about her talents; offer to help her get started again; provide practical support like supplies or workspace
- **Skill Development**: Offer mock interviews; help with resume review; share interview tips and experiences; connect them with others in their target field
- **Community Building**: Make the introduction and offer to attend the first meeting together; share information about opportunities; help them overcome initial hesitation
- **Experience Sharing**: Schedule dedicated time to share your story; offer ongoing support; connect them with others who've had similar experiences; provide practical advice

Question 5: What did you learn from your 30-day gratitude and outreach challenge?

Former Student Responses:
- "I learned that people really appreciate being acknowledged - several people told me my messages made their day."
- "I discovered that I have more people in my life who care about me than I realized."
- "I found that expressing gratitude actually made me feel happier and more connected."
- "I learned that reaching out to people I hadn't talked to in a while often led to meaningful conversations."
- "I discovered that I was taking a lot of relationships for granted and not expressing appreciation enough."
- "I found that being intentional about gratitude changed how I see my relationships."

- "I learned that small gestures of appreciation can have a big impact on relationships."

Possible Solutions:
- **Positive Impact Recognition**: Continue the practice beyond 30 days; make gratitude expression a regular habit; notice how it strengthens your relationships over time
- **Support Network Awareness**: Reach out to supporters more regularly; express appreciation for their presence in your life; reciprocate their support when possible
- **Personal Happiness Boost**: Maintain a gratitude practice as part of your daily routine; use gratitude as a tool for improving mood; share this discovery with others
- **Meaningful Reconnections**: Schedule regular check-ins with people you've reconnected with; make reaching out to old friends a monthly practice; maintain the connections you've renewed
- **Appreciation Awareness**: Make gratitude expression a weekly habit; be more mindful of others' contributions to your life; practice noticing and acknowledging support as it happens
- **Relationship Perspective Shift**: Continue viewing relationships through a gratitude lens; practice appreciation as a way to strengthen bonds; help others see the value of gratitude
- **Small Gesture Impact**: Incorporate small acts of appreciation into daily life; encourage others to practice gratitude; use this knowledge to be more intentional in all relationships

Universal Solutions Across All Chapter 8 Questions:

Practice Reciprocal Support: Actively look for ways to both give and receive help, ensuring your relationships are balanced and mutually beneficial.

Express Gratitude Regularly: Make appreciation a consistent practice rather than a one-time event; specific, heartfelt gratitude strengthens all relationships.

Address Imbalances Directly: Have honest conversations about one-sided relationships rather than letting resentment build over time.

Be a Connector: Use your network to help others by making introductions, sharing resources, and facilitating opportunities for growth.

Create Support Systems: Build circles of mutual aid where everyone contributes and benefits from the collective strength of the group.

Practice Vulnerability: Share your own struggles and needs to allow others the opportunity to support you and deepen the relationship.

Celebrate Others' Growth: Take genuine joy in others' successes and progress, creating an environment where everyone feels encouraged to grow.

Maintain Consistency: Regular, small acts of support and gratitude are more powerful than occasional grand gestures.

Take Action

- Complete the 30-day gratitude and outreach challenge if you haven't already.
- Identify one relationship that needs more reciprocity and take a specific action to rebalance it.
- Choose one person to support or encourage this week in a meaningful way.
- Express specific gratitude to someone who has supported you recently.
- Create a system for regularly acknowledging and appreciating the people in your life.

Chapter 9 – Navigating Change, Conflict, and Life Transitions

Adapting Relationships Through Life Changes

Change is inevitable—whether it's a move to a new city, a career shift, a marriage or divorce, or the arrival of a child. Each transition brings both opportunity and challenge to your relationships. Some bonds will grow stronger as you weather change together; others may fade or need to be redefined. The healthiest relationships are those that adapt, allowing for growth and new circumstances on both sides.

When you face a major life change, communicate openly with the people who matter most. Share your hopes, fears, and needs. Invite others into your process, and be willing to listen to theirs. Recognize that transitions can be stressful for everyone involved, and give yourself—and others—grace as you adjust. Sometimes, relationships will naturally shift in priority or intensity; that's not a failure, but a normal part of life's ebb and flow.

Repairing, Letting Go, and Grieving Lost Connections

Not all relationships are meant to last forever. Sometimes, distance, misunderstandings, or simply the passage of time can cause connections to weaken or end. When this happens, it's important to allow yourself space to grieve what was lost, even as you honor the good that the relationship brought to your life.

Repair is often possible—and worthwhile—when both parties are willing. Reach out with humility, acknowledge your part in any conflict, and express your desire to rebuild trust. If repair isn't possible or healthy, practice letting go with compassion. Closure can come from honest conversation, a written letter (even if never sent), or a simple ritual of farewell. Remember, letting go of a relationship that no longer serves you creates space for new, life-giving connections.

Conflict as an Opportunity for Growth

Conflict is not a sign that a relationship is failing; rather, it's a natural part of any meaningful connection. When handled well, conflict can deepen understanding, strengthen trust, and spark growth for both people involved. The key is to approach disagreements with curiosity, respect, and a willingness to listen.

Use these steps to navigate conflict constructively:

1. **Pause and Breathe:** Give yourself a moment to calm down before responding.

2. **Use "I Statements":** Focus on your feelings and needs, not accusations. ("I felt hurt when...")
3. **Listen Actively:** Let the other person share their perspective without interruption.
4. **Seek Common Ground:** Look for areas of agreement or shared goals.
5. **Collaborate on Solutions:** Work together to find a way forward that respects both parties.

Handled with care, conflict can be a catalyst for greater intimacy and resilience in your relationships.

When to Hold On, When to Let Go: Discernment and Self-Care

One of the hardest decisions you'll face is whether to keep investing in a struggling relationship or to let it go. There's no simple formula, but some guiding questions can help:

- Does this relationship support my growth, values, and well-being?
- Is there mutual respect, effort, and willingness to repair?
- Do I feel safe, heard, and valued most of the time?

If the answer is consistently no, or if the relationship is marked by ongoing harm, it may be time to step back. Letting go is not a sign of weakness or failure—it's an act of self-care and discernment. Trust that by releasing what no longer serves you, you make space for healthier, more supportive connections.

Practice: Conflict Resolution and Closure Scripts

Here are some practical scripts to guide you through tough conversations:

Conflict Resolution Script: "I value our relationship and want to understand your perspective. When [describe the event], I felt [your feeling]. What was your experience? How can we move forward together?"

Repair Script: "I realize I hurt you when I [describe action]. I'm truly sorry. I want to make things right. What do you need from me to rebuild trust?"

Closure Script: "I appreciate the time and experiences we've shared. I feel our paths are diverging, and I wish you well. Thank you for being part of my life."

Use these as starting points, adapting them to your voice and situation. The goal is to communicate honestly, listen deeply, and act with integrity—whether you're repairing, redefining, or releasing a relationship.

Chapter Summary

- Life transitions—moves, career changes, family shifts—require relationships to adapt and evolve.
- Not all connections last forever; repair when possible, and let go with compassion when necessary.
- Conflict, when handled well, is an opportunity for growth and deeper understanding.
- Discernment and self-care are essential in deciding when to hold on and when to move on.
- Scripts and practical tools help you navigate tough conversations with honesty and grace.

Reflection Questions

Question 1: What is one relationship in your life currently being tested by change or transition?

Former Student Responses:
- "My marriage is being tested by my new job that requires travel and long hours."
- "My friendship with my college roommate has become strained since I moved to a new city."
- "My relationship with my teenage daughter is changing as she becomes more independent."
- "My work relationships are shifting since I got promoted to a management position."
- "My friendship with my workout partner changed when they got injured and couldn't exercise anymore."
- "My relationship with my parents is evolving as they age and need more care."
- "My connection with my book club friends has weakened since I started graduate school."

Possible Solutions:
- **Work-Life Balance Strain**: Communicate openly with your spouse about the challenges; schedule dedicated family time; find ways to stay connected during travel periods

- **Geographic Distance**: Make regular video calls a priority; plan visits when possible; find new ways to share experiences virtually; accept that the relationship may naturally evolve
- **Parent-Teen Dynamics**: Respect their growing independence while maintaining connection; find new activities you both enjoy; practice active listening without trying to fix everything
- **Professional Relationship Changes**: Be transparent about your new role; maintain friendships while establishing professional boundaries; seek mentorship on managing former peers
- **Activity-Based Friendship**: Find new shared activities; offer emotional support during their recovery; explore different ways to connect beyond exercise
- **Aging Parent Relationships**: Have honest conversations about changing needs; involve siblings in caregiving decisions; seek support groups for adult children of aging parents
- **Time Constraint Issues**: Communicate your current limitations; suggest modified ways to stay involved; prioritize the relationships that matter most during busy seasons

Question 2: Are there any connections you need to repair, release, or grieve?

Former Student Responses:
- "I need to repair my relationship with my brother after a family argument six months ago."
- "I should probably let go of my friendship with someone who consistently drains my energy and creates drama."
- "I need to grieve the loss of my mentor who passed away last year - I haven't processed it fully."
- "I want to repair my relationship with my former business partner after our company dissolved badly."
- "I need to release my expectation that my mother will ever be the supportive parent I want her to be."
- "I should grieve the end of my marriage and stop trying to maintain a friendship with my ex-spouse."
- "I need to repair my relationship with my adult son after years of conflict over his life choices."

Possible Solutions:
- **Family Repair**: Reach out with a simple message acknowledging the rift; focus on the relationship rather than who was right; suggest a neutral meeting place for conversation
- **Toxic Friendship Release**: Gradually reduce contact; stop initiating plans; redirect your energy toward healthier relationships; practice self-compassion about the decision
- **Grief Processing**: Allow yourself to feel the loss; create a ritual to honor their memory; consider counseling if grief feels overwhelming; share memories with others who knew them
- **Business Relationship Repair**: Acknowledge both parties' contributions to the conflict; focus on learning from the experience; approach with humility and a genuine desire to understand their perspective
- **Expectation Release**: Accept your mother as she is rather than who you wish she were; find maternal support from other sources; set boundaries around what you share with her
- **Divorce Grief**: Allow yourself to mourn the relationship that was; accept that friendship may not be possible; focus on co-parenting if children are involved
- **Parent-Adult Child Repair**: Approach with unconditional love; listen to understand rather than to change; focus on accepting them while maintaining your own boundaries

Question 3: How do you typically handle conflict, and what could you do differently to foster growth?

Former Student Responses:
- "I avoid conflict at all costs and just hope problems will go away on their own."
- "I get defensive immediately and start arguing my point without really listening."
- "I tend to shut down emotionally and give people the silent treatment."
- "I bring up past issues and grievances instead of focusing on the current problem."
- "I try to fix everything immediately and don't give the other person space to process."
- "I take everything personally and assume people are attacking my character."
- "I get overwhelmed by emotions and either cry or get angry, which shuts down productive conversation."

Possible Solutions:
- **Conflict Avoidance**: Practice having small, low-stakes difficult conversations; remember that avoiding conflict often makes problems worse; use "I" statements to express needs
- **Defensive Reactions**: Pause before responding; ask clarifying questions; practice reflecting back what you heard before defending your position
- **Emotional Shutdown**: Communicate when you need processing time; set a specific time to return to the conversation; practice expressing feelings before they build up
- **Past Grievance Patterns**: Focus only on the current issue; address patterns separately from specific incidents; practice forgiveness and letting go of old hurts
- **Over-Fixing Tendency**: Ask if the person wants solutions or just wants to be heard; give people time to process; resist the urge to solve everything immediately
- **Personal Attack Interpretation**: Separate the issue from your identity; ask yourself, "What is this really about?"; practice not taking things personally
- **Emotional Overwhelm**: Take breaks when emotions run high; practice calming techniques; communicate your emotional state rather than acting from it

Question 4: When was the last time you had a closure conversation? How did it feel?

Former Student Responses:
- "I've never really had a formal closure conversation - I usually just let relationships fade away."
- "I had one with my ex-boyfriend last year, and it was really healing for both of us."
- "I tried to have closure with my former best friend, but she wasn't receptive to the conversation."
- "I had a closure conversation with my dying grandmother, and I'm so grateful I did."
- "I attempted closure with a toxic family member, but it turned into another argument."
- "I had closure with my former boss when I left my job, and it helped me move forward positively."
- "I've been avoiding a closure conversation with my estranged father because I'm afraid of being hurt again."

Possible Solutions:
- **No Closure Experience**: Start with a less emotionally charged relationship; practice writing what you would say; remember that closure can be one-sided if necessary
- **Positive Closure Experience**: Use this as a model for future difficult conversations; share your experience with others who might benefit; continue practicing vulnerable communication
- **Rejected Closure Attempts**: Accept that you can only control your part; find closure through other means like journaling or therapy; focus on your own healing process.
- **Meaningful Closure**: Honor the memory of that conversation; use the experience to encourage others; recognize the gift you gave each other
- **Failed Closure Attempts**: Learn from what went wrong; consider whether the timing was right; accept that some people aren't ready for closure conversations
- **Professional Closure Success**: Apply these skills to personal relationships; recognize the value of ending things well; maintain professional relationships when possible
- **Avoidance Due to Fear**: Consider what you have to gain versus lose; prepare for different possible outcomes; remember that you can't control their response, only your own actions

Question 5: What boundaries or self-care practices can help you discern when to hold on and when to let go?

Former Student Responses:
- "I need to trust my gut feelings more instead of always giving people the benefit of the doubt."
- "I should set a time limit for how long I'll work on repairing a relationship before accepting it's not working."
- "I need to pay attention to how I feel after spending time with certain people."
- "I should stop making excuses for people's behavior and accept what they're showing me."
- "I need to ask myself if this relationship aligns with my values and supports my growth."
- "I should consider whether the relationship is reciprocal or if I'm doing all the work."

- "I need to practice self-compassion and remember that letting go isn't giving up."

Possible Solutions:
- **Trusting Intuition**: Practice mindfulness to tune into your body's signals; journal about your feelings after interactions; ask trusted friends for their observations
- **Time Boundaries**: Set specific timeframes for repair efforts; create measurable goals for relationship improvement; accept when you've done your part
- **Energy Awareness**: Rate your energy before and after time with different people; notice patterns over time; prioritize relationships that consistently energize you
- **Reality Acceptance**: Practice seeing people as they are, not as you wish they were; stop making excuses for harmful behavior; believe people when they show you who they are
- **Values Alignment**: Regularly review your core values; assess whether relationships support or undermine what matters to you; make decisions based on alignment
- **Reciprocity Assessment**: Track who initiates contact and plans; notice who asks about your life versus only sharing their own; evaluate the balance of giving and receiving
- **Self-Compassion Practice**: Remember that healthy boundaries are acts of self-care; recognize that some relationships have natural endings; focus on what you can learn from each experience

Universal Solutions Across All Chapter 9 Questions:

Accept Change as Natural: Understand that relationships naturally evolve as people grow and circumstances change; this doesn't always indicate failure.

Practice Honest Communication: Address issues directly rather than hoping they'll resolve themselves; use "I" statements and focus on specific behaviors.

Develop Conflict Skills: Learn to see conflict as an opportunity for growth rather than something to avoid; practice staying calm and curious during disagreements.

Honor Your Feelings: Allow yourself to grieve losses, feel anger about betrayals, and experience joy about repairs without judgment.

Set Clear Boundaries: Know your limits and communicate them clearly; protect your energy while remaining open to genuine connection.

Seek Support: Don't navigate difficult relationship transitions alone; use friends, family, or professionals to help you process and make decisions.

Practice Discernment: Learn to distinguish between relationships worth fighting for and those that need to be released for your well-being.

Focus on Your Growth: Use relationship challenges as opportunities to develop better communication skills, emotional intelligence, and self-awareness.

Take Action

- Identify one relationship that needs attention and decide whether it needs repair, release, or grieving.
- Practice one new conflict resolution skill in your next disagreement.
- Have a closure conversation with someone if it would bring you peace.
- Set one boundary that will help you better discern which relationships deserve your energy.
- Seek support from a trusted friend, family member, or professional as you navigate relationship transitions.

Chapter 10 – Your Relationship Mastery Plan

Synthesizing Your Insights: Relationship Audit, Mapping, and Goals

Now that you've explored the foundations of connection, communication, boundaries, community, and support, it's time to bring everything together into a practical, personal plan. Start by reviewing your relationship audit and mapping exercises from earlier chapters. Who are your champions, challengers, collaborators, companions, and catalysts? Where are the gaps, energy drains, or missing connections in your network? What patterns do you notice about who lifts you up, and who may be holding you back? Based on these insights, set clear relationship goals. Do you want to deepen your bond with a family member, reconnect with an old friend, expand your professional network, or find a new community? Be specific. The more clearly you define your intentions, the more likely you are to take meaningful action.

Setting Relational Intentions (Cross-Reference to Goals That Matter)

As you learned in *Goals That Matter*, meaningful change starts with intention. Write down your top 2–3 relational intentions for the next 90 days. For example:
- "I will schedule a monthly lunch with my sibling to rebuild our connection."
- "I will join a local hiking group to expand my circle of companions."
- "I will express gratitude to one person in my network each week."

Make your intentions SMART: Specific, Measurable, Achievable, Relevant, and Time-bound. This gives you a clear target and a way to track progress.

Scheduling Connection (Cross-Reference to Time That Matters)

Intentions become reality when you make space for them in your life. Use your calendar as a tool for connection, not just productivity. Block out time for regular check-ins, phone calls, or community events. Protect these appointments as you would any important commitment, because relationships are the foundation of a life that matters.
For example:
- Add a recurring reminder to call a friend every Sunday evening.

- Block out one evening a month for a "gratitude dinner" with people who energize you.
- Schedule a weekly walk or coffee with a mentor or mentee.

Building Habits for Reciprocity, Gratitude, and Regular Check-Ins

Strong relationships are built on small, consistent actions. Develop habits that keep your connections vibrant:

- **Reciprocity:** Make it a habit to offer help, encouragement, or resources without expecting anything in return.
- **Gratitude:** Start a gratitude journal focused on your relationships, or send a thank-you note each week.
- **Regular Check-Ins:** Use a habit tracker to ensure you're reaching out to key people in your network consistently.

These habits compound over time, creating a network of trust, support, and mutual growth.

Creating a 90-Day Relationship Growth Plan (Template)

Here's a simple template to guide your next steps:

Goal/Intention	Action Step	Frequency	Who/With Whom	Scheduled Date/Time	Progress Notes
Reconnect with a sibling	Monthly lunch	Monthly	My sister	1st Sat each month	
Expand community	Join a hiking group	Weekly	Local hikers	Sundays, 9am	
Practice gratitude	Thank-you note/email	Weekly	Different person each	Fridays	
Deepen mentorship	Coffee & goal review	Monthly	Mentor	3rd Wed each month	

Customize this plan to fit your priorities, and review it at the end of each month to celebrate progress and adjust as needed.

Reflection: What Does Your Ideal Relationship Ecosystem Look Like?

Visualize your ideal network. Who is in your inner circle? What kinds of communities are you part of? How do you feel after spending time with the people in your life? What roles do you play in supporting others? Take a few moments to write or sketch your vision. This will be your compass as you build and sustain your social wealth.

Take Action: First Steps and Accountability

1. **Choose one relationship goal to act on this week.** Schedule the first step in your calendar now.
2. **Share your intentions with an accountability partner**—someone who will encourage you and check in on your progress.
3. **Track your actions and celebrate small wins.** Each connection, conversation, or act of gratitude is a building block for your relationship mastery.

Remember, mastery isn't about perfection—it's about consistent, intentional effort over time.

Chapter Summary

- Synthesize your relationship insights into clear goals and intentions.
- Schedule connection as a priority, not an afterthought.
- Build habits of reciprocity, gratitude, and regular check-ins.
- Use a 90-day plan to create momentum and track your growth.
- Reflect on your ideal relationship ecosystem and take the first steps with accountability.

Reflection Questions

Question 1: What are your top three relationship goals for the next 90 days?

Former Student Responses:
- "I want to reconnect with my college roommate whom I haven't spoken to in over a year."
- "I need to have a difficult conversation with my manager about my career development and growth opportunities."
- "I want to join a local hiking group to meet people who share my love of outdoor activities."

- "I'd like to strengthen my relationship with my teenage son by having weekly one-on-one time together."
- "I want to set better boundaries with my mother-in-law, who calls constantly and creates drama."
- "I need to find a mentor in my industry who can guide my professional development."
- "I want to start hosting monthly dinner parties to bring my friend group together more regularly."

Possible Solutions:
- **Reconnection Goals**: Send a simple message like "I've been thinking about you and would love to catch up"; suggest a low-pressure video call or coffee meeting; be prepared to acknowledge the gap in communication without making excuses
- **Professional Conversations**: Schedule a formal meeting; prepare specific examples of your contributions; research growth opportunities within the company; practice your talking points beforehand
- **Community Building**: Research local groups on Meetup or Facebook; attend one event as a trial; introduce yourself to at least three new people; follow up with connections made
- **Family Relationships**: Schedule specific weekly time in your calendar; let your son choose the activity sometimes; put away devices during this time; focus on listening rather than lecturing
- **Boundary Setting**: Practice specific phrases like "That doesn't work for me right now"; limit call frequency by not always answering; communicate your availability clearly
- **Mentorship Seeking**: Identify potential mentors through professional associations; reach out with specific questions rather than general requests; offer value in return for their time
- **Social Hosting**: Start small with 4-6 people; choose simple menus; focus on creating a connection rather than perfect entertaining; establish a regular schedule

Question 2: How will you make space for connection in your schedule?

Former Student Responses:
- "I'm always too busy with work and family responsibilities to maintain friendships."
- "I want to prioritize relationships, but I don't know how to fit them into my packed schedule."

- "I tend to cancel social plans when work gets busy, which damages my relationships."
- "I need to be more intentional about scheduling time for people, not just tasks."
- "I realize I spend more time on social media than actually connecting with people in real life."
- "I want to create regular rituals for staying in touch with important people."
- "I need to stop treating relationship time as optional or something I'll do when I have time."

Possible Solutions:
- **Time Scarcity**: Audit your current time usage to identify where relationship time could fit; replace some solo activities with social ones; combine errands with friend time (walking meetings, grocery shopping together)
- **Intentional Scheduling**: Block relationship time in your calendar like any important appointment; use recurring calendar events for regular check-ins; schedule social activities during your peak energy times
- **Work-Life Balance**: Set boundaries around work hours; communicate your availability to colleagues; protect weekend time for relationships; practice saying no to non-essential work requests
- **Priority Alignment**: Treat relationship time as non-negotiable; schedule important relationships first, then fit other activities around them; remember that relationships support all other life goals
- **Digital vs. Real Connection**: Set limits on social media time; use technology to facilitate in-person meetings rather than replace them; have phone-free meals and gatherings
- **Connection Rituals**: Establish weekly coffee dates, monthly dinners, or quarterly check-ins; create traditions like birthday celebrations or holiday gatherings; use habit stacking to attach relationship activities to existing routines
- **Mindset Shift**: Recognize that relationship time is an investment, not an expense; understand that strong relationships actually save time by providing support and resources; view connection as essential self-care

Question 3: What habits will you build to nurture reciprocity and gratitude?

Former Student Responses:
- "I'm good at helping others but terrible at asking for help when I need it."
- "I forgot to express appreciation to people who support me regularly."

- "I tend to take my closest relationships for granted and don't acknowledge their contributions enough."
- "I want to be better at following up on conversations and remembering important details about people's lives."
- "I need to practice being more vulnerable and sharing my own struggles, not just listening to others."
- "I want to celebrate other people's successes more enthusiastically."
- "I realize I'm always the one reaching out, and I want to create more balanced relationships."

Possible Solutions:
- **Asking for Help**: Start with small requests to build comfort; practice specific phrases like "I could use your perspective on something"; remember that letting others help strengthens relationships
- **Gratitude Expression**: Set weekly reminders to thank someone; keep a gratitude journal focused on relationships; send handwritten notes or voice messages; express appreciation in the moment rather than waiting
- **Appreciation Habits**: Create a "wins folder" for positive feedback you receive; regularly acknowledge others' contributions publicly; practice specific rather than general praise ("Thank you for listening when I was stressed about my presentation")
- **Follow-Up Skills**: Keep notes about important conversations; set reminders to check in about things people mentioned; ask about updates on situations they shared with you
- **Vulnerability Practice**: Share one genuine challenge or feeling each week; practice the phrase "I'm struggling with..." or "I could use support with..."; balance listening with authentic sharing
- **Celebration Habits**: React enthusiastically to others' good news; offer to celebrate achievements together; share others' successes on social media (with permission); remember important dates and milestones
- **Reciprocity Balance**: Track who initiates contact and plans; practice letting others reach out sometimes; communicate your needs clearly rather than expecting others to guess

Question 4: Who will support you and hold you accountable as you grow?

Former Student Responses:
- "I don't really have anyone who understands my relationship goals or would hold me accountable."
- "My family is supportive, but they don't really get why I want to expand my social circle."
- "I have friends who would support me, but I'm embarrassed to admit I need help with relationships."
- "I'd like to find someone who's also working on building better relationships so we can support each other."
- "I think a professional coach might be helpful, but I'm not sure if it's worth the investment."
- "I want accountability, but I'm afraid of disappointing someone if I don't follow through."
- "I need someone who will be honest with me about my relationship patterns, even when it's hard to hear."

Possible Solutions:
- **Building Support Network**: Join online communities focused on personal development; attend local meetups for people interested in growth; consider starting a small accountability group with like-minded individuals
- **Family Communication**: Help family understand how relationship growth benefits everyone; ask for specific support, like reminding you to reach out to friends; share your wins and challenges regularly
- **Friend Support**: Choose one trusted friend to share your goals with; frame it as mutual support rather than one-sided help; start with small, specific requests for accountability
- **Peer Partnerships**: Find someone with similar goals through social media groups, classes, or workshops; create structured check-ins with specific questions and timelines; celebrate each other's progress
- **Professional Guidance**: Research coaches who specialize in relationships or social skills; consider it an investment in your overall well-being and success; look for coaches who offer group programs for affordability

- **Accountability Fears**: Start with low-stakes commitments; choose supportive rather than judgmental accountability partners; focus on effort and learning rather than perfect execution
- **Honest Feedback**: Ask trusted friends for specific observations about your relationship patterns; create safe spaces for difficult conversations; practice receiving feedback without defensiveness

Question 5: What does your ideal relationship ecosystem look and feel like?

Former Student Responses:
- "I want to feel like I belong somewhere and have people who really know and accept me."
- "I'd love to have a diverse group of friends who challenge me to grow and support me through difficulties."
- "I want relationships where I can be completely authentic without fear of judgment."
- "I envision having mentors who guide me, peers who collaborate with me, and people I can mentor in return."
- "I want to feel energized rather than drained after spending time with the people in my life."
- "I'd like to have a strong sense of community where people look out for each other."
- "I want relationships that feel balanced - where I give and receive equally."

Possible Solutions:
- **Belonging Creation**: Join communities aligned with your values and interests; participate regularly in group activities; be vulnerable and authentic to invite deeper connections; create traditions and rituals with your chosen community
- **Diverse Network Building**: Intentionally seek connections across different demographics, industries, and life stages; attend events outside your usual circles; practice curiosity about different perspectives and experiences
- **Authentic Relationships**: Practice sharing your true thoughts and feelings gradually; choose relationships where vulnerability is welcomed; set boundaries with people who judge or criticize your authentic self
- **Multi-Generational Connections**: Seek mentorship opportunities; offer to mentor others in areas where you have expertise; join professional associations or community groups with mixed age ranges

- **Energy Management**: Regularly assess which relationships energize versus drain you; prioritize time with energizing people; set boundaries with energy drains; practice self-care to show up fully for others
- **Community Investment**: Contribute actively to groups rather than just consuming; organize gatherings or activities; offer help and support to community members; participate in mutual aid or support networks
- **Reciprocal Relationships**: Practice both asking for and offering help; track the balance of giving and receiving; communicate your needs clearly; appreciate others' contributions to your life

Universal Solutions Across All Chapter 10 Questions:

Create Specific, Measurable Goals: Transform vague relationship desires into concrete, actionable objectives with clear timelines and success metrics.

Schedule Relationship Time: Treat connection as a priority by blocking time in your calendar and protecting it from other demands.

Build Sustainable Habits: Develop small, consistent practices for gratitude, reciprocity, and connection that compound over time.

Seek Mutual Accountability: Find others who share your commitment to relationship growth and create structured support systems.

Design Your Ideal Network: Envision the relationships you want and take specific steps to create that reality through intentional choices and actions.

Practice Patience and Persistence: Understand that building meaningful relationships takes time and consistent effort; celebrate small progress along the way.

Focus on Quality Over Quantity: Prioritize deep, authentic connections over superficial networking or social media metrics.

Integrate Relationship Goals with Life Goals: Recognize that strong relationships support all other areas of personal and professional growth.

Take Action

- Complete your 90-day Relationship Growth Plan using the template provided.
- Schedule your first relationship-building activity within the next week.
- Identify one person who can serve as an accountability partner for your relationship goals.
- Begin implementing one small daily habit that supports connection and gratitude.
- Share your relationship vision with someone you trust and ask for their support.

Congratulations on completing your journey through Relationships That Matter. Your commitment to building social wealth will create ripple effects of positive change that extend far beyond what you can imagine. Keep investing in the people who matter most; they are your greatest asset for a life of meaning, connection, and impact.

Final Reflection

Key Questions for Ongoing Relational Growth

As you reach the end of *Relationships That Matter*, take a moment to reflect on your journey and set your intention for the path ahead. Use these questions to guide your ongoing growth:

- Who are the people currently shaping your life—and how do they influence your mindset, energy, and direction?
- Which relationships energize and support you most? Which ones need boundaries, repair, or release?
- What new connections or communities would enrich your life right now?
- How can you practice gratitude, reciprocity, and vulnerability more consistently in your relationships?
- What habits or rituals will help you nurture your social wealth in the weeks and months ahead?
- Where do you want to invest more time, attention, or care—and what's one small step you can take today?

Keep these questions handy and revisit them regularly. Your relationships will keep evolving as you do.

How Relationships Amplify the Results of Change, Goals, and Time Management

Throughout the About Things That Matter series, you've learned that lasting change, meaningful goals, and effective time management are all deeply influenced by the company you keep. Relationships are the multiplier for every other pillar of personal growth:

- **Change** is easier and more sustainable when you have encouragement, accountability, and honest feedback from people who care.
- **Goals** become more achievable when you share them with others, seek mentorship, and celebrate milestones together.
- **Time management** is more effective when you protect space for those who matter and align your schedule with your values and social commitments.

Social wealth is the connective tissue that binds your progress together. The stronger your relationships, the greater your capacity to adapt, achieve, and thrive in every area of life.

Invitation to Join the About Things That Matter Community

You don't have to walk this journey alone. The *About Things That Matter* community is here to support you as you continue to build a life anchored in meaning, momentum, and connection. Share your wins, struggles, and insights with fellow readers. Access exclusive resources, templates, and new tools. Ask questions, offer encouragement, and celebrate progress together.

Visit aboutthingsthatmatter.com to join the community, download worksheets, and find updates on future books and events. Your story can inspire others, just as theirs will inspire you.

Keep Moving Forward

Thank you for letting us be part of your story. The best is yet to come. Keep learning, keep growing, and keep investing in the things—and people—that matter most. Every step you take, no matter how small, is a vote for the life you want to create.

"The journey of a thousand miles begins with a single step." – *Lao Tzu*.

Appendices & Resources

Relationship Audit Worksheet (Printable/Digital)

Purpose: To help you take stock of your current relationships, assess their quality, and identify areas for growth.

How to Use:
- List your key relationships (family, friends, colleagues, mentors, community).
- Rate each on a scale from 1 (draining) to 10 (energizing).
- Note the role they play (champion, challenger, collaborator, companion, catalyst).
- Identify relationships to nurture, boundaries to set, and gaps to fill.

Sample Table:

Name	Role	Energizing (1–10)	Notes/Next Step
Alex	Champion	8	Schedule regular catch-up
Jamie	Draining	3	Set boundaries
Priya	Collaborator	7	Explore a new project

Relationship Mapping Template

Purpose: To visualize your relationship ecosystem and spot strengths, gaps, and opportunities.

How to Use:
- Place yourself at the center of the map.
- Draw circles for different layers: inner circle (closest), professional, community, and digital.
- Add names and note their primary role.
- Use different colors or lines to indicate relationship strength or frequency of contact.

Downloadable:

Available as a printable PDF or editable digital template (compatible with Canva, Google Drawings, or Miro).

Conversation Starter and Listening Guide

Purpose: To move beyond small talk and foster deeper, more meaningful conversations.

Conversation Starters:
- "What's been the highlight of your week?"
- "What's something you're looking forward to?"
- "What's a challenge you're working through right now?"

Listening Guide:
- Give full attention (put away devices).
- Reflect back what you hear ("It sounds like you're saying...").
- Validate feelings ("That sounds tough/exciting.").
- Ask open-ended follow-ups ("Tell me more about...").

Boundary-Setting and Conflict Resolution Scripts

Purpose: To help you communicate your needs and resolve disagreements with clarity and care.

Boundary-Setting Scripts:
- "Thank you for asking, but I can't commit to that right now."
- "I need some time to recharge this weekend, so I'll have to pass."

Conflict Resolution Scripts:
- "When [event], I felt [emotion]. Can we talk about how to move forward?"
- "I realize I hurt you when I [action]. I'm sorry—how can I make this right?"

Community-Building Templates

Event Planner:
- Event name, date, purpose, invite list, logistics, follow-up notes.

Gratitude Journal:
- Daily/weekly space to record who you're grateful for and why.
- Prompts: "Today I appreciate...", "A small act of kindness I received was..."

Support Circle Tracker:
- List of people in your support network, how you support each other, and check-in frequency.

Recommended Books, Podcasts, and Online Communities

Books:
- *The Art of Gathering* by Priya Parker

- *Dare to Lead* by Brené Brown
- *Never Eat Alone* by Keith Ferrazzi
- *Radical Candor* by Kim Scott

Podcasts:
- *We Can Do Hard Things* (Glennon Doyle)
- *The Science of Happiness* (Greater Good Science Center)
- *Unlocking Us* (Brené Brown)

Online Communities:
- Meetup.com (find local interest and support groups)
- Lunchclub (professional connections)
- Reddit: r/relationships, r/DecidingToBeBetter

Digital Tools Directory (Apps for Intentional Connection)

Tool/App	Best For	Platform	Features
WhatsApp	Private messaging/groups	iOS/Android/Web	Text, voice, video, group chats
Marco Polo	Asynchronous video chat	iOS/Android	Video messages, group threads
Zoom	Virtual meetups/calls	All	Video, screen sharing, breakout
Meetup	Finding local groups	Web/App	Events by interest/location
Slack/Discord	Community and projects	All	Channels, DMs, integrations
Gratitude App	Practicing gratitude	iOS/Android	Daily prompts, journaling

30-Day Relationship Challenge Tracker

Purpose:

To help you build momentum by practicing gratitude, outreach, and connection daily for a month.

How to Use:
- Each day, write the name of the person you reached out to and what you did (thank you note, call, coffee, support).
- Reflect weekly: What did you learn? How did your relationships shift?

Sample Tracker:

Day	Person	Action	Notes/Reflection
1	Mom	Thank-you text	She was surprised!
2	Colleague	Praised project	Built a stronger rapport

How to Access and Use These Tools

- All templates and worksheets are available for download at [your series website] or via QR codes in this book.
- Print them for handwritten use or edit digitally on your device.
- Use them regularly to review, reflect, and strengthen your relationships.

Bibliography

- **Major Research Foundations Referenced**
- Harvard's Grant Study – 80-year longitudinal study on human flourishing.
- Stanford University research – Growth mindset and achievement, notably work by Dr. Carol Dweck.
- MIT – Studies on habit formation and behavioral change.
- Organizational psychology research – high-performance teamwork and support.

- **Explicitly Cited or Recommended Books**
- The Art of Gathering by Priya Parker
- Dare to Lead by Brené Brown
- Never Eat Alone by Keith Ferrazzi
- Radical Candor by Kim Scott
- As a Man Thinketh by James Allen (cited for foundational life philosophy)

- **Recommended Podcasts**
- We Can Do Hard Things with Glennon Doyle
- The Science of Happiness (Greater Good Science Center)
- Unlocking Us with Brené Brown

- **Digital Tools and Online Communities**
- Meetup.com – Find local and interest-based groups and events.
- Lunchclub – Build professional connections.
- Reddit – r/relationships and r/DecidingToBeBetter.

- **Apps for Intentional Connection**
- WhatsApp, Signal – Secure, private messaging and groups.
- Marco Polo – Personal, asynchronous video chat.
- Zoom, Google Meet – Virtual meetups and group calls.
- Slack, Discord – Community and project-based communication.
- Gratitude app – Journaling and daily gratitude prompts.

- **Research Literature & Classic Works**
- Grant, G., et al. (Harvard's Grant Study)
- Dweck, C. S. – Mindset research
- Goleman, D. – Emotional intelligence and social psychology

- **Series Cross-References**

- Books from the *About Things That Matter* series provide foundational pillars and are referenced throughout for integrated personal growth:
- Change That Matters – JC Ryan
- Goals That Matter – JC Ryan
- Time That Matters – JC Ryan
- The Connection Code – JC Ryan

- **Notable Quotes/Influences**
- Jim Rohn on the influence of your closest relationships ("You are the average of the five people you spend the most time with").
- Brené Brown on vulnerability and connection.

Your Journey Continues

As you reach the end of this book, remember: the true value lies not just in what you've learned, but in what you choose to do next. Growth is not a single event; it's a lifelong journey, built on small, consistent steps and fueled by your willingness to keep moving forward, even when progress feels slow.

The principles and practices you've explored here are meant to be lived, revisited, and refined. Some days will be easier than others. There will be setbacks, doubts, and moments when old habits resurface. This is all part of the process. What matters most is your commitment to begin again, each day, with compassion and courage.

You are now part of a larger community of readers and learners who, like you, have decided to focus on the things that truly matter. The *About Things That Matter* series is your ongoing companion, offering new tools, fresh perspectives, and encouragement for every stage of your journey.

As you close this book, ask yourself:
- What is one small action you can take today to move closer to the life you envision?
- Who can you invite to join you on this path, offering support and accountability?
- How will you celebrate your progress, no matter how incremental?

Thank you for letting us be part of your story. The best is yet to come. Keep investing in yourself. Keep daring to create change that matters. Keep learning, keep growing, and keep moving forward, one meaningful step at a time.

The next chapter of your story is yours to write, one intentional step at a time.

Stay curious. Stay compassionate. Stay committed to the things that matter.

Share your journey: Tell a friend or accountability partner what you've learned and what you plan to do next.

Choose the next book that fits your current needs, or read the whole series for the most powerful results. Visit http://aboutthingsthatmatter.com

Please take 2 minutes to give us your feedback https://bit.ly/3ZZjERJ

The Complete Transformation System

The complete "About Things That Matter" series provides a comprehensive, science-based system for transforming every area of your life while reclaiming the fundamental human capacities that have become luxuries in our modern world.

Each book builds on the previous ones, creating a compound effect of growth and transformation. You don't need to read them in order, but starting with your biggest challenge area will create the most immediate impact.

The Research Foundation:

Harvard's 80-year Grant Study on human flourishing
Stanford's research on the growth mindset and achievement
MIT's findings on habit formation and behavioral change
Decades of organizational psychology research on high performance

Foundation Building

Book 1: Change That Matters
Stop Drifting. Start Directing.

Master the psychology of lasting personal transformation through 8 proven principles that turn intention into achievement.

What You'll Gain:
The neuroscience-based principles that make change stick
A systematic approach to breaking limiting patterns
Proven strategies for overcoming resistance and fear
The mindset shifts that accelerate personal growth

Readers report feeling more in control of their lives within the first week of implementation.

Book 2: Goals That Matter
Turn Dreams into Done.

Create and achieve meaningful goals through purpose-driven planning that delivers real fulfillment, not just external success.

What You'll Gain:
- The SMART goals framework increases achievement rates by 42%
- How to align goals with your deepest values for sustained motivation
- Systems for maintaining momentum through obstacles and setbacks
- The art of celebrating progress to fuel continued success

Goal completion rates increase by 65% when shared with others using these methods.

Book 3: Time That Matters
Make Every Moment Count.

Transform your relationship with time through proven systems that create freedom, focus, and alignment with what matters most.

What You'll Gain:
- The 80/20 principle applied to daily and weekly planning
- Energy management strategies that multiply your effective working hours
- Digital tools and analog systems that enhance rather than distract
- The art of saying "no" to create space for what matters most

Users gain an average of 8-12 productive hours per week within 30 days.

Book 4: Relationships That Matter
Build Your Social Wealth.

Create deep, meaningful connections through authentic communication and relationship skills that enrich every area of your life.

What You'll Gain:
- The five essential relationship roles that every successful person needs
- Communication skills that transform surface connections into deep bonds
- Digital relationship strategies for authentic connection in a virtual world
- Community-building skills that create belonging and mutual support

Noticeable improvements in relationship quality and communication effectiveness within the first conversations.

Skill Development

Book 5: Emotional Intelligence That Matters
Feel Deeply, Respond Wisely.

Master the art of understanding and managing emotions to enhance relationships, decision-making, and personal effectiveness.

What You'll Gain:
- Advanced emotional awareness and regulation techniques
- Skills to read and respond to others' emotions effectively
- Tools for transforming emotional triggers into growth opportunities
- Leadership abilities rooted in emotional wisdom

Improved emotional responses and relationship dynamics within days of applying core techniques.

Book 6: Happiness That Matters
Choose Joy, Create Fulfillment.

Discover the science of sustainable happiness and build daily practices that create lasting contentment independent of circumstances.

What You'll Gain:
- Evidence-based strategies for cultivating genuine happiness
- Tools to break free from comparison and external validation
- Gratitude and mindfulness practices that rewire your brain for joy
- How to find meaning and purpose in everyday moments

Measurable improvements in mood and life satisfaction within two weeks of consistent practice.

Book 7: The 24-Hour Miracle That Matters
Transform Your Day, Transform Your Life.

Design perfect days that compound into an extraordinary life through intentional morning, work, and evening routines.

What You'll Gain:
- Hour-by-hour blueprints for days that energize rather than drain

Morning routines that set you up for success and clarity

Evening practices that restore and prepare you for tomorrow

Weekend rhythms that rejuvenate and reconnect you to purpose

Dramatic improvements in energy, focus, and life satisfaction within one week of implementation.

Book 8: From Stressful to Successful
Stress Less, Achieve More.

Transform stress from a life-draining force into a success-driving advantage through proven resilience and performance strategies.

What You'll Gain:
Stress reframing techniques that turn pressure into performance fuel

Resilience-building practices for bouncing back from any setback

Peak performance strategies used by top athletes and executives

Recovery and restoration methods that prevent burnout

Significant reduction in stress levels and improved performance under pressure within days.

Advanced Integration

Book 9: The Connection Code
Crack the Code to Meaningful Relationships.

One-line Summary: Master advanced relationship dynamics, conflict resolution, and influence techniques that create lasting bonds and positive impact.

What You'll Gain:
Advanced empathy and emotional attunement skills

Conflict transformation strategies that strengthen rather than damage relationships

Influence and persuasion techniques rooted in genuine care

Leadership approaches that inspire and unite rather than divide

Enhanced ability to navigate difficult conversations and deepen existing relationships immediately.

Book 10: Procrastination
Stop Putting Off Your Potential.

Overcome procrastination forever through understanding its root causes and implementing systems that make action inevitable.

What You'll Gain:
- The psychology behind procrastination and how to interrupt the cycle
- Environmental design strategies that make good choices automatic
- Motivation techniques that work even when you don't feel like it
- Completion systems that turn started projects into finished successes

Immediate breakthrough on stuck projects and tasks that have been delayed for weeks or months.

Book 11: Self-Esteem That Matters
Build Unshakable Confidence from the Inside Out.

Develop authentic self-worth through proven strategies that transform self-doubt into genuine confidence and self-respect.

What You'll Gain:
- Tools to overcome negative self-talk and limiting beliefs
- Habits that reinforce your sense of worth daily
- Assertiveness skills to express needs and set boundaries
- The ripple effect of healthy self-esteem on relationships

Noticeable shifts in self-talk and confidence levels within the first week of practice.

Book 12: Thoughts That Matter
Your Brain Is Not Your Boss.

Harness the neuroscience of conscious living to master your mind, emotions, and purpose through proven mental training protocols.

What You'll Gain:
- How to rewire your brain for resilience, clarity, and growth
- Digital detox strategies to reclaim your attention
- Emotional intelligence tools for wise decision-making
- Daily practices to align thoughts with purpose

Mental clarity and emotional regulation improve within days of implementing the core exercises.

Your Gift

Don't forget your gift: the first book in the series **About Things That Matter**.

This book is exclusive to my readers. You will not find this book anywhere else.

You're invited to pause, reflect, and reconsider what truly defines a meaningful life. In a world conditioned to chase money, status, and material achievements, this book challenges the conventional yardsticks of success. Through incisive insight and refreshing authenticity, it guides readers to shift their focus from external validation to the internal foundations that cultivate real fulfillment, purpose, and enduring happiness. It's a call to eliminate distractions, clarify values, and build a life anchored in what matters most.

Visit this link to download your free copy of [About Things That Matter](https://BookHip.com/HLAJBFP) or type this address into your browser https://BookHip.com/HLAJBFP

Also by JC Ryan

Rex Dalton K9 Thrillers

Here's what readers are saying about the series:

"A great read, started and couldn't stop until the end!!!"

"Just gets better and better. Can't wait to read the next in the series."

"Rex and Digger return. The continuing story of Rex Dalton and Digger is a suspenseful and intriguing work."

"What's A Dog To Do? 5 stars. I love reading about Rex Dalton's exploits, but my favorite character has to be Digger, his military-trained super-intelligent dog."

"JC Ryan scores again. I was not a fan of the first Rex Dalton book, but I plunged ahead with the second, hoping JC Ryan would not disappoint. I loved it. Now here I am after reading the third book in this series. I had a hard time putting it down and found myself wondering about it when I was not reading. Rex has added several new ports of call to this adventure. He sure gets into more trouble than any person I know who just wants to become a sightseer. With the help of Digger (his new comrade-in-arms), we are once again trying to correct the wrongs inflicted on the weak."

Visit The Rex Dalton Series Page http://viewbook.at/RexDaltonSeries

The Rossler Foundation Mysteries

http://myBook.to/RosslerFoundation

Here's what readers are saying about the series:

"A brilliant series by a master of the techno thrillers turning old much debated mysteries into overwhelming modern engrossing sagas of adventure, heroism and a sense of awe for the many mysteries still unexplained in our universe. Enjoy!"

"I LOVED this series! It's readily apparent that the author drew from a large body of knowledge in writing this series. It's just believable enough to think it could happen someday, and in fact, aligns quite well with some of the current relationships that exist between present-day countries and the USA."

The Carter Devereux Mystery Thrillers

myBook.to/CarterDevereux

Here's what readers are saying about the series:

"Omg, this series is awesome. Full of adventure, action, romance, and suspense. If you start reading, you are hooked. Carter and all characters are awesome, you will fall in love with all of them they become like family. I love the way J C weaves the human and animals together in the story. Try it you will love it."

"The best! What a joy to read these four books about Carter and Mackenzie Devereux and their adventures. A very good read. I will look for more of JC Ryan's books."

"Suspenseful! Fabulous just fabulous! I enjoyed reading these books immensely. I highly recommend these books. Bravo to the author! You won't regret it."

"What a wonderful and intriguing book. Kept me glued to what was going to happen next. Not a normal read for me. But a very enjoyable series that I would recommend to everyone who likes adventure and thrills."

Satire and Humor

https://www.amazon.com/dp/B0FTLMH2BN

In a world where words are outlawed, news is tranquilized, and history is bubble-wrapped, The Snark Files dares to ask the questions everyone else is too comfortable to touch. Each "case file" is a darkly comic record of society's most absurd attempts to outlaw reality, rebrand common sense, and algorithm-proof the obvious.

From professors fired for quoting Aristotle, to news anchors forced to deliver "comfort reports," to bureaucrats panicking over a lost Manual of Common Sense, the series exposes the hilarious fragility of a culture addicted to feelings, euphemisms, and spin.

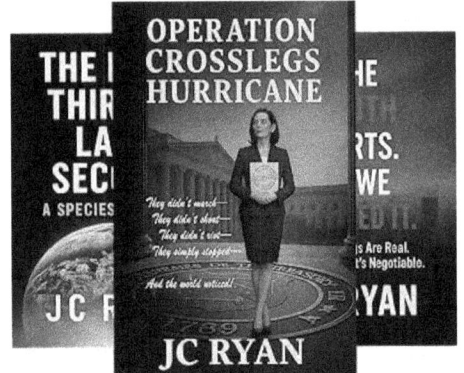

Wry, biting, and disturbingly plausible, The Snark Files read like classified documents accidentally left on the copier—records of a civilization so desperate to protect itself from offense that it banned the very tools of truth.

Think Orwell with a laugh track. Swift with Wi-Fi. Douglas Adams at a government hearing.

If you've ever wondered how far nonsense can go before it collapses under its own contradictions, this is your front-row seat.

About JC Ryan

JC Ryan is a bestselling author renowned for his intricate espionage, archaeological thrillers, and conspiracy mysteries. With over 30 acclaimed novels, including the popular Rex Dalton K9 Thrillers, Rossler Foundation Mysteries, and Carter Devereux Mystery Thrillers, Ryan has captivated readers around the globe.

Drawing from his diverse professional background—as a military officer, lawyer, and IT manager—Ryan creates compelling narratives that skillfully blend historical accuracy with thrilling adventure. He is celebrated as a master storyteller, known for crafting riveting plots, meticulous historical details, and engaging, multidimensional characters. Ryan's meticulous research lends authenticity and depth to each story, immersing readers in richly constructed worlds filled with intrigue, suspense, and adventure.

Fans of David Baldacci, Lee Child's Jack Reacher, Tom Clancy's Jack Ryan, Nelson DeMille's John Corey, Vince Flynn's Mitch Rapp, Mark Greaney's Gray Man, Gregg Hurwitz's Orphan X, Robert Ludlum's Jason Bourne, Daniel Silva's Gabriel Allon, Brad Taylor's Pike Logan, Brad Thor's Scot Harvath, James Rollins' Sigma Force, Steve Berry's Cotton Malone, and Dan Brown's Robert Langdon will find JC Ryan's novels equally compelling and unforgettable.

When not writing, Ryan enjoys spending time with his college sweetheart, whom he married in 1978. They are proud parents of two daughters, have two sons-in-law, and are grandparents to two grandchildren.